MY SECRET MOTHER

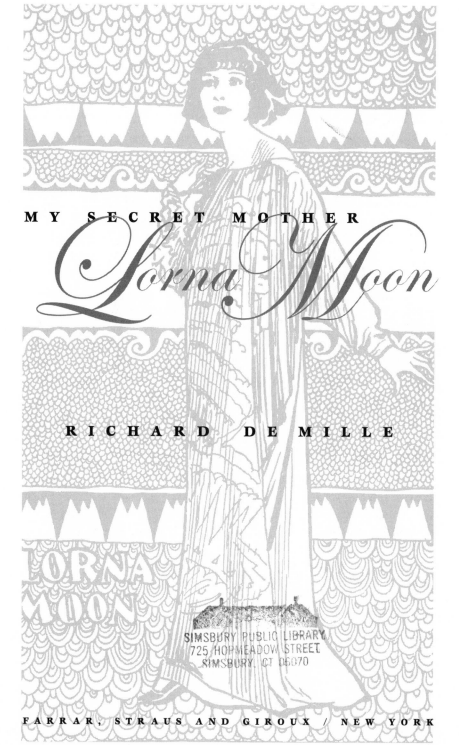

MY SECRET MOTHER

Lorna Moon

RICHARD DE MILLE

FARRAR, STRAUS AND GIROUX / NEW YORK

Farrar, Straus and Giroux
19 Union Square West, New York 10003

Copyright © 1998 by Richard de Mille
All rights reserved
Distributed in Canada by Douglas & McIntyre Ltd.
Printed in the United States of America
Designed by Abby Kagan
First edition, 1998

Library of Congress Cataloging-in-Publication Data
De Mille, Richard, 1922–
    My secret mother : Lorna Moon / Richard de Mille.
        p.   cm.
    ISBN 0-374-21757-2 (alk. paper)
    1. Moon, Lorna, 1886–1930—Biography. 2. Women novelists,
American—20th century—Biography. 3. Women screenwriters—United
States—Biography. 4. Women journalists—United States—Biography.
5. Birthmothers—United States—Biography. 6. De Mille, Richard,
1922–   —Family. I. Title.
PS3525.0498Z64   1998
813'.52—dc21
[B]   97-48280

The works of Lorna Moon and Mary Moon are owned by Richard de Mille.
For other rights and permissions, inquire of publisher.

Contents

The Bobbs-Merrill Company, Publishers

Memorandum for: Publicity   **Date:** December 29, 1928

Subject: QUESTIONS TO ASK LORNA MOON

2.   Names of some of her better-known motion pictures.

~~3.   Who were her husbands.~~

7.   How did she happen to leave Scotland?

10.   What newspapers did she work on?

13.   Did she become ill here or abroad?

14.   How much of DARK STAR is her own story?

16.   Would her son give us his impressions of his mother?

A WOMAN OF MYSTERY

These are some of the questions Lorna Moon's publisher wanted to ask her. Reconsidering Question 3, the publisher crossed it out, believing it would only invite more playful Lorna moonshine about a childhood marriage in Scotland, quickly followed by wartime loss of a second husband in France, soon replaced by a third husband in Canada, to say nothing of several anonymous children tucked away in secret corners. One doesn't know whether Question 16 was ever put to Lorna, but this book is the answer to that question and the others.

MY SECRET MOTHER

Lorna Moon

His Father's Boy

Late one school-day afternoon in the spring of 1930 Tommy Runyon said to me:

"I know something about you you don't know."

We were coming home in the bus from Carl Curtis School. I was in the third grade, he was in the fourth.

"What?" I said.

"I'm not supposed to tell you."

"Why not?"

"You're too young."

"No, I'm not."

"Yes, you are. My mother says you are. Your parents will tell you when you're older."

"Tell me *now!*"

"I can't. Go ask your mother. She can tell you if she wants to."

If that were not enough, he started singing his song about me, *"The little Dickey bird is sitting in a tree . . . ,"* a very dumb song. He sang it for blocks. On the other hand, when we got to his house we went up to his room and he showed me his Benjamin pump, a beautiful thing. He wouldn't let me shoot it. You could put someone's eye out. You had to be strong to pump it. All I had was a BB gun.

Tommy's mother, Mrs. Runyon, was a tall dark woman with a face like a hawk. Talking on the telephone, Mother called her Cornelia. They had been friends for years. Later Cornelia became a sculptor. Agnes de Mille's book *Portrait Gallery* has a very nice essay about Cornelia and her sculpture. There's also a chapter about the brothers William and Cecil de Mille, Agnes's father and uncle—mine too in a different arrangement—and how different they were. Before it was published, Agnes sent me the manuscript for comment. That pleased me because for the previous sixty years she hadn't sought my opinion. I suggested numerous changes and she made nearly all of them—which was a surprise, since she was seventeen years older and a well-known author noted for her definite opinions. But with Agnes art came first.

Mrs. Runyon lived at 2018 North Hobart, on the west edge of Laughlin Park. Almost every day after school I would go through Tommy's back yard, climb the bank to Betty's house, sneak along the gardener's path behind the pittosporums, examine the goldfish in Mrs. Wood's pond, slog up her steep lawn, squeeze through a hedge, and come out on DeMille Drive. Ten years later my sister Katherine's first baby set off on his first adventure, along the drive, through the hedge, and pell-mell down that lawn. Nobody knew where he had gone. After a frantic search they found him floating among the lily pads. Katie was very brave about it. She retired from the movies and gave her husband, Anthony Quinn, three daughters and another son. She took care of the house and raised the kids. In 1947 she went back to make her last two films. One was Father's *Unconquered*, in which she played the mistreated Indian wife of a white gunrunner, her soft sad eyes and noble countenance more beautiful even than thirteen years before, when she had played the fiery jealous wife of Pancho Villa. The other film was *Black Gold*, in which she played the loyal, devoted wife of an oil-rich Indian. The husband was played by Tony Quinn. It was the only time they worked together in a film, five years before Tony's award-winning *Viva Zapata!* and seventeen years before his image-defining *Zorba the Greek*. Katie said:

Black Gold was my favorite picture, playing opposite Tony. Much as I loved Father, I didn't like working in films for him. He was too theatrical. He didn't know how to tell an actor to be simple and real. I learned a lot about that from Tony.

But kids grow up too fast. When Katie's fifth child was nine, Tony felt compelled to start a second family in Rome. "The house was too quiet," he told a reporter. "Nobody yelling 'Daddy! Daddy!' when I came home. I gotta have small children running around." A man who has small children is still young and strong; his children are his future life, the more of them the better. A woman of fifty, no matter how loyal and devoted, can't give a man any more children. Zorba the Virile found four new women to bear him eight more children, three in Italy, one in France, two in Germany, two in New York. Playing Zeus on TV at seventy-nine, he told the infant Hercules what to do about women. "Take a *lot* o' them!" he roared. He named his twelfth child Antonia and taught her to say she was Toni Quinn. He said they would enter the next century together. No use taking chances with your immortality.

When I was eight it was Katie, after Father, I wanted to be with. She took me with her to the beach and to see Johnny Weissmuller swing and yodel from tree to tree. On the way home I asked her if she thought Tarzan was real. She laughed. I said I was pretty sure he was. She didn't say he wasn't. She wrote me funny letters when I was in boarding school and came with Mother to see me. Then she came with Tony Quinn. He was almost as exotic as Tarzan. She asked me if I liked him. I said I liked him, and I did. I didn't say I wanted her to marry him. Or anybody. She loved him for sixty years. That was simple and real.

I found Mother arranging flowers in the living room and asked her what Tommy had been talking about. She looked serious and we had to sit down on the couch.

"Tommy must have heard his mother say that you are adopted."

"What's adopted?"

"It means that Father and I didn't get you till you were nine months old. You were at Castelar Creche. The minute I saw you I wanted to bring you home. Then Miss Pickrell called and said you had whooping cough and I'd better come right down. I went down and brought you home, and now you are a member of the family, just like John and Katherine."

"What about Cecilia?"

"Cecilia is not adopted. She was born in the family. Most parents have only the children God gives them, but some lucky parents can adopt other children they want. After Cecilia was born, Father and I wanted more children, so we picked John and Katherine and you."

That sounded pretty good. They had to take Cecilia, but they wanted John and Katherine and me. I could see why they wanted Katie. I wasn't sure about John. Castelar Creche was a home for babies that had lost their parents. Mother went there for meetings, and when I got whooping cough she brought me home. Lucky I got it when I did.

I had sometimes wondered why I didn't have a middle name. All the others had middle names. Cecilia had Hoyt, John had Blount, Katie had Lester. I had nothing. That was odd. My name looked empty with nothing in between. Father said:

"You were named after your Uncle Richard." He showed me a picture of Uncle Richard with a long white beard and let me sit on Uncle Richard's awkward antique chair. Later I found Uncle Richard's season ticket to the Paris Exhibition of 1855 and learned that he was Father's great-uncle, Richard Mead De Mill, born in 1828. *He* had a middle name. They could have given me that.

The name de Mille did not begin as "De Mill" but as "de Meld." In his book on the Gallic War, Julius Caesar wrote about the Meldi, or the Melds, a Celtic tribe on the coast of what is now Belgium, where in 55 B.C. he built forty ships to sail against the Britons. The *e* at the end of "de Mille" makes the name look French, which would mean "of thousand," but it is not French. It is Dutch, meaning "the Meld," a person descended from the Melds. The *e* was added in a moment of foolish Francophilia by my great-grandfather William Edward De Mille, and now we can't get rid of it. Another misleading sign is the choice of capital *D* or lowercase *d*, which has been chronically inconsistent. Some critics, including Agnes, have made much of William de Mille's supposedly modest small *d* and Cecil DeMille's apparently grandiose large *D*, but it was a question of what would work on the movie screen. Father believed that audiences would pay more attention to a large *D* than a small one and would feel more at home with the name DeMille all in one piece. Off-screen Father signed his name "de Mille," like the rest of us.

Our family came to America in 1658, when Anthony de Mil and Elisabeth van der Liphorst, born in Haarlem, Holland, and married in the Protestant Dutch Reformed Church, sailed six weeks on the *Gulden Bever* (the *Gilded Beaver*) from Amsterdam to New Amsterdam, debarking from the East River at the foot of Wal Street (named for the stockade built along it in 1653 by order of Peter Stuyvesant to stop British and Indian invaders from the north). Anthony was a baker, son of Isaac de Mil, dean of bakers at Haarlem, where de Melds, de Melts, and de Milts had come to be de Mils and to dust themselves with flour for a hundred years. Anthony de Mil baked bread in New Amsterdam until 1664, when the British seized the burg and changed its name to New York. Anthony baked bread in New York until 1673, when the Dutch came storming back and made him *Schout* (that is, Sheriff) of New Amsterdam. A year later the British returned and put the *Schout* in jail for being disloyal to George I, a German who didn't speak English but, as happens over there, was somehow King of England.

Anthony's son Pieter baked bread in New York and was appointed Sheriff like his father. He added an *l* to his name and capitalized his *D*. He married Maria van der Heul, who bore him five boys and five girls in twenty-two years. Three of the boys died young, and so did three of the girls. In New York, De Mill men married women with names like Steenbeecke, Provoost, de Baets, and van den Vyver, but in 1713 Pieter and Maria moved to Stamford, Connecticut, where they joined the Episcopal Church and De Mills began to marry women with names like Arnold, Banks, Mead, Price, and Blount. Peter De Mill, son of Pieter and Maria, married Abigail Banks of Greenwich. In sixteen years she bore nine children, four of whom survived. One survivor was Joseph. When Joseph was thirteen, George II, another German King of England, founded a college in Manhattan near the red-light district, naming it, of course, King's College. Joseph didn't go to King's or any college, but when he was forty-three, George III by the Grace of God was thrown out of New York by force of arms, and King's College became Columbia, which would be attended by five de Milles—Richard Mead, Henry C., William C., William's daughter Margaret G., and Richard who had no middle name.

In 1795 Joseph De Mill's son Peter married Sophia Mead, and the family returned to New York. In sixteen years she bore ten children, nine of whom survived. Sophia's son Thomas Arnold De Mill married a southern girl named Caroline Elizabeth Price. Though Thomas and Caroline lived in Brooklyn, their five children were born in Washington, North Carolina, by the banks of the river Pamlico, where Caroline went to be with her mother whenever a baby was due. Thomas and Caroline's eldest son, William Edward De Mille, my great-grandfather who added the unnecessary *e*, settled in Washington, North Carolina, where he built a thriving business, married Margaret Blount Hoyt, served as mayor of the town, and was a pillar of the Episcopal Church. Union cavalry captured him during the War Between the States, and while he was in prison, his wife bought a tobacco farm with Confederate money and supported the family till he got back.

William Edward's younger brother, Richard Mead De Mill, stayed in Brooklyn with their father, Thomas. Richard attended Columbia College before it moved uptown, graduated at nineteen, and went on to study law. Practicing in Brooklyn, he laid up earthly treasure, but his heart was in the Gospels and his eyes were fixed on heaven. He read the New Testament every day in the original Greek and quarreled with previous translations and interpretations. When Richard was about fifty, the Lord afflicted his body for the sake of his soul, and he spent the next twenty-five years in sickly but productive retirement composing what he called "a manuscript of considerable size, entitled *The Purpose of the Aeons*." I don't know what happened to that manuscript, but it must indeed have been of considerable size, because a condensation of it prepared by the author with "necessary brevity" fills four hundred finely printed pages. "This little volume," as Uncle Richard called it, is found today in seminarian libraries under the title *The Foundation and the Superstructure, or the Faith of Christ and the Works of Man*. It is a solemn, devout, often eloquent dissertation on many fine points of theology, including the following distinction between sin and sinfulness:

While that which is pardonable comprises all sin and blasphemy, it is the Sinfulness from which they spring, which is caused by the evil spirit within man, which is unpardonable.

Contrite sinners forgiven, yes. Deals with the Devil, no.

Uncle Richard's eloquence, reverence, and learning greatly impressed his nephew Henry C. de Mille, eldest of the ten children born over twenty years to Margaret Blount Hoyt and William Edward De Mille. Henry first studied Greek out of Uncle Richard's well-worn New Testament and would spend his short life emulating Uncle Richard's piety and charity. At thirteen he played a role on the stage at school and ever after felt himself torn between the pulpit and the theater. At Columbia University on a religious scholarship he earned an A.B. and a master's degree. He taught school for small pay while studying for the ministry, but he could never quite bring himself to renounce the stage. He married an actress, an Englishwoman, Matilda Beatrice Samuel, daughter of a prominent merchant family in Liverpool, where her great-grandfather Ralph (Raphael ben Samuel) had helped to found the Ashkenazi Hebrew Congregation. Loving Henry more than religion, Beatrice joined the Episcopal Church and raised her sons as Christians.

When Henry was thirty, his first play opened in Madison Square Theatre and closed after six nights. His second three years later did better but not much. Then he began to collaborate with the great David Belasco, who added theatrical spice to Henry's moral uplift. It was a winning combination. De Mille and Belasco achieved a national reputation. Henry produced his last play when he was thirty-seven. Titled *The Lost Paradise*, it portrayed a struggle of workmen for fair treatment. Though it was written without Belasco, audiences liked it. Flushed with his success, Henry took a year off to build his family a large Victorian house at Pompton Lakes, New Jersey. He called the house "Pamlico." As Senior Warden of Christ Church, where the congregation was too poor to pay a clergyman, he conducted services every Sunday morning and read over the graves of fellow parishioners. At home on Sunday afternoons he held a Bible class for men and every evening read the Bible to his wife and sons. Henry was a man of faith, charity, and courage. Once when a little boy stricken with diphtheria was

struggling for breath, Henry with his own mouth sucked the
phlegm from the child's throat to restore his breathing. Established
in his new home, he set to work on a sequel to *The Lost Paradise*
but suddenly fell ill. The doctor said it was typhoid fever. In February 1893, Henry died at thirty-nine. Son William was fourteen,
son Cecil was eleven.

The indomitable Beatrice started a school in her husband's
name in the house called "Pamlico," where girls from good families came to stay and do such meritorious things as compose English prose, recite Milton's "Il Penseroso," prove the propositions
of Euclid, discuss the politico-economic teachings of Henry
George, sketch from nature, honor Nathan Hale, mark the mach-
inations of Bismarck and Disraeli, converse at table in French or
German, translate Homer from the Greek and Virgil from the
Latin, enact roles in amusing skits to gratify proud parents, sew
plain and fancy garments, enter a drawing room with proper carriage and expression, keep accounts, type letters, and trim their
girlish figures boating, bicycling, skating, sleighing, dancing the
polka and minuet, and swatting tennis balls. Tuition and board
came to five hundred dollars a year, but fencing lessons were extra
even when conducted by the principal's younger son, Cecil, home
on leave from military school.

Beatrice raised her boys to be gentlemen like their father, sacrificed her luxuries to send them to good schools, told them they
were champions, and urged them on to great achievement. Early
in the twentieth century son William married Anna, daughter of
Henry George, and became a Broadway playwright. Son Cecil married Constance, daughter of Judge Frederic Adams, and became
an international household word for the movies. Shortly after
World War I, between flappers and flaming youth, I joined the
family and began to call Constance Mother.

One thing Mother and I had in common was liking flowers.
When I was a little child, much of her day and mine was spent
inspecting the work of gardeners. Treading lightly along the rows
between the old brown barn and the tennis court, I marveled at
the spicy sweetness of the pink carnations. Circling Mother's white
rose garden and Father's red rose garden, I pressed my unforbid-
den nose into every tender bloom. Mother's roses were pale and

delicate; Father's roses were dark and delicious. I crouched by
steaming pansies under the noonday sun and stared into a thousand vivid, worried feminine faces. Gathering as many as I could,
I took them to my room. Frank, our horticulturist, reported to
Mother that a vandal had destroyed the pansy bed. Her deep theatrical voice shook with righteous anger. Pansies in their innocent
glory felt things she didn't dare to feel—desire, abandonment,
ecstasy, surrender. She spanked me with a hairbrush. I pinched
her shin and spoiled her stocking. It was the only time we came
to blows. By afternoon the pansy bed seemed to be forgotten. Only
Frederick the butler said any more about it. He told me I was a
very naughty boy. I didn't care what *he* thought.

Mother didn't like people to suffer, especially children. After
she and Father were no longer penniless actors skimping and
scraping and doing without she contributed to many good causes
—the Castelar Creche, where I had been, the Los Angeles Or-
phans' Home, where she had found Katherine, Children's Hospital, the Children's Protective Association, and the Boys' and
Girls' Aid Society. In a typical year she gave to a wide variety of
good causes, from the Tuberculosis Association to the Veterans of
Foreign Wars to the Albanian-American School of Agriculture. At
the same time she routinely sent checks to her less affluent relatives, all this of course with Father's consent and usually his approval. Father too was generous. Neither of them made a public
show of giving, and often they gave in secret as Jesus recommended. A displaced Italian aristocrat known as the Countess Li-
gura came to tea with Mother and went away with a modest sum
to tide her over. The record shows that Mother sent two 1930
dollars to a certain Wilfred E. Racker at the Utah State Prison. I
don't know what his story was.

Referring to Mother's treatment of those close about her, Agnes
said: "Aunt Constance is a saint, an infinitely loving open-armed
woman." Except as noted below, no one has ever denied that.
Mother's saintly love fed me, clothed me, housed me, took me to
the doctor, tended me when I was sick, and bought me books and
toys. She took me shopping at Robinson's, which had a wonderful
toy department. On the way downtown she fiddled with her hair-
pins and stuck her elbow in my face. I hated it when she did that.

At Wetherby-Kayser shoe store I stood at the fluoroscope watching my toe bones wiggle inside my new high shoes, an early video entertainment not yet banned as radiation hazard, child endangerment, and health crime. I sat on a small blue wicker chair that played marvelous tunes when anyone sat upon it. I didn't want to get up and leave the shoe store. Mother bought me a chair just like it to sit on in my room. Another time she gave me a carved wooden frog that played the march from *Aida*. I still have the works. She supported my habit, which was reading. She kept an orderly, tranquil house where routines were dependable and there were few unpleasant surprises. When I came home from school she said:

"Hello, my little kitten." I answered:

"I'm not a kitten."

Kind and generous as she was, I was not drawn to Mother. I didn't want to sit in her lap. If she lifted me up, I would wriggle off. Before long she stopped trying. Not much has been written about infinitely loving open-armed women rejected by their little boys. Once after a scolding I accused her of adopting me just so she could be mean to me. This was quite unfair and, if I had only known it, the opposite of the truth. I was drawn to a different kind of woman. Just across DeMille Drive lived Hamlin Garland, author of *A Son of the Middle Border* and *Forty Years of Psychic Research*. Next door to him lived his daughter Connie, Mrs. Joseph Harper, a lush, blond, pretty young matron who read fortunes in lucky palms and pulsed with psychic power. To be near Connie was enchantment. To be touched by her was to hear strange, distant music. (Later Joe Harper married Cecilia; I guess he couldn't hear the music.) When fear of infantile paralysis was keeping kids out of school and away from swimming pools and barbershops, Connie cut my hair at her house. I wished my hair would grow faster. And of course I was drawn to Katie. When Katie was seventy-four we had one of our last pre-Alzheimer's conversations. I asked her about her childhood.

R: Did you feel loved in the family?

K: *Yes!* By Father. I adored him.

R: What about Mother?

K: I loved her. She was sweet.

R: *You* loved *her*. But how did she feel about you?

K: [Sigh] It was very hard to tell. Mother was— [Sigh] Oh, I know she loved me. She was precious. I lov—I liked her, but I can't remember ever having any deep communication with her. I'm not sure if she even knew how. Do you think she knew how?

R: No, I don't. She was a sweet, kind person, but she didn't know how to make you feel her love.

K: No, she didn't.

R: And he did.

K: Yes, he *did*!

R: He didn't have to do much actually.

K: No!

R: He sort of looked at you, and you felt included.

K: *Yes!* That's very strange. I'm glad you felt that too.

Now and then I wondered who my real parents had been, the ones I had somehow lost. Did they die? Were they in prison? Did anyone know their names? Did they speak English? Could they read? What was wrong with them anyway? In our family you weren't supposed to ask about some things. There was no list of forbidden questions, you were just supposed to know what you shouldn't ask. I didn't know, so I didn't ask anything. I waited and watched and listened. I read the Sunday comics and felt a bond of sympathy with Skeezix of *Gasoline Alley*.

Skeezix was born on 12 February 1921, a year to the day before me, and he too was adopted. Someone left him in a basket on the small-town doorstep of a bulky bachelor named Walt Wallet. A note in the basket said: "I have never seen you but I have seen your picture. I know you are kind-hearted. Please care for and give baby a good home." Skeezix grew to manhood not knowing who his real parents were, but someone must have known, because "Uncle" Walt said he "had it on good authority" that Skeezix had been two days old when he landed on the doorstep. Just who this "good authority" was no one ever said. As the years went by, Skeezix and I lived parallel lives, growing up, going to school, serving in the war, marrying, getting a job, having a child, and growing old, all on the same schedule. One odd thing about Skeezix. Though he was adopted and no one knew who his mother was, he looked exactly like his adoptive "Uncle" Walt.

In 1931 Mother and Father went to Russia to see the Workers' Paradise firsthand. They left Ammama in charge. Ammama was Mother's stepmother, Ella King Adams, widow of Judge Frederic Adams of the New Jersey Court of Errors and Appeals. She was tight-strung and constantly frowning. To calm herself she smoked Sweet Caporals and drank coffee all day long. When she died of bladder cancer, suffering great pain, she took my hand and held it. Her hand was cold and thin and white.

Ammama liked to win at solitaire, either Patience or her favorite, Fooley Ann or the Idiot's Delight. She catalogued all of Father's books. She did crossword puzzles without looking anything up. That summer we played a word game in which we packed a suitcase for a trip to a desert island. Ammama said she was going to take Eggs and Apples. They were allowed. I said peaches and plums, but they were disqualified. Ammama said Emus and Aardvarks, and they went right in. I said Rabbits and guinea pigs. Rabbits went in, but guinea pigs were thrown out. It was a puzzle. Ammama filled her suitcase with Elephants and Anteaters, Epiphanies and Angels, Emblems and Allegories. All I had in mine was Rabbits. If I had remembered that her real name was Ella Adams, I could have packed Rabbits and Ducks, Ropes and Drums, Riddles and Dreams.

Ammama wanted me to be a happy, smiling child. That summer I frowned and fidgeted. She told me not to waggle my foot. It could make me sick. I said:

"Do you know who my real parents were?" She looked solemn and said:

"You mustn't worry about that. Your parents were *fine* people. I knew them both very well, and you are *all right!*" I suppose with Father and Mother way off there in Russia and Queen Victoria dead for thirty years Ammama thought it would be safe to drop one little hint of the great store of kind and reassuring facts cruel but wise necessity had withheld from me. I felt better on the spot. Somebody actually knew my parents, and I was *all right*. I didn't tell anyone what she had said.

Aunt Rebecca Adams, Mother's maiden sister, came for the summer to keep us company. Aunt Rebecca lived in New York, where she taught weaving to Bellevue Hospital psychiatric patients and had a friend named Gisela Richter, who knew all about Greek art. I liked hearing Aunt Rebecca say "Ghee-se-luh" in German. She spoke in a soft and spooky voice and drifted about the circular gardens filling a basket with wilted roses. She told me flowers were most beautiful when they were dying. She set up her loom in the West Wing, stretched the warp, and shuttled the woof. As I stood by watching her, she turned to me with a twinkle.

"*I* know something about *you*!" She didn't say what it was, and of course I didn't ask her. Whatever it was, I knew by then that I was *all right*. Let her keep her spooky secrets.

Like me, brother John was of unknown origin. Unlike me, he was dark and handsome. All I knew about him for sure was that he was nine years older, had a middle name, and was a Spaniard. "John's a *Spaniard*!" Mother would say, her eyes alight with dashing dragoons and tuneful toreadors. He did bellow in the bath— not *Carmen* but *Wagon Wheels* and *Anchors Aweigh!* It was awful to hear him. He never got anywhere near the tune.

Katherine's origin was known. She remembered both her parents and knew how she had lost them. Her father had died in France from battle wounds when she was six, her mother two years later of tuberculosis. At first Katherine was a docile, round-faced little girl, but all of a sudden at eighteen she was a glorious princess dazzling as the Snake-Tsarevna in whose lap the evil dragon laid his smoking head while she told him bedtime stories. Oh to be that evil dragon! Or the fearless Cossack who rescued Princess Katherine. When I looked into the mirror, I didn't see a fearless Cossack or even a tone-deaf Spaniard. I certainly didn't see Valentino, who was the ideal. I hated the way I looked. I was pale and ordinary, rather like Father's father, Henry C. de Mille, whose picture hung on the wall in Father's room. Being *all right* didn't cure that.

In the servants' dining room, where antique plates hung on the wall, Frederick the butler and Hilja the maid and Emilie the cook and Einar the kitchen boy gossiped about the doings of the household. Master Richard isn't satisfied with his own Christmas tree.

Now he wants a canary up in his room. Haven't we got a big enough mess with the ones downstairs? Mrs. Chase is coming tomorrow to alter Mrs. de Mille's dresses. It's a shame she's putting on so much weight. Mr. John lost all his money playing blackjack in Ensenada. His mother had to send him twenty dollars to get home. He takes money out of her purse and she doesn't tell his father. I can't keep anything in the liquor cabinet.

Only Hilja spoke like us, with an American accent. She had come from Finland as a baby. She sipped her coffee through a lump of sugar, which made her sweet. Frederick was Norwegian. He tinted his hair blond and curled it with an iron. His friend Harold, a ballet dancer, came to help him serve at parties. I liked Harold. He was cute. Emilie was a plain-faced Czech with a very big chest. She brought the coffee to a boil and cleared the grounds with an egg. She fried the cornmeal mush crisp and brown the way I wanted it. One day she cried into the peas and left us to have a baby. Mother was upset. Einar Isaksen from Sweden packed the ice and salt around the tank of vanilla cream and turned the crank while singing *Three O'Clock in the Morning*. Einar had a magnificent voice, and he would take requests. Passing through the backstairs hall, I heard the servants talking. Frederick was the opinion maker.

"John's his mother's boy," he said. "Richard is his father's boy."

I didn't know what that meant, but I liked the sound of it.

CHAPTER 2

A Marriage Made on Earth

Father was kind to all his children, but he treated them differently, according to his understanding of what was right, what was fair, what was suited to their capacities. Cecilia was his firstborn child, his natural child, his female child. It was a winning combination. Father followed the old tradition that said an eldest child had a primary claim on property and position. He believed it would be unfair to treat a natural child as though she were only adopted. He thought a woman who showed ability to manage wealth should inherit wealth, while a man should go forth boldly into the world and make his fortune. Easy money was bad for men. Men should struggle, contend, and provide. Women were the preservers. A man unpressed by necessity would waste his substance in riotous living, marry a fortune hunter, or substitute wealth for achievement, clipping coupons at the bank, drinking highballs at the club, and never amount to anything he could have amounted to.

When Father died, some in the family were disappointed by the terms of his will, under which firstborn, natural, female Cecilia (and her three children, good kids really, none of them adopted) skipped off with ninety-five percent of the estate and (to some it seemed) of the decedent's love. Worse things could have happened. I, for example, could have been born the cherished, favored only son of Nicholas the Last and shot in a basement at thirteen by order of Comrade Lenin. As it was, I barely made it out of the womb in one piece. Doctor's advice and parents' convenience both ran against me. A wise child does not look a gift life in the mouth.

Father hadn't really wanted to adopt any children. That was Mother's idea. It went back a long way. In the fall of 1900 Cecil B. de Mille, a minor player in a traveling repertory company, a brashly confident nineteen-year-old pampered from the age of eleven by a widowed mother, heir to a well-known theater name left by his dead father, possessor of boundless energy and enthusiasm if not so boundless acting talent, was standing backstage when he saw a shapely pair of ankles come twinkling down a staircase followed by an hourglass figure and a handsome English face set off by beautiful long brown hair. Many an actress could have done that, but matters took a serious turn as soon as Cecil realized that this particular young woman, Constance Adams, of Orange, New Jersey, was also gentle, understanding, capable, and refined. The eldest child of an eminent judge, she had managed her father's household, looking after the younger children when their mother died. She was just the wife an eager, penniless upstart in the theater needed to help him forge ahead, a lady he could count on to maintain his social standing, listen sympathetically to his plans, fulfill his husbandly desires, and look after him like a mother. On the last night of the century, sitting together on the steps of a Boston theatrical boardinghouse, the two plighted their troth. In 1902 they were married at her father's house in Orange. The bride carried lilies of the valley.

Difficulties soon arose. Cecil was barely twenty-one, an impetuous, hot-blooded Edwardian ladies' man. Constance was already twenty-nine, a cool, restrained Victorian matron. During their first season on the road as man and wife, Boston to San Francisco, Biloxi to Montreal, Constance was quietly dismayed at Cecil's luxurious notion of marital bliss. She yearned to give him all he wanted, but it went against her nature and against her background. Disappointed by her restraint, he accepted invitations from more excitable young women ready to give and glad to receive sharper if less loving pleasures. Constance went home to her father. Judge Adams told his favorite child she must make a decision. Either break with Cecil completely or come to terms with him and go back, and if she went back she must not thereafter quarrel or complain. She must take him the way he was. In spite of the terrible way he was and the sorrow he would cause her, she was helplessly in love, they had exchanged their marriage vows in the sight of God and man, and she couldn't bear to give him up. No other man had come into her life and none ever would. She made her decision for all time and hardly ever after that thought of changing it. She exacted only one condition: as long as she remained alive there would never be another Mrs. Cecil B. de Mille. Cecil gratefully agreed.

After six years of marriage their daughter Cecilia was born in Judge Adams's house. Cecil assisted the doctor. It was a long, difficult, dangerous delivery. Giving birth for the first time at thirty-five, Constance endured torment, terror, and despair. The doctor sternly advised Cecil not to risk her life again. She was both relieved and disappointed. She loved looking after children but lived in fear of pregnancy and shuddered at intimate demands. To keep her gallant husband at home she did her duty as well as she could, while he attempted to teach her the joy of sex. She wasn't ready for such joy, so dangerous even with protection, so emotionally uncontrolled, so far beyond what nice people would do—and Cecil wanted the lights on! He would try in vain to please her, then he would take her like a lion. Sometimes he almost frightened her. Throughout the ordeal she kept her composure. Afterwards he was always sweet.

In December 1913, having utterly failed to make his mark in the New York theater, Cecil de Mille, thirty-two, went West to begin a new career in something called the movies. Elder brother playwright William said it was the height of folly and would lead to poverty, shame, and degradation. (The following year he ate his words and went West to write scenarios under the confident command of his little brother.) Clicking along on the Atcheson, Topeka & Santa Fe from Albuquerque to Gallup, Cecil took out a pencil, opened a ruled pad, and scribbled eleven pages to his forty-year-old wife, trying once more to explain to her how their all but perfect marriage could be made complete. He called her by a pet name she had borne in a play:

Dearest Gretchen—

All day long, in fact ever since the train left western Kansas, I have been looking for a permanent home for us. For, in spite of my harem numbering hundreds of the most beautiful women in the land, I love you.

1st because you are you, generous, good, self-sacrificing, and lovable in more ways than I have time or space to write.

2nd because you love me, with all the strength and bigness of a big heart, a loving nature, and a sharp mind. And the next glorious thing to loving is being loved.

3rd, well the third shouldn't be written. It should only be suggested on nights when the moon is wonderfully clear and that strange throb that passes the heart of all living things is felt. Or when it is storming terribly and that cozy feeling of warmth and snugness comes to us sitting before a fire dry and warm. I said it shouldn't be written, but it has occurred to me that by writing it I can forever frustrate any intention on your part to publish this letter after I am dead and famous. Third, then, I love your body. I like your cool solid flesh. I like your strong pretty legs. I like the round firmness of your breasts. I love the passion in you. I love the thought of your body taught by me for me. I love the thought that it is mine and never has been nor could be another's. I love to have you want me and to show me that you want me. I love the deep look that comes into your eyes when you are mine this way. I know that no one on earth has ever seen that look, or ever will see it, but me. It gives me a barbaric desire to hurt you— that's when I pull your hair.

I love to feel your body next to mine and pressing close and to hear what you and I only know and to feel a kiss far from the ordinary kiss on my lips. So do we cut the strings of all reserve from all the senses. I believe there is nothing more improper than mentioning these terrible things to one's wife. These little tributes are always kept for the mistress. She alone hears such shameful words. But what am I to do? I find myself in the unique position of preferring my wife's body to that of any other woman. Here then is a predicament. I must teach my wife those things the mistress usually provides. But, shrieks the horrified god of morals, she is a good woman, she is pure, she has no right even to know that such things exist, to feel such violent and evil passion.

Then weakly I reply, But it is *her* body I want to feel pressed close to mine. It is her passion I want to feel respond to mine. It is her breath I want to feel warm and quick against my cheek. It is the sound from her lips I want to hear when for a heavenly moment she is transported onto the heights of passion.

You libertine! replies the god of morals. Would you so debase your wife? It is for this I have created the mistress. Then I look the god straight in the face and laugh. You two-faced idiot! I call him. I don't care what other women feel. It's what *my* woman feels that pleases me. Let other men go in to their wives in the dark and steal silently and with hallowed dignity their frigid nights of love and save themselves and their passion for their mistresses. My wife's my mistress and I'll teach her all a mistress knows. And we'll have light, liberty, and passion with our love. And to our heart's content. And I'll pull her hair to *my* heart's content, and you can go to the devil with your morality and your mistresses. Horrible! gasps the god. I shall hide my face from you forever. You can't, I call as he departs, for if you turn your back I see your double face.

That, little mother, is the third way I love you, the way that should never be written.

Constance kept the letter locked in a boudoir drawer for fifty years, but she couldn't change herself any more than she could change her husband. Agnes remembered a time in 1927 when Aunt Constance tried to console her about her own father's straying outside his marriage: "She told me she believed that sex had little to do with love, that one did not require the other. I was shocked, but she said, that's the way it is, and no use breaking your heart over it."

Cecil's fantasy of romance featured the bodily and emotional conquest of a reluctant beauty by a dominating master, as in the once popular lines of William Ernest Henley:

I saw, I took, I cast you by,
I bent and broke your pride.

In Henley's purple scenario (which made a brief appearance in DeMille's *Male and Female*, 1919) a king in Babylon notices a good-looking slave girl, commands her presence on the royal couch, and enjoys what were then called her favors—at first proudly withheld, then given in wild abandon. The unfortunate girl has, it seems, fallen head over sandals in love with the royal rapist, who, being accustomed to wasting young women, then callously discards her. Seduced, abandoned, and brokenhearted, she curses her gods and dies.

The scene shifts to London in the nineteenth century, where exploiter and victim are reincarnated as Victorian man and wife. The ruthless monarch is now a devoted English husband, but the cast-off slave is nursing a four-thousand-year-old grudge. Her new status as Christian lady and Good Woman helps her to suppress her animal desires and punish her betrayer by lying in the marriage bed like a suffering corpse. Needless to say, his feelings are hurt.

The pride I trampled is now my scathe,
For it tramples me again.
The old resentment lasts like death,
For you love, yet you refrain.

Divining in his frigid wife the once burning concubine, he takes grim satisfaction from the secret knowledge that long ago he *did* enjoy the blazing passion she now withholds from him. And he wouldn't change a thing:

Yet not for an hour do I wish undone
That deed beyond the grave,
When I was a king in Babylon
And you were a virgin slave.

This is far from logical, for if the poor frustrated fellow could undo his ancient mistreatment of the slave, today's wife would have no reason to withhold her passion. Beneath the illogic and bravado lurks the poet's bitter acknowledgment that this tantalizing Englishwoman is not now and never was a lustful Babylonian but is in truth a Victorian prude, and nothing he can ever do will turn her into the eager lover he once dreamed of marrying.

In his own marriage Cecil faced the same bitter truth about the maidenly woman he loved, but, being a man of action, he didn't count on poetry to bring relief. In 1914 Gladys Rosson, twenty-three years old, came to be his secretary. She worked for him for the rest of her life. In 1915 Jeanie Macpherson, twenty-seven, began to write his scenarios. Her last credit was for *The Buccaneer*, 1938. In 1917 Julia Faye, twenty years old, played a handmaiden in *The Woman God Forgot*. Her last role was in *The Ten Commandments*, 1956. On the sleeping porch at home Constance set her single bed close to Cecil's, where he slept almost every night, when he wasn't working at the ranch or on the yacht. She treated the other women with unfailing cordiality, and they treated her with scrupulous respect. In a business plagued by exposés—comedian Fatty Arbuckle called in papers across the land "the sex-mad maniac from Hollywood," director William Desmond Taylor slain in the love nest where he had dallied with actress Mabel Normand and Golden Girl Mary Miles Minter, *and* Mary Miles Minter's mother, who was the prime suspect—Cecil B. DeMille, producer-director of beauties in bathtubs and Moses in the desert, an inviting target for gossipmongers, was never touched by scandal. The mistresses he chose, not for their beauty but for their affection, trustworthiness, and discretion, loved him and protected him, surrounding him in a close-knit conspiracy of propriety. In turn he didn't cast them by like a king in Babylon but gave them enduring loyalty. In 1946 I went with him to the hospital to visit Jeanie Macpherson a few days before she died. He held her hand and told her they would surely meet in the next world. She murmured that they would. On the way back to the studio he was very quiet. When Gladys died he was gray and taut. During his own last days, Julia came to sit with him. She lived out her life in a house he had lent her, and when Cecilia inherited it, Julia said, "Well, Cecilia, I guess you've inherited me too." Cecilia honored the commitment.

On every anniversary lilies of the valley came for Constance

with a card from Cecil. An early card called her by another pet
name from a play: "My true, sweet, dear bully Mrs. McGucken."
It was signed "Cizzle." A late card said: "Only a saint could stand
30 years with a Satyr." At seventy-four, Constance wrote:

My Darling One
The dear lilies of the valley carried me back to that night in
Boston when we watched the century come in. For forty-five
of these years we have been married. It has been a thrilling,
exciting, adventurous life. You have brought me great
happiness. Whether through sunshine or occasional shadow,
my love has grown stronger. Today is a day for presents, but I
can only give you again what I gave you many years ago,
which has been the strongest thing in my life. All my love.

Her last note says:

Forty-six years ago I hitched my wagon to a star. Sometimes it
was a shooting star, but always one that burned brightly. I
watched it and loved it. Its light is my life and always will be.
Constance

CHAPTER 3

The Intellectual of the Family

Cecil de Mille was a storyteller. Henry, his father, and William, his brother, were social reformers who told stories to lead the people toward a better world. They are remembered in history books. He lives in legend. They had no trouble at all with spelling. He never got the hang of it. At nine Cecil was writing stories. One of them his mother saved. Like his movies, it is packed with action.

MY HUNTING STORY

When I was nine I had a verry small gun. I whent out to see what I could shout. I was about five miles from home when it began to snow. I found no game, one little bird. It was snowing verry fast when I started for home. I had to pas by a house that had a verry saveg dog. It was no fun to here that big dog barking in the snow. Some years ago I had a fine mastif pup. I only had it about four months, when it was stolen. I had nat senn him for three years. And so the dog came running for me, and I mistoke his joy for hate, and shot. He gave a yelp and quickened his speed. I drew my knife and waited for him, when suddenly I huerd a noise behind me. I turnd half round to see a large Panther crouching behind me. On came the dog, but to my joy he sprang past me and caut the Panther by the throat and speedily put an end to him and then turnd to receve my knife blow. When he fell deing at my feet I saw to my sarowe that it was my pup come to my aid. I neeld down by him. He looked up in my face and liced my hand, but I could not save him. He deid a minnit affterwrod from my gun shot. I thrwe him ofver my back and carid him home. And now he stands in are parler in the same possichon he was in when he saved my life.

In high school Cecil played right guard on the football team. In youth he boxed with novelist Albert Payson Terhune. Out West he hunted bear in the sierra, blew up in a speedboat, and raced his Curtiss biplane round and round above a track against a Chevrolet. William, three years older and to all appearances generations wiser, fenced and won track medals in college, set sportfishing records at the Tuna Club, and played tennis into his seventies. Both boys had good voices and could sing on key. Though Agnes would one day look down on their limited taste in music, they knew what they liked and they liked it very much. After going to school in Germany, William taught his little brother about *Der Ring des Nibelungen*. In Wagner's themes Cecil heard the dragon Fafnir roaring flame, saw the hero Siegfried dripping dragon's blood, beheld the battle maid Brünnhilde riding boldly down the sky or sleeping in the ring of magic fire. Wagner didn't waste your time with "deedle-deedle" string quartets. Every note advanced the story. "Wagner is *all* music!" Cecil said.

Cecil barely graduated from Pennsylvania Military College, which was in fact not a college but a boarding school. In his algebra book he scribbles: "Oh, the long and dreary winter! Oh, the cold and cruel winter!" Next to *auxiliary unknown quantity* he demands to know: "What in pink hell is the meaning of *this*?" Under *binomial formula* he complains: "If x = my dinner, and y = the cavity my dinner should fill, then x is negative and y is very possitive." Already in his algebra book he renders conflict in pictures. Just offshore from *Theory of Equations* a cartoon naval ship explodes and bodies hurtle in all directions, as they will again at the Battle of Actium in Cecil B. DeMille's *Cleopatra*. He learns to control his temper. Within plain view of *Horner's Method* two cartoon schoolboys duel with swords. One is fatally wounded. The other is promptly hanged from a gibbet. "Let not your angry passions rise!" warns Cadet de Mille. Staking an early claim to fame, he writes his name on twenty-two pages of his algebra book. To pass the course and graduate Cecil needed a score of sixty. Boyish charm made up the deficit. "Mr. de Mille," his teacher said, "I *can't* give you a score of sixty, but I have given you fifty-nine and ten tenths."

Henry de Mille implored his sons to avoid the theater and get into something solid. Headstrong Cecil followed his heart straight into the theater but the more prudent William set out to be an engineer. After three years of honors in math, materials, and stresses at the Columbia School of Mines, he couldn't resist the footlights any longer. He studied with Brander Matthews, America's first university drama professor, graduated in 1900 from Columbia College and in 1901 from the American Academy of Dramatic Arts, where he was soon a popular teacher. Success came early in his life. Audiences applauded his well-constructed, psychologically observant, often funny plays, and hardly ever felt oppressed by his social conscience. In 1905 at twenty-six he had a hit on Broadway. His play *Strongheart* deplored the unkindness and stupidity of race prejudice. In private he reflected that prejudice was a hard thing to get rid of, admitting with regret that only after brief hesitation could he shake hands with a Negro. Strongheart, the object of prejudice in his play, is not a Negro but an impeccably literate, urbane American Indian, captain and hero of the Columbia College football team. The "cruel law of race" forbids Strongheart to marry the woman he loves, or dance with her, or make love to her (which in 1905 means: tell her that he loves her), but it does allow him to correct silly fair-skinned girls at college teas with the same dignified, some would say haughty, irony that was known to mark author William's conversation.

MAUD: Tell me, how do you like America?
STRONGHEART: My people have always been fond of the place.

In 1911 William's play *The Woman* exposed businessmen as selfish hypocrites sorely in need of moral guidance and proposed that democratic government elected and populated by good and thoughtful people should firmly guide businessmen into unselfish ways. The de Mille family of that era were Episcopalians, and therefore good and thoughtful people, even if one or two of them didn't entirely believe in God. Henry de Mille, a complete believer, saw good government as God's moral agent, but William, an ardent humanist, saw God as a mere uplifting idea, a symbol of ethical aspirations, possibly useful to social-reforming playwrights and politicians. A nineteenth-century political idealist, William imagined a government of honest, selfless public servants competent to make the big moral and economic decisions which, one regretted to say, unenlightened moneygrubbers were making incorrectly. Though he called himself a Jeffersonian Democrat, he didn't always remember Jefferson's indispensable warning: Government is a dangerous beast and must be chained.

When it came to the goring of his own ox, William was for laissez-faire. Unlike his daughter Agnes, who in her day would loudly demand tax money for the arts, he quoted Goethe on the failure of the state-endowed theater at Weimar: "It is a bad thing for the drama not to be dependent on the takings at the door." For himself he rejected every kind of interference from authorities official or unofficial. Legislators and bureaucrats might teach morals to businessmen, but prudes had no business dictating standards of decency to playwrights. In his play *The Woman*, considered daring in 1911, an understanding husband forgives his wife for going to bed with another man—two years before they met. Scandalized by this attack on the ideal of the virgin bride, the Drama League of Chicago refused to endorse the play. William struck back savagely with a one-act satire titled *The Stork*, in which, he said, the laws of nature had been suitably revised to fit the rules of good taste. The plot runs as follows:

> After two years' absence, John comes home to Eva, his wife, who tells him they have a two-week-old baby, brought by the stork. Nagged by a mean suspicion that the baby may not be his, John refuses to look at it. Long ago his father told him babies are *not* brought by the stork but by the doctor in the little black bag. Joe, the family doctor, used to be John's friend, but ever since John caught him kissing Eva's photo-

graph, John has hated him. It isn't enough that Eva now turns the photo to the wall when she is alone with Doctor Joe. A two-year absence is no excuse for her naming the baby Joe. Eva tells John that if he doesn't trust her she must leave him. To save the marriage, Doctor Joe is about to take the baby away in the little black bag, when on the front steps he finds a stray stork feather. Convinced by this merciful proof that the baby is his own, John embraces wife and friend, and tasteful harmony is restored.

Whether in comedy or in drama William was a perfectionist, who took great care with every detail of plot, dialogue, set design, and production. Each story was tightly woven and moved with inexorable logic toward a convincing climax. Cecil's plots raced ahead too fast for logic to leak in. In December 1912 he wrote a sketch titled *The Royal Mounted*. William, the established playwright, gave his struggling brother a boost—and risked his reputation—by signing on as co-author. It's clear he had nothing to do with the writing. In one short act *The Royal Mounted* boils with conflict, leaps with courage, sinks into despair, glows with love, and shines with honor, but its thrilling climax teeters on a logical contradiction.

As the play opens, we are on the Great Elk River in the Canadian Northwest. Rosa hurries to the cabin of her brother, trapper Sam, to warn him that a telegram has gone downriver reporting the murder of the unpleasant stranger named Jed Brown. Lieutenant O'Byrne of the Mounties is on his way to arrest the killer. This brings on a family crisis. Lieutenant O'Byrne wants to marry Rosa, and she wants to marry him, but Jed Brown was killed by trapper Sam, who caught him trying to rape sister Rosa. While O'Byrne is questioning Sam and Rosa, U.S. Marshal Hicky arrives on the trail of a certain Snake Butler, wanted for robbing trains. Mountie Sergeant Radly finds Jed Brown's body in a snowbank, and the bullets in it match Sam's gun. Because he loves Sam's sister, Lieutenant O'Byrne lets Sam escape. Whereupon Sergeant Radly regretfully arrests his superior for treason. At the last minute

Marshal Hicky comes back from examining the body to announce that, far from being a murderer, trapper Sam has earned a reward for killing Snake Butler, wanted dead ($5000) or alive ($2000). All live happily ever after, except of course Snake Butler, alias Jed Brown.

A satisfying denouement, but one question remains. If Jed Brown's body wasn't discovered till Sergeant Radly found it in a snowbank, who would have sent a telegram downriver to the Mounties? In 1940 when *The Royal Mounted* was reborn as Cecil B. DeMille's *North West Mounted Police*, the storyteller had mastered his craft and the plot was watertight, as William would have wanted it to be. By that time William wasn't writing stories anymore.

Despite his early success on Broadway, William had from the start resented producers who thought they knew what audiences wanted better than playwrights did. Instead of bearding them in their offices, he poked fun at them onstage. In one of his comic sketches, Mr. Stork, a playwright, brings a new play to Mr. Fox, manager of the prospective star, a cow named Marigold Mooley. The text of the play is: "Hey, diddle, diddle, the cat and a fiddle." By demanding more and more revisions, manager Fox step by step builds up Miss Mooley's part at the expense of everything else in the play. One by one, cat, dog, dish, moon, diddle, fiddle, sport, and spoon are written out of the script, until at last the text becomes: "Hey, cowdle, cowdle, the cow and the cowdle." This hilarious jape no doubt had theatergoers rolling in the aisles, but arrogant managers and producers went right on mutilating the brainchildren of supercilious playwrights. In his memoir, *Hollywood Saga*, William explains why he left New York in 1914: "I . . . had reached the point where nothing I wrote pleased me." But surely *The Woman*, a well-written play popular with audiences, had pleased him in 1911. Suddenly in 1913 the critics rejected his comedy *After Five*. Not one critic said a good word about it. William was stunned. He dreamed of "a theater of the whole people," where the dramatist's powerful voice would lead and elevate his audience, "a new social force . . . revealing the peoples of the world to one another . . . encouraging international fraternity." He didn't want critics and moneymen standing between him and the people, who he said were the "real owners of the drama," and whom, after years of applause, he trusted to like his work. At that crucial point Cecil offered him a share in a risky business where they would be the bosses—Cecil, of course, a bigger boss than William—telling stories directly to the people not only in New York but in every city, town, and hamlet of the world. William left the theater "to stay with the audience." He went West "for six months" and never came back to Broadway except to see the new plays.

From 1914 to 1932 William made movies in Hollywood, first as writer, soon as director. His films sold fewer tickets than Cecil's but got more respect from highbrow reviewers. He liked to transform stage plays into living cinema. His best-known work, *Miss Lulu Bett*, was a play by Zona Gale adapted for the silent screen by Clara Beranger, who wrote nearly all of William's scenarios after 1921. *The New York Times* called it "pictorially dynamic." Today his few surviving films are admired by film historians. One historian, having praised Cecil's "whirlpool storytelling," compliments William on naturalistic acting and emotional reality, but adds: ". . . good as he is with actors, William invariably lacks dramatic intensity. . . . he is too self-consciously the New York intellectual to be an exciting filmmaker." Another refers to his "intellectual operas."

In temperament the brothers were wholly different. Cecil was an adventurer, William was a philosopher. Cecil was fearless, William was cautious. Cecil fared forth every day girded for mortal or business combat; William preferred to rise above the fray. If an obstacle blocked his path, Cecil stormed over it or found a way around it; William withdrew to a hilltop and looked down on it with disdain. When Adolph Zukor took away Cecil's power and status at Paramount, Cecil promptly started a studio of his own, the DeMille Studio, where he made *The King of Kings*, his most memorable silent picture; seven years later he was back at Paramount with status and power restored. In contrast, after eighteen years in the business, during which he had been elected president of the motion picture Academy, William was directing his fifty-sixth film, when a Johnny-come-lately Paramount production supervisor gave him some friendly pointers on how to make his scenes more effective and sent assistants to the set to check up on him. Though William would later write that it was impossible to do creative work with anti-artistic spies creeping around the set, he didn't take the intruders by the scruff of the neck and throw them into the company street but simply commented wryly: "Now we not only have supervisors, we have supervisors' mice." It was the last picture he directed. Though he had helped to form the art of the film, the business of film had no further need of his services. He lacked the energy, flexibility, innovation, and determination to keep imposing his work on studio executives as his undauntable brother would do for the next twenty-five years.

"Cecil was tough," Agnes said. "He was a fighter. Father was not."

To William the early days of Hollywood were "those magic years" when moviemakers were pioneers "held together in the fraternal bond of a common purpose," inspired by "the vision of an audience of millions." To have felt the "keen thrill" of directing movies in that happy time "was to have lived." The magic lasted fourteen years. Then sound came in. It wasn't the technical difficulties; they were rapidly overcome. It wasn't the despair of friends who fell in an instant from heights of stardom into depths of obscurity because of foreign accents, bad voices, or poor speech. It was money. Sound movies cost so much to make that Hollywood was overrun by "masterminds of finance," whose "superior intellects" quickly began to govern writers and directors. William no longer felt himself "an eager, young explorer." "Those gay, adventurous days were gone forever." There was "a general leveling down, a fatal standardization." "Within two years our little old Hollywood was gone, and in its place stood a . . . terrifying city . . . less friendly . . . much more cruel."

A different kind of trouble appeared in the mid-twenties, when William's marriage began to fall apart. Everyone was fond of Anna George de Mille, a cute, bright, delightful, adorable little dynamo. Christmas Day, when I was five, Aunt Anna burst into our house calling out: "Merry Christmouse, everybody!" I thought she was very funny. In her own house, Agnes wrote, she drove everybody crazy, demanding perfection in all things, urging daily self-improvement, exhorting child and husband to greater effort. At eighty Agnes still felt guilty if she read fiction in the daytime. "She was the spur in Father's flank, the gall under his saddle." After twenty years William got fed up with his wife's chaotic household, ceaseless uproar, and well-meant harassment. He longed for order, peace, and freedom.

Another source of discord was Anna's constant preoccupation with the teachings of her famous father. Henry George, author of *Progress and Poverty*, had sought to end economic injustice by taxing away all the rent landholders could charge others for using their private land. Since nothing else would be taxed, Henry George's tax on land was called the Single Tax. Three generations of de Milles—Henry, William, and Agnes—would be disciples of Henry George, but Anna George de Mille was more than a disciple; she was her father's prophet on earth. She lived to bring his message to the people of the world, including those that came to tea. The writer Beulah Marie Dix said Henry George was an unseen guest at all of Anna's social gatherings and turned up in every conversation. Not that William ever doubted his father-in-law's ideas. He had made speeches to promote them and wanted to write a play about them when the time was right. The two families were old friends. A shared belief in Georgism, along with a pair of intense blue eyes, long red hair, milky skin, and her tenacious interest in him had drawn William to Anna. But after years of making room for a famous invisible intellectual rival in his house, William wished his dear wife might be engaged a little less in the teachings of Henry George and just a little more in the thoughts of William C. de Mille. During Anna's prophecies he would retire to his study with one of the gentlemen guests to talk about tennis tournaments, sportfishing, or the art of the film. Once on returning to the living room, William said he wished he had "a long and plumy tail to drape across one arm for making entrances."

All this was taking place against a melancholy and unmentionable background of disappointment in the bedroom. In 1903, just before their wedding, William was both pleased and disconcerted to discover that his innocent fiancée, already twenty-five, had not the slightest notion of what she was letting herself in for by marrying a man. Maternal instruction, girlish gossip, conversation

among the ladies, even the otherwise comprehensive teachings of
Henry George, not one had treated the topic of carnal knowledge.
As politely as he could, William explained the brutal facts. Anna
was horrified. She said of course as a married woman she would
do her duty. William hoped that wifely duty would soon give way
to marital bliss as his bride learned to feel the same burning desire
for him that he felt for her. To make a sad story short, she didn't.
It was love's old bittersweet Victorian song once more. She loved
her husband very much, enough to want to make him happy even
in that way, but animal passions and erotic arts were culturally and
personally beyond her. At fifty she would still be proud of knowing
"nothing about sex." Dutifully, devotedly, unresponsively she
gave him what she thought he wanted and didn't understand why
he often seemed unhappy. William didn't know what to do. He
knew she loved him with all her heart, as he loved her in return,
and love, he thought, even in marriage to a gentle lady would
welcome, exalt, and glorify those powerful, primitive feelings one
couldn't really talk about to a gentle lady. At first he was hurt,
then he was enraged. In Hollywood (if not before) he discovered
what modern women did in marriage or out of it, with or without
love, about primitive feelings.

In moviemaking, William wrote, "a close bond should exist between writer and director." He didn't go on to say that if the writer
was a woman the bond could be especially close. Before Clara
Beranger came from New York to be the last of his lady writers,
nine of William's films had been written by Olga Printzlau, a small,
round, artistic woman, who made charcoal drawings of pretty feminine faces and was raising a little daughter without a visible husband. An accomplished scenarist, Olga was in demand at several
of the studios and wrote some of William's better films, including
Conrad in Quest of His Youth.

When William's liaisons became known to Anna, she was distraught. Arguments crackled behind closed doors, where the children couldn't hear. She told him that if such a thing ever became
common knowledge, she would have to leave him. She wasn't
going to compromise. She would never put up with mistresses the
way Constance did—entertaining them in her house! Then William fell in love with Clara Beranger, and for the first time it wasn't

just an affair. Clara was his refuge, understood him, brought him peace. Anna said he must choose between them. The three of them met in anguish to sort it out. Clara told Anna her marriage had obviously come to an end and she should give it up gracefully. Anna told Clara that her husband continued to share her bed and was her frequent lover. Clara felt betrayed. The man she had thought she was rescuing was sleeping with his supposed tormentor!

Anna took her daughters, Agnes twenty, Margaret seventeen, and went to Europe—"a sad and dreadful journey," Agnes recalled. When they came back, William met them at the train. He told Anna he had given Clara up, he had given all other women up, he would be her faithful, loving husband from now on. For a year William and Clara didn't work together, and Anna was very happy. "But the galling old differences continued," Agnes said. Neither of them could change. And Clara, he knew, was waiting for him—the calm, able collaborator, who loved him exactly as he was and didn't try to drive him every day to greater heights, who was no other man's prophet, who shared his thoughts and welcomed his primitive feelings. He didn't want to live the rest of his life without her.

To the day of her death twenty years later Anna didn't understand what had gone wrong with her marriage, how she had driven her husband away. "Indeed," Agnes said, "she never learned anything about human living." After William left her, Anna never spoke to him again. William remembered their early love and often felt the pain and guilt of the separation. Years of psychoanalysis didn't heal his daughters' wounds, though Margaret put on a good front. It wasn't enough that their father had always wanted a son, that until they were nine he had called them "the boys" in letters to their mother—"How are my fellers? Kiss my boys good night." Now he had abandoned them altogether. For two years Agnes also didn't speak to her father, and it was never the same between them. She felt he had never had time for her, had never loved her enough. No father would ever love her enough. She was alone in the world with her mother and her ballet career.

In 1927, using his light-tackle Vom Hofe rod and reel, Uncle William caught a fifty-five-pound albacore, still a record at the

Tuna Club in Avalon, where sportfishing history began. I saw it
there on the wall sixty-six years later, and his yellow dolphin fish,
another record at thirty-two pounds. In honor of his angling and
of their brotherly affection, Father ordered a special Christmas
present for William, a white marble ashtray big enough for his
cigars—he always smoked cigars—with three red metal tuna
swimming above its edge. Christmas 1928 Uncle William and our
new Aunt Clara came to the house along with many friends and
family members. I was glad to see them. I had seen Uncle William
only a few times before. He didn't say anything to me, but I liked
to watch him and listen to his mellow voice and smell the aroma
of his fine cigars. Among the guests was Billy Buckland, son of
Wilfred Buckland, Belasco's art director in New York and Father's
in Hollywood. At seventeen Billy had grown suddenly tall and
handsome. "Hello, Billy," everyone said. "Hello, Billy." Smiling
modestly, Billy stood in front of the fireplace, next to Uncle William. As a boy, Father had called his brother Billy. In the age-old
manner of elders who don't put themselves into children's shoes,
Father pressed the precious fraternal token into my hands, saying:
"This is a present for your Uncle Billy. You can take it over to
him."

Though I was only six, I was not a dunce. I knew my own Uncle
William from the fresh-faced youth standing next to him, who was
apparently now to be called not simply Billy but Uncle Billy—to
whom I straightway presented the year's most significant gift.
"This is for you, Uncle Billy," I said.

Two or three persons looked up in alarm. Stammering and
blushing, Billy said it wasn't for him—but one of the marks of the
gracious hostess is that she tries to put every guest at ease. To put
blushing Billy at ease, Mother graciously declared that the unique
trophy was indeed intended for him—known as a skillful tennis
player, never seen to catch a fish or smoke a fine cigar, quite unlike
the champion fisherman standing next to him smoking a cigar—
and he should happily accept it. Powerless to reverse this triumph
of etiquette over good sense, several persons stared in dismay. I
knew I had made a mistake. Helplessly, Billy took the ashtray,
said how beautiful it was, and set it down gingerly on a table.
When he departed, he tactfully forgot to take it with him.

From the first ripple of this barely detectable disturbance on the surface of Christmas cheer, Uncle William, as was his wont, rose above the embarrassment, studiously ignoring both a nephew's surprising failure to recognize his uncle and a brother's loving—and in better circumstances heartwarming—tribute, which rested unclaimed on that table all during my childhood and was there decades later on the day when Uncle William died from smoking many fine cigars without it. I felt a twinge whenever I saw it. Why, I wondered, couldn't my mistake be corrected? A hearty laugh all round at the foolishness of a child should have been enough. No one answered that question. No one spoke of the ashtray again. Father, and Uncle William, must have been very disappointed.

The Cat That Walks by Himself

Sometimes I felt like a stranger in the house. Brother John wouldn't sing on key. Sister Cecilia said "Goodbye" when I sat down next to her. For my fifth Christmas they gave me a yellow airplane to ride in. The steering chain was installed wrong. When I turned right, the plane went left. When I turned left, the plane went right. I flew into a rage, got off, and never got on again. No one tried to fix the chain. No one peered into the works. No one asked why I didn't ride in my yellow airplane. No one noticed that I didn't. I was too proud to ask for help.

Natalie came on the train from Chicago with a big box from Marshall Field. She and Katie were best friends at the Hollywood School for Girls. They brought the box to my room and stood together in the doorway eagerly watching as I took the lid off. Inside was a toy Swiss village—little houses, little trees, little people, little carts. Instead of branches, twigs, and leaves the trees had diminishing circles of wood painted shiny green. I sat on the floor and cried. Natalie was a very nice girl but I didn't want Art Deco trees. I wanted someone I could talk to the way Tommy Stubbins could talk to Doctor Dolittle, the way Urashima had talked to the Princess under the Sea. They took the village away. Mother was disappointed. She said, "Marshall Field has such wonderful toys."

I liked to play with John's old toys. They wouldn't give me his pre-Depression four-hundred-dollar wide-gauge electric train which covered a floor twelve by fourteen feet with bridges, switches, flapping signals, two giant engines, and foot-long cars for passengers and freight, but I could play with his World War I tank, which roared across the carpet till it came to the end of its cord and pulled the plug out of the wall. From that battered old sparking tank I had my first hundred-and-ten-volt shock, more impressive by far than puny little twelve-volt tingles from my dinky electric train. With my train transformer and some carbons Father brought me from the studio I rigged a carbon arc and stared in admiration at its blinding brilliance. My central vision came back in less than half an hour. At 6 a.m. on the Fourth of July I lit salutes and cherry bombs and blew great holes in the lawn without losing even a finger. Father, who was a patriot, didn't say I had started too early. I climbed to the top of a redwood tree and shouted hello to Mother. She told me to "come down this *instant*!" She said it was very dangerous to do that. Next time I didn't shout.

Father shaved with murky brown water brought in gallon jugs from the harbor at San Pedro where the water was soft and just right for shaving. He lathered his face with a brush and pot and hardly ever cut himself. One day stepping out of the bath he saw me staring at his penis. He said I shouldn't do that. He said men didn't look at other men's private parts. He knew, of course, that some male persons liked to look at other male persons' parts, but he didn't call such persons men. Ashamed, I looked at the floor. To a child Father's taboo organ (even in repose) seemed wondrously large. Sixty-five years later my opinion of it hasn't changed. I have been told by a lady whose opinion I respect that women don't care about that sort of thing, but a popular female psychologist on the radio declares emphatically they do, so I'm documenting Father's organ for whatever credit it may bring him.

According to Agnes both de Mille brothers, Uncle William and Father, suffered from nineteenth-century bad taste in visual art, aggravated in Father's case by a failure to outgrow adolescent sexual fantasies. We dare not take this judgment lightly. Agnes was the outstanding aesthete of the family and had been to a psychoanalyst. In Father's bedroom hung a painting of the Lorelei, a

plump, toothsome, naked nymph perched on a mossy rock by a
Viennese painter named Hans Makart. Sharing Father's regrettable
immaturity and bad taste, I stood and looked at that dear girl and
longed to meet a girl just like her. Cecilia despised her as a whore
and urged Father to show good taste by throwing her out of Mother's house. He declined to do so. Downstairs on a wall of the living
room hung a post-Rubens portrayal of Silenus, a fat, drunken, naked old roué menacing a pitiful, naked young woman, on whom
he had apparently fathered a pair of naked, suckling twins. She
was lovely, they were cute, he was repulsive. Cecilia hated that
picture and what it said to her about the most loved, least con-
trollable, most annoying man in her life, but randy old Silenus
stubbornly stood his ground, a daily affront to Cecilia and to the
modest Dutch housewife quietly sewing on a nearby wall (painted
by Jozef Israels but sold to Father as a Vandyke). Cecilia didn't
collect paintings. She took pleasure in owning stallions. They were
headstrong randy brutes over whose sex life she had complete
control.

Glued to my Brunswick radio, I followed the ingenious career
of Rajput the Hindu Detective, sponsored by Dr. Strasska's tooth-
paste, which came in clove and cinnamon. I sent in box tops from
Post Toasties and received in the mail my Inspector Post Detective Kit, using which I searched for clues all about the house. A
coup occurred when I was eleven. Mother neglected to block my
view while opening the wine vault. Indeed, she asked me to hold
the flashlight, a security violation Father would never have permitted. As she spun the dial, I memorized the combination. After
that I opened the vault and went in whenever I liked. Nobody
saw me. One day Mother mislaid her copy of the combination, and
I told her the numbers. With an edge in her voice, she asked how
I had learned them. I said I had watched her turning the dial. One
of the ladies who came to tea complimented Mother on what a
smart boy I was. Mother said she thought I might be a little too
smart for my own good. Frederick the butler overheard and
couldn't resist the fun of repeating the comment to me. I was
annoyed. How could anyone be too smart for his own good? (I
found out at boarding school.) Aunt Rebecca said I was the cat
that walks by himself. That was better.

Four newspapers came to our house and twenty-five magazines: *Spur, Sportsman, Sportologue, Vogue, Vanity Fair, Harper's Bazaar*; shiny pages on house and garden, deserts, igloos, Scottish glens, bare brown jungle boobs, painting, sculpture, architecture, theater. Humor was my specialty, and I studied the cartoons in *Judge, Ballyhoo,* and *The New Yorker.* Some were easy, some were hard, some had me stumped. No one offered guidance, and I didn't ask for any. This was in the years with Ross, Gardner Rea, Rea Irvin, Gluyas Williams, Sidney Hoff, O. Soglow, R. Taylor, Charles Addams, William Steig. In the gentle society spoofs of Helen Hokinson I recognized Mother and Aunt Rebecca. Peter Arno pioneered sex education. James Thurber and George Price were masters of absurd family relations. I took them all as my teachers.

Cecilia came back from Italy and reported that *Mew-saleeny* had made the trains run on time. I told her it was *Moose-oleeny.* She wouldn't change the way she said it. She claimed to have heard an *ear-curdling* shriek. I said, "You mean a *blood-splitting* shriek, don't you?" She didn't even smile. Not that she didn't have a sense of humor. Gladys Rosson's brothers, Arthur and Hal, were movie directors. They looked alike, and I never knew which was which. After Arthur died, I was afraid to speak to Hal for fear of calling him Hal if he was really Arthur. "That's no problem," said Cecilia. "Hal is here, Arthur is absent." She smiled a tiny, careful smile. At dinner Mother announced, "For dessert we are going to put cheese on apple." It was fingernails on the blackboard. I said it should be a *piece* of cheese on a *piece* of apple. She continued to say "put cheese on apple." Father said socialist professors were *swaydo-intellectuals.* No one corrected *him.*

At sixteen I put my solitude into verse and proudly showed the lines to Mother. She read them intently. Then she said:

"Where did you get this?"

"I wrote it."

"You couldn't have written this," she said. "Only a much older person could have written it. You must have copied it from a book."

I pushed her out of my room. She complained to Father. He came to my room and said that if I wanted to go on living in that house I would treat Mother with respect. It was a shock. I had seen Father's terrifying histrionic explosions of temper at the studio, a deliberate leadership technique picked up from Belasco, but he didn't do that at home, and in sixteen years he had never spoken angrily to me. I was afraid to defend myself. I didn't tell him about the poem or how Mother had insulted me. I nodded humbly and said I would. "How do you feel about your mother?" he asked. I mumbled that I loved her. It was a lie. Father said that was good, and I should make sure she knew it. I said I would.

At school I read *The Three-Cornered Hat*, a charming comic Spanish novel, which had seemed rather naughty to Spanish ladies of 1873, the year Mother was born. I bought a copy, had it bound in red leather, and gave it to her without warning. She was surprised. She was touched. She said it was sweet of me to give it to her. She read it and said she liked it very much. She said she would always treasure it. After that I loved her a little, but I never showed her anything more I had written. By the time my first story was published, she could no longer read.

In the midst of directing *Union Pacific*, Father was rushed to the hospital, where at fifty-seven he was rudely separated from his prostate gland. For a short time he did his directing from a stretcher. For a much longer time he complained about the surgeon. From the drift of his complaints I gathered that his taboo organ was no longer up to snuff, an inference never confirmed to me by any lady in a position to know. The following year, a large, round, sinister lump appeared practically overnight on his index finger. The surgeon (not the same one) said it had to come right off, or Father might lose his finger or his life. As it happened, he didn't lose either, but these close encounters with weaknesses of the flesh and bone turned his attention to loose ends needing to be tied up. One morning I was visiting him in the bathroom. (Father held conferences in the bathroom. Mr. Treacy, who kept track of Father's stocks and bonds, would come every weekday morning from his office in the West Wing to stand in the doorway giving the latest market prices, while Father in the bathtub would balance the risks and allocations.) From the tub Father told me he had instructed Neil McCarthy, his lawyer since 1914, to draw up adoption papers, so that if anything happened to him I would have legal status in the family. This was completely unexpected, and

when Neil filed the petition, a reporter asked the question I had
been too polite to ask: Why had he waited so long? Neil explained
that I had become "so much a part of the family" that the legal
formalities had simply slipped their minds. Hearing this ridiculous
excuse, the reporter missed his chance to ask: Why didn't they do
it right away, *before* it slipped their minds?

A social worker came to the house and asked me whether I had
been mistreated there in any way. Discounting minor molestation
by Frederick the butler when I was four (fully but tastefully described elsewhere), I said I hadn't. Mother and Father and I sat
before Judge Scheinman of the Superior Court, while Neil Mc-
Carthy solemnly averred that the aforesaid minor had been deserted without identification, and therefore consent of his parents,
whoever they may have been, was not required. Ammama could
easily have told the judge the names of the missing parents, two
fine people, both of whom she had known very well, but she had
died the previous November. Judge Scheinman didn't ask why the
matter had waited so long. Declaring that the Court was now fully
informed, he decreed that from now on I would be treated in all
respects as Mother and Father's lawful child and my name would
be Richard de Mille. As it had been for eighteen years.

Father didn't urge me to go to any particular college, but after
I picked Columbia he revealed that his father and his brother and
his great-uncle Richard had all gone to Columbia, where they had
won honors. He said he was sure I would follow in their footsteps.
He said: "You're like your Uncle William. He is the scholar of the
family."

At college my hairline receded a bit. Father said it was bound
to happen. He pointed to his own bald pate. He said his father
and his brother had lost their hair early in life. "You'll be bald at
twenty-five," he told me. The implication was clear: I was related
to him by blood. Perhaps he was even my father. I wondered
which of his lady friends could have been my mother. I hoped it
wasn't one of the three I already knew about—not that they
weren't all very nice—but I had in mind someone more like Gloria
Swanson, Blanche Sweet, or Leatrice Joy. Sad to say, Claudette
Colbert, smashing as Cleopatra, was a bit too young.

One day during World War II, while I was still living at home,

I found the glass door to the West Wing locked. The view into Father's office was shrouded by a sheet. Banging and scraping could be heard. I was only a little surprised. A secret construction project was quite in keeping with our custom of releasing information only to those with a need to know. There was a lot of sensitive information in our family, especially in the West Wing, where Gladys managed Father's personal affairs. Father and Gladys, of course, needed to know everything. Mother and Cecilia needed to know most things. John and Katherine and I and the servants needed to know very little. This made perfectly good sense as a security policy, but I never liked it and, applying the skills I had learned from Rajput the Hindu Detective and Inspector Post, I kept a sharp lookout for gaps in security.

After several days Father's office was open once more. Inside everything looked normal. Shelves, books, boards, panels, ceiling, floor, windows—nothing was amiss. I went out to the patio and noticed a bush covered with white dust. A stucco wall looked brighter. Otherwise—but wait. I saw a bulge in the wall where fuchsias used to grow. I went inside and matched the bulge with an ornately carved panel. I grasped the carving and pulled. The panel swung out. Behind was a black steel door. Behind that was an empty safe. I sat down at Father's desk, penned a message on a pad printed with his name, laid the message in the safe, and closed everything up tight. Monday morning Gladys proudly took Joe Harper in to see her brand-new super-secret safe. Because he was now Cecilia's husband, Joe had a need to know about it. As the steel door swung back, they caught sight of an impish face peering over a wall and a motto popular with our troops: *Kilroy was here.* Joe couldn't stop laughing, but Gladys didn't think it was funny. She never mentioned it to me, and we remained good friends, but Joe said she never put anything into that safe.

At twenty-four, after the war, I wanted to work for Father as a writer, but he wouldn't have it. He didn't approve of nepotism. Katherine had done very well in her profession without his help, and he wanted me to do the same. There were other reasons. He thought I was too analytical to have dramatic ideas. He knew I wasn't submissive enough to work for a man like him. Father was known for giving his writers hell, and he didn't think I would stand for that. He didn't want to ruin everything between us.

At thirty-three I married the beautiful, talented Margaret Belgrano, whose cousin General Manuel Belgrano was a founder of Argentina. We saw Cousin Manuel in Genoa last year, sitting on his horse in Tommaseo Square, but we haven't been down to see him in Argentina. Maybe there is still time. At the wedding Father was best man. Mother, eighty-two, was there with a companion. After the ceremony, Mother gripped the hand of the startled bride, stared into her widening eyes, and said in that still deep theatrical voice: "You've *stolen* my *son*!" Despite being the cat that walked by himself, I was still her little kitten. Carefully prying her fingers open, I was surprised at how strong they were.

CHAPTER 5

The Funeral

After the movie business gave Uncle William up, he and Aunt Clara lived in a Spanish California house on the seaward slope at Playa del Rey, where they enjoyed a commanding view of Santa Monica Bay. I was in their house three times. The first time, when I was a boy, Uncle William played his Bert Williams records for me. Bert Williams was a Negro vaudeville comedian popular in 1903, when the world had been Uncle William's oyster pleading to be opened by his dramaturgic pen. Sounding a bit like Louis Armstrong, Bert Williams sang: "I'll lend you my coat, I'll lend you my hat, I'll lend you anything I've got—'cept my wife. And I'll make you a present of her!" Uncle William laughed. He wasn't thinking of Aunt Clara.

Clara's father, Benjamin Strauss, had immigrated from Germany. He and two brothers opened a dry-goods store in Indiana. As they were telling the painter what name to put on the sign, the painter said: "*Strauss*—what kind of name is that?" Benjamin answered indignantly: "Simple—it rhymes with mouse." Later when they went outside to inspect the sign, it said *Strouse's Dry Goods*. The newly named Benjamin Strouse gave his name to Fannie Kahn, and soon they went to Baltimore, where their daughter Clara was born and where Strouse's Department Store made a lot of money, some of which Clara would inherit. Clara married Albert Berwanger and had a daughter named Frances, but the marriage didn't last. When Clara began to write, she changed Berwanger to Beranger. In 1921 Clara went to Hollywood, where Frances, twelve years old, met her future stepfather and liked him right away. I didn't see Frances at Playa del Rey, because by then she was full-grown, a tall gorgeous brunette actress playing the other woman (feminine leads were played by blondes) on the New York stage.

During the 1930s William's hard-won movie fortune was cheerfully confiscated by the very public servants he had counted on to teach unselfishness to businessmen. A government democratically elected by the people (one doesn't know whether or not they were good and thoughtful like William) "took away all his savings, every penny," Agnes said. Cecil, in contrast, didn't trust the government and hired lawyers to protect him from its lessons in economic justice. After a long legal fight, which ended in the Supreme Court, he managed to beat off the government's relentless and unflagging—though, of course, selfless and high-minded—attempts to teach him it was selfish, greedy, and unfair for a mere private citizen to accumulate capital, thumb his nose at central planning, and provide nongovernment jobs for electricians, technicians, carpenters, painters, cowboys, Indians, seamstresses, and actors. Father couldn't seem to get this idea through his head, and never really understood that he was doing wrong. In his heyday William could have hired the same lawyers, but he trusted the people's democratic government and took no defensive measures. In consequence, a dire confluence of divorce, Depression, career failure, and unchained revenue enhancers brought him to financial ruin. Clara had plenty for both of them and was glad to pay the bills, but William didn't like taking a single dollar he hadn't earned. He felt quite bad about it.

In other respects William wasn't nearly so hard on himself. "He always did just what he wanted to do," Frances remembered.

In the late thirties, when William was writing *Hollywood Saga*, he and Mother took a house on the New Jersey shore at Mantoloking. I was in New York, and used to come on weekends. Cornelia Runyon lived close by, and she invited the three of us to a cocktail party. William hated parties and refused to go. Mother and I went to the party, and Mother told Cornelia William was sorry he couldn't come, but he was working so hard on his book. During the party Cornelia walked out on her back porch, and there was William on the beach surf casting. He was mad about surf casting. Cornelia thought it was very funny, but Mother said, "Oh *God*!"

After *Hollywood Saga* was published, William had no prospects. On her own, Clara appealed to Father, who suddenly discovered that he needed William to write a scenario for *The Queen of Queens*, a story about the Virgin Mary in a family setting. William was not the obvious choice to write about the Mother of God. He only tolerated transcendent, supernatural beliefs, like the divinity of Christ, whom he humanistically if politely called "one of the world's greatest philosophers." William's visions of Paradise were immanent and earthly, like the just society or theater owned by the people. *The Queen of Queens* was never produced, because Catholic prelates objected to showing the Blessed Virgin as the mother of several children, all but one conceived in the ordinary way. I was disappointed, having hoped to see the angelic Loretta Young in the role.

The following year William entered on a new career that would employ his skills as teacher and director and suit his lately lowered expectations of wealth and fame. He was appointed chairman of the new Drama Department at the University of Southern California, where Clara taught screenwriting. Cecil, who helped to create the post by endowing the department, had mixed feelings about it, which he didn't mention to William. On the one hand, he pitied William for his impracticality and reluctance to fight for his place in the sun. On the other, he admired him for his intellect and learning. He often said, with a self-depreciating smile: "If I had William's mind, there is nothing I couldn't do." On the surface it was a compliment, but lurking beneath was the proud if sad implication: If my dear intellectual brother had my warrior spirit and rigorous self-discipline, he wouldn't be teaching in a college; he would be conquering the world, as I in my modest way am doing, even with the poor mind I've got, which apparently, if the truth be told, isn't so bad after all.

Putting the world behind him, William immersed himself in the academic life. He taught two courses, one in the structure of drama, the other in acting. Directing two plays a year, in the Belasco tradition with a touch of movie technique, he favored traditional plays. He didn't care for experiments like theater in the round. He didn't think Tennessee Williams was really a playwright. To the students William was a fascinating antique, imparting soon to be lost wisdom from an earlier time. He did just what he wanted to do, and enjoyed doing it. He took great pride in his meticulous productions, where he had complete control and didn't have to put up with movie supervisors or their creeping mice. Every day he smoked eight or ten cigars. Before lunch he had a double martini, after lunch a beer. It didn't seem to interfere with his work in the afternoon. At home, he complained that Clara was measuring out the martinis with an eyedropper. He did get one or two worrisome traffic tickets. Feeling some discomfort, he went to Clara's brother, Dr. Solomon Strouse. Even after the radium pellets were inserted in his throat, he insisted on having his highball and cigar. Clara hid her tears and gave him what he wanted.

William was a perfectionist, which is right for an artist, but he lacked the iron will that sustains the flagging spirit, the boldness that beats down opposition, the wily persistence that flanks the enemy line. He fell back. He settled for less. "Spoiled rotten by his mother," Agnes said, but that hardly explains it. Cecil was pampered and praised by the same mother. A key may be found in Agnes's description of the artist: The successful artist submits himself to "relentless discipline." He is "driven without respite." He finds happiness in the "untiring race." His life is ruled by his purpose, and his purpose is his work. He is subject to good and bad luck but doesn't count on either. He asks no guarantee of success and gives no excuse for failure. He believes in himself. He doesn't give up. And, of course, he has talent. William had talent and believed in himself, but he didn't submit to relentless discipline, was not driven without respite. Beneath his courtly restraint, he was immensely proud. He saw himself as a prince of the pen, and when the "masterminds of finance" neglected to kneel before him, he abdicated and went into academic exile. Except for double martinis with a beer chaser, he gave no sign of discontent, of longing for past glories. Lunching with a colleague during thirteen pleasant years, he didn't talk about the past. He talked about current politics and needed social reforms. Boating in the channel, he lured and landed albacore, yellowtail, and bass. He played remarkably good tennis. He made brilliant, amusing after-dinner speeches and received the instant reward of laughter and applause. He didn't try to write anything new, not a history, not a novel, not a movie, not a play. Agnes said: "He sank into self-indulgence and never again made the grand effort toward his real work."

Cecil was a stoic. He suffered slings and arrows with small surprise and brief indignation. He didn't sulk in his tent. He said: "The more I see of people, the better I like dogs." He took the world as he found it and did his best in it every day, going from triumph to defeat and back again to triumph. He lived his life at full speed. From youth William played the role of the wise old man, but in some respects he was not so wise as his vigorous, flamboyant, resolute little brother.

One battle William did wage. After three years of beating the enemy back, he was resting at his beloved Avalon. Boats were bobbing in the harbor. Chimes were ringing from the hill. His pen glided across the paper. For the first time in thirty-five years, he wrote to his brother, he would not be going out sportfishing. At the university, he would take a lighter load. He hated to give up directing plays, but he was forced to recognize that cancer is a tricky enemy. He had been deeply touched by Cecil's affectionate letter, which showed him that the steady bond between them had not been weakened through those many years by superficial differences of opinion or by the frequent attempts of others to put them into opposition. More than ever he felt that they were working for the same end, a free and secure America. What did it matter that they were taking slightly different roads? He was grateful that time and circumstance had been powerless to change their fraternal ties, which meant so much to him.

Who were those who had so frequently tried to put William and Cecil into opposition? They were William's friends on the left. In 1952 America was torn by a war of political ideas and by fear of terrible new weapons. In only four years the Soviets had managed to build an atom bomb. How could they have done it so quickly without help from traitors in the United States? A Democrat in the White House had imposed a loyalty oath on decent American citizens. The Un-American Activities Committee would hold hearings in Los Angeles. According to Agnes, Cecil telephoned William more than once "to alert him about Reds on his faculty and order him to fire them forthwith."

"Oh *heavens*!" Frances said. "I don't think Cecil *ever* told William what to do! I mean, he would *never* do that, any more than William would."

But Cecil had a commanding way about him and a stern view of the nation's enemies. William was only mildly alarmed by excesses of the Communist Revolution. He had faith in the Russian people—"as Russia settles into her stride"—to conduct their social experiment in "a less insistently propagandist" way. To Cecil the Soviet Union was a land of two hundred million hungry, ragged political prisoners working long hours to provide roast lamb, warm coats, and private bedrooms for two million unelected bureaucrats. The main difference Cecil saw between the Soviets and the Nazis was that the Nazis were gone and the Soviets were still here. On the domestic front, William believed in listening to all sides of an argument, confident that truth would prevail in the marketplace of ideas. Cecil believed that Communists in America were not qualified to teach in a university because they preferred doctrine to truth, advocacy to scholarship, fake constitutional republics to real ones, and a hostile foreign power to the United States. William returned to the university just in time to see his production assistant, Janet Stevenson, named before the Committee as a member of the Communist Party. Frances had worked with Janet Stevenson in one of Hollywood's progressive political organizations:

I knew Janet very well, but I didn't know she was a Communist. I mean, I was never on the *left*. I was very active in the Democratic Party. I served on the State Central Committee and was a district chairman in both Stevenson campaigns. I was quite startled to learn that anyone *I* knew was a real live Communist. I guess I was naive. Janet once asked me at a meeting if I would join the Party, and like an idiot I

said, 'What party?' I do know William was very relieved when
she resigned of her own accord. I think William and Cecil
sidestepped their political differences and always treated each
other with respect and affection. William may have thought
it was silly of Cecil not to pay the dollar to the radio union,
but he respected him for his principles. I remember his saying that.

When it became clear that Uncle William was not going to defeat his final enemy, Father urged me to go and see him, along
with my son from my first marriage, a boy I had named William
Cecil after both of them. It wasn't a cheerful meeting, because my
uncle was fatally ill and young William, nine years old, had mus-
cular dystrophy and was in a wheelchair. Soon after that, Margaret
Belgrano agreed to marry me. Father was delighted with his prospective daughter-in-law and told her in confidence that I was "a
real de Mille," something he had also said to my first wife. He
didn't tell either of them just what "a real de Mille" was or how
I had become one. He called Uncle William and told him the good
news. Sick as he was, Uncle William wanted to meet Margaret.
Clara said we could stay with him only a few minutes. We climbed
the stairs to his study, where we found him sitting in an armchair.
Though he wasn't smoking, the air smelled of tobacco. He looked
us over carefully and smiled. He welcomed Margaret into the family. He asked me about my plans. He didn't allude to his illness.
We didn't play his Bert Williams records. He didn't bring up the
incident of the white marble ashtray. He made some kindly wise
old comments. Clara appeared in the doorway, and it was time to
go. In March 1955 Uncle William died at seventy-six. The last
person to see him alive was Frances's seven-year-old son, who
reported that Poppi had said: "They tell me it's a nice day"—
fitting words from a man who loved life and knew it would go on
without him.

Father asked me if I wanted to go to the funeral with him. I
said I didn't like funerals. He was disappointed, but he left it up
to me. I had my reasons, all of them bad. I didn't want to be
oppressed by religious folderol. I knew my son wouldn't live, and
I didn't want to hear pious talk about God's mercy. Though I had

always liked Uncle William, I had never been close to him. I wasn't thinking of Father. He had lost his only brother, the companion and teacher of his youth, the comrade of his pioneer days. He wanted me to come with him and pay my respects and be seen to pay them. He was right, and I was wrong. He didn't say I was wrong, and he didn't hold it against me.

Services were at Pierce Brothers Mortuary in Inglewood. Two hundred people crowded the small chapel. Hollywood notables included Father's friend Jesse Lasky and William's friend Joseph Mankiewicz. University colleagues were led by Chancellor Rufus B. von KleinSmid and Vice President Albert Raubenheimer. Father's lawyer, Neil McCarthy, was there. Frank Reicher, the actor, William's chum since 1906, leaned over and whispered to Frances: "An excellent house. William would be pleased." Brief words were spoken by the pastor of Christ Church Unity, Clara's church. Next day the ashes were placed in an urn at the Cecil B. DeMille Memorial in Hollywood Cemetery. Some years before, when establishing the memorial, Father had telephoned William in Playa del Rey. William came back from the phone, struck a dramatic pose, and announced to Clara and Frances: "Well, I've got it made at last! Cecil invited me to be buried in the family plot."

At graveside, Frances and her husband stood with Clara, Agnes, Father, and Cecilia. Agnes had come out from New York. Years later Frances told me about it:

Cecilia turned to me and said: "The de Milles certainly have longevity." I said something dumb like "Yes, and continuity of love." Agnes snapped: "Well, *you* should *know!*" I was stunned. After the ceremony Frank Reicher and Dr. Raubenheimer came back with us to the house. Mother went upstairs to rest, and Rauby poured us all a drink in the living room. He put his arm around me and said: "We shall miss him—I as a friend and colleague, and you as his daughter." I think he just forgot that Agnes was in the room. She banged her drink down on the table, stalked out, and slammed the door. Later she heard me refer to William as "Poppi." It was a Chekhov thing, the way she exploded at me. "I know you

care about him," she said, "but you're not really his daughter,
and I am his firstborn." I was already in a state of shock, and
that finished me off. She was frigid to me for years. I realize
now that she had plenty to feel frigid about. I had been in
the nest a long, long time, many years when she would have
liked to be there. I was a real pain in the neck when I was a
teenager, and William was marvelous to me. I used to go into
his study and talk about my inner life, and he understood
me. She didn't have much of that. He wasn't as good a father
to her as he was to me.

R: He was older and happier in his second marriage.
F: Yes, and he was a tremendous person. I wish you could
   have known him better.
R: And you were an easier daughter than Agnes.
F: *That's* hard to believe! [Laughing] I was *wild*. We won't go
   into *that*.
R: How did you make peace with Agnes?
F: Well, she wanted it. I was in New York and called her up
   as usual, just as a gesture. This time she sounded wistful,
   as if she'd like to see me. So I went to see her. Later,
   when she had her stroke, I think it made her more mellow. She came to San Francisco and called me from the
   Clift Hotel and asked me to come over. There were just
   the two of us in this big empty dining room. We talked for
   a long time. And once she gave me a photograph of herself
   on which she had written, "For Frances, who has been
   through the wars alongside me, in tribute to her fidelity
   and courage, with lifetime love." I have it on the wall.
R: She wished it had really been that way.
F: I think so. We buried the hatchet, more or less. But I was
   never close to her the way I was to Maggie [William's
   daughter Margaret]. Maggie was a love.

A few months after William died, his heartbroken widow died.
This time Father and I went to the funeral together. I was glad
to go. We had talked in the meantime about some family matters.

Soon after Uncle William's funeral, I found Father sitting at his desk in the West Wing.

"Stay a moment," he said. "I want to tell you about your parents."

That was a surprise. Except for the adoption proceeding, when I was eighteen, my lost parents hadn't been mentioned since Ammama told me not to worry about them when I was eight. Now I was thirty-three.

"Before you were born," Father said, "your Uncle William and I agreed that whichever of us died first, the other would tell you about your parents. Your father was your Uncle William. Your mother was a writer. This is a book she wrote." He handed me a slim black volume. The title was odd: *Doorways in Drumorty*. Inside was an inscription: "To my friend William de Mille, very tenderly, Lorna Moon." It wasn't a name I recognized or remembered hearing before.

CHAPTER 6

Twilight of DeMille

Father told me very little about Lorna Moon. She was my mother. She was dead. She had written a book. He didn't tell me many things he knew perfectly well—for example, that she had come to Hollywood at his invitation to join his writing staff a year before I was born. To be fair, I wasn't ready to learn it. In a few seconds my whole family had stepped through the looking glass to the other side, where everything worked backwards. Father, whose boy I wanted to be, whose boy I often suspected I was, had now become my uncle, and Uncle William, whom I barely knew, was now my father. Sister Cecilia was now my cousin, but sister Katie was still my sister because we were both adopted. Agnes and Margaret, cousins for thirty-three years, were now my sisters, and I hadn't even begun to reckon up my aunts.

Once more I felt angry about being kept in the dark, an understandable reaction but not a correct position from a security standpoint. For his time and place, Father lived an unconventional life, and it was our duty not to give aid and comfort to gossip-mongers. In turn, Father was protecting the members of the family, me as much as anyone else. Early in 1921 Lorna Moon had helped Jeanie Macpherson and Beulah Marie Dix write *The Affairs of Anatol*, a spicy boudoir comedy "suggested by" Arthur Schnitzler's play and featuring flaming vamps like "Satan Synne, the wickedest woman in New York." The day the picture opened in New York, eight thousand persons in Los Angeles were viewing the body of pretty Virginia Rappe fatally injured at an orgy hosted by Paramount's Prince of Whales, comedian Fatty Arbuckle. Ten days before I was born, Paramount director William Desmond Taylor was murdered in his porno-cocaine love nest. William de Mille helped carry the coffin. A real DeMille born on the wrong side of the flaming camera would if discovered by the press be stripped to his blushing birthday suit and ritually circumscribed with painful, cutting headlines.

DEMILLE WRITER CONCEIVES SHORT SUBJECT
NINE MONTHS IN THE MAKING
Anatol Didn't Have All the Affairs

Naked truth would be swaddled in romantic falsehood.

C. B. DEMILLE ADOPTS OWN SON!
MATERNAL MOONSHINER BOOTLEGGED BOY
Abandoned Baby Concocted by Lawyer

Father's later, religious films would only make things worse.

BIBLE BARNUM'S MORALS PROBED
MOSES FORBIDS, ZUKOR RETHINKS
Busted Commandment Could Break Contract

Family relations would be strained.

C. B. DENIES SINFUL PATERNITY!
BROTHER WAS FATHER, LAWYER REVEALS
No Flies on Us, Says Showman's Daughter

The reckless would be called to account, the innocent would suffer, the betrayed would take a righteous stand.

PLAYWRIGHT WANTED SON, NOT BABY
SONLESS EX-WIFE IN HEART ATTACK
Boy Still Cousin, Dancer Says

Uncle William had not always trod the straight and narrow any more than Father had. Aunt Anna would have been devastated to learn that he had a son with another woman. Mother was an Adams and above reproach, but Cecilia was spooked by the sexual conduct of the de Mille men and feared for their and her good name. She was president not only of the Junior League but of the Thoroughbred Breeders Association. She specialized in breeding and reputation. Anyway, why should I complain about being kept in the dark? I was living in the movie *Great Expectations*, a marvelous mystery story, and here was another exciting reel. All the same, I was not pleased. I said:

"I hope you won't mind if I go on calling you Father."

"I *am* your father!" he said. Well, that was settled. In a way.

Perhaps he would have told me more about my mother if I had asked. Was she a blonde or a brunette? How did Uncle William meet her? Did she die in childbirth? But I knew the family rule. If you didn't see it posted on the bulletin board, you didn't need to know it, and you shouldn't ask about it. I wasn't going to beg. And what did it have to do with me? I had heard of Lorna Doone. I didn't remember Lorna Moon. We were strangers, really, two people who had briefly met in a delivery room and gone our separate ways. I may as well have been brought by the stork.

It was easy to see why I hadn't been told before. Father wasn't going to tell a seven-year-old boy his secret mother lay on her deathbed a few blocks away and he could read all about it in the evening *Herald*, where the headline said:

DEATH NEAR FOR LORNA MOON
Scenario Writer Spurns Sympathy

A seven-year-old would be looking for the comics. If he saw his mother's name, he wouldn't recognize it. If you told him her name, he would be bound to blurt it out in the wrong place, at the wrong time. Now it was twenty-six years later. Lorna Moon was gone and forgotten. Constance had lost contact with the outside world. Cecilia had known the story for years. William was dead. Anna was dead. Agnes and Margaret were grown women. Richard, at thirty-three, was more or less grown up. Balancing his security needs against the pleasures of living drama, Father decided to risk it. One day in a weighty but casual tone he said:

"I have Mary *Moon* at the studio." People didn't just *work* for Father. He *had* them—for the picture or at the studio.

"Mary Moon?"

"Lorna Moon's daughter. Next time you come to the bungalow, I will introduce you. She doesn't know about *you*." He looked at me significantly. I got the point. *Brother* Richard would stay out of sight on the dark side of Lorna Moon. That was how we did things in *Great Expectations*. But if Brother couldn't resist coming round into the light, Father was ready for whatever headlines might appear after all this time. I knew I had to see her at least. Sister Mary wasn't just a character in a story or a name from the distant past. Older or younger, pretty or plain, raven-haired or platinum, she was a living, breathing woman. If I didn't like what I saw, I didn't have to say a thing.

Would my sister look like me? Striding down the hall of the bungalow on our way to lunch at the commissary, Father and I stopped at an open door. A pretty, red-haired woman not in the least like me looked up at us brightly. "*Hell*-eo!" she said—in an English accent. We spoke a few words about this and that, I to a British stranger, she to the Boss's son. I didn't see her again for four years. Lorna's book rested unread on the shelf. I was about to remarry and enter graduate school. I wouldn't have time to read short stories by a woman I didn't remember or to worry about an unaccountably English, possibly inconvenient sister.

And there was Father's health to consider. I didn't want to do anything to complicate his day. The previous year, at seventy-three, he had gone to Egypt to open the Red Sea and deliver the Children of Israel from the hand of Pharaoh for a second time. To check a camera angle, he ran up a hundred-foot ladder just as though he were back at Guadalupe Dunes on the California shore, where he had delivered them thirty years before. Reaching the platform at the top, he felt sharp pains in his chest. Whether or not brought by God into the land of Egypt, Max Jacobson was on hand at the bottom of the ladder ready and willing to inject certain highly restricted experimental medicines, which put Father back on his feet and saved the shooting schedule. (Max, alias Dr. Feelgood, lost his license a few years later for giving President Kennedy speed.) *The Ten Commandments* was released in 1956, and Father was asked about his future plans. "Another picture," he said, "or another world."

In June 1958 Father was asked to testify before a congressional committee amending the labor laws. It was a contentious hearing. Congressman Wier scolded Father for wanting to put the divisive question of compulsory membership directly to the people instead of trusting the duly elected officers of the union to act in the people's interest. Father said he trusted the people to act in their own interest. Congressman Wier said Father was audacious, bitter, biased, and carrying a grudge, but he hoped Father didn't think he was trying to embarrass him. Believing Congressman Wier was a lackey of power-hungry, monopolistic economic wreckers, Father replied that he wasn't in the least embarrassed and knew exactly why Mr. Wier spoke as he did. Congressmen Holland said his own father had suffered more than Father's father, and Father had never been poor enough to have an opinion about freedom. Father recalled that he had walked seventy-two blocks home from the theater every night to save a nickel to buy milk for his baby daughter, Cecilia. Congressman Kearns said Father had made an outstanding contribution to improving the labor laws, and Father said he was proud and happy to do his duty. He came home, and three days later had a second heart attack.

One thing Father refused to be was an invalid. He worked in his hospital bed. He returned to the studio. He traveled down to New Orleans, as he had promised to do, to promote Tony Quinn's first (and last) venture in movie directing, a flashy but often tedious remake of DeMille's 1938 whirlpool of storytelling, *The Buccaneer*. It was Father's last excursion. Confined to his bed at home, he worked on his next project, received staff and family visitors, and consulted with his doctors. To keep him alive he had Dr. Schiff, a reputable physician. To raise his spirits he had Max Jacobson. Forbidden by Dr. Schiff to inject any more highly re-

stricted experimental medicines, Max penetrated the patient's
fears with his X-ray eyes and caressed the patient's hopes with his
rumbling voice. None of it brought relief.

Father complained about tasteless food salted with a substitute
that had lost its savor. He called for bigger pillows at the bottom
of the bed to keep the covers from oppressing his toes. He neglected to say, as he used to do when turning out the light:
"*Aaaah!*—the pleasures of bed—*alone.*" There were no pleasures
left to him in bed or out, alone or otherwise. Father sighed long
and deep. He read often in the Bible, underlining as he read. In
the Psalms, King David's cry:

> Be not thou far from me, O Lord, for trouble is near, and
> there is none to help.

In the Red Letter New Testament given to him by Jeanie Macpherson, its cover tattered and torn, its pages marked in better
days for sacred dialogue in *The King of Kings*:

> I have fought a good fight, I have finished my course. I have
> finished the work which thou gavest me to do.

He asked God whether he had finished the work he was meant to
do. He waited for the answer, not so patiently as Job.

Others waited in sorrow and dread, scores in his employ, hundreds who had worked for him and hoped to do so again, many
that loved him, some that didn't, a few who could hardly imagine
life going on without him, who didn't know what they would do
after he was gone. The Boss's yacht was outward bound on the
final voyage, the DeMille Gate would be walled up, workmen
would carry away the sign, the files would go to Utah to be dusted
by Mormon librarians, the two-tone chiming pocket watch which
had struck the hour, the quarter, and the minute in the dark pro-
jection room would be sold at auction in New York. In the pavilion
on the hill the old chief lay dying, and there was none to take his
place. The days of chieftainship were over. Soon the tribe would
scatter, and no one would remember how it was before, in the

time of origin, when Hollywood was new and giants left their foot-
prints on the sands of Guadalupe.

The deepest mourner was Cecilia, she who had never been seen
to cry, except one time when her stallions died in a fire. Father
had sometimes written addressing me as "my son," but Cecilia
was the child of his body, his first and only born, his "Baby
Bonzo," his brave girl, who had ridden at fourteen fearless down
the dunes, scattering sand in all directions, shaming the timid cowboys of Pharaoh's West Coast cavalry. She was the loyal successor
and heir he trusted to carry on in his name, even without his name.
It was a heavy burden, which she accepted gratefully. Wife,
mother, Thoroughbred breeder, did any of it count as much as
being the worthy daughter of that great and famous man who had
walked seventy-two blocks home from the theater to save a nickel
to buy milk for his Baby Bonzo? Yet as a child she had felt he
never had time for her, the same complaint Agnes would make
about William. I asked Katie about Cecilia.

R: Did Cecilia love you?
K: Did she love *me*?
R: Yes.
K: I tell you, I'm always remembering when I first came into
   that family. I was down by the swimming pool. You re-
   member, where the swings were?
R: Yes.
K: And there was a little room where you changed your
   clothes.
R: Yes.
K: And I remember—oh, I don't suppose I had been in the
   family more than a few days—Cecilia came out of that
   room, and she was sucking her thumb.
R: Really! How old was she?
K: I was nine, so she was twelve. They had to tape her
   thumb to try to stop her. And I remember feeling that
   somehow it was my coming into that family that was making her . . . because I remember her being so *shy*. And
   when you think of all she was able to do for so many
   years, the brilliant, capable woman she is—but that shy-

ness is still there, and when I think of that, it almost makes me cry, because I see how many veneers, how many walls she put up. And this is where Joe Harper was so important in her life, bless his heart.

R: He brought her out a bit.

K: Yes, he did.

R: And did she love you?

K: Oh, I think . . . it must have . . . I haven't any *idea*. To this *day* I wouldn't know whether Cecilia loves me. But I know that she is such an honorable lady that she would do everything that is right, even if she despises me. She has a stiff spine of righteousness. And I remember when she grew up, she was so sure of herself, and so attractive. I would go into her bedroom while she was getting dressed to go to dances, and I would say "Oh!" because she was so glamorous. It's nice to reminisce.

R: Did you ever have any doubt that I loved you?

K: *No!* [Laughing] Listen, *should* I?

In our house two blocks west of Laughlin Park the telephone rang in the night. Joe said, "Your father died a few minutes ago. Cecilia would like you to come up."

I got dressed quietly, so as not to wake baby Cecil Belgrano de Mille. Margaret was crying. At the big house the nurse was tying the dead man's ankles together.

"It was five past five," she said. "You can tell when they take the last breath." Cecilia had gone down to her house at the foot of the hill and locked herself in the bathroom, where no one could see her and only Joe would hear. I stayed alone with the strangely quiet figure. I thought of times when I had disappointed him. Despite the gibes of Congressman Wier, Father didn't hold grudges. He had forgiven Zukor for saying in 1925, "Cecil, you have never been one of us," and Jesse Lasky for lacking the courage to stand up for him. He had forgiven Belasco for taking nearly all the credit for *The Return of Peter Grimm*, a play Father wrote for Belasco and Belasco improved. He forgave those who trespassed against him as he had been forgiven for laying waste his mother's Jerusalem artichokes, believing he was the Champion Driver cutting down the enemies of the true and the good. I had no such excuse.

When I was nine, I thought it would be a nice gesture to make Father a highball. At three in the afternoon he hadn't asked for a highball, but he tasted the one I made, four parts scotch, one part soda. He said it was a waste of good liquor.

When Father was eleven his father died, leaving behind a gold Swiss watch with his picture in it. Since 1893 the watch had been kept safe and sound in a velvet-lined box, along with keys to wind and set it, first by Father's mother, then by Father. It was stored in a cabinet in the bathroom. One morning when I was eleven, I asked to see it. Father handed me the box and turned back to his shaving. The bathroom floor was paved with small white hexagonal tiles. As I opened the watch to look at my grandfather's picture, the precious heirloom slipped from my fingers and crashed on the tiles in front of me. In a panic, I snatched it up and said, "I'll fix it! I'll fix it!" Father took it from my hand and put it away silently. It never ran again. Whenever I opened the dented case, I saw my grandfather staring sadly at the motionless hands, pretending not to notice his unworthy grandson.

When I was thirteen, I saw *The Informer*, directed by John Ford. It was a very good picture. I told Father John Ford was my favorite director. Father said:

"He's a good director."

I know he forgave everything, but one wishes (in vain) not to have hurt one's father.

The undertakers came before dawn. They laid the fallen hero on the battle bier and carried him down the long flights to the hearse. I walked behind. Except for a few early birds, one dead man, and three alive, the new day was empty. They put him in and locked the door and glided silently away, westward down the hill toward the Hall of the Slain Warriors. Upstairs Hilja stood distraught in her robe and nightcap.

"Is your father dead?" she whispered.

"Yes," I said.

She put her arms around me. "What are we going to *do*!" she wailed.

"Cecilia will manage everything," I said.

A newspaper reporter rang the doorbell. Pencil poised, she asked: "What was his favorite possession?" I said it was his family. She didn't find that newsworthy.

When I was little and Father was fifty, he used to box with a punching bag in his dressing room. The bag was on a vertical rod held upright by powerful springs. Father would punch it to the floor, and it would spring back savagely, trying to return the blow. He would duck and weave and dance and leap about the room, as the silverware and crystal tinkled downstairs in the pantry. Father nearly always won. He was strong and he was fierce. His chest was broad and hairy. It was fun to watch him. I was glad it was the punching bag he was mad at.

Some time after the funeral, I had a vivid dream. I was standing in the arbor under the platform where Father used to sunbathe. He would open the French windows and go out from his room. Sweating out there in the sun, he read most of Sienkiewicz's *Quo Vadis?* As I stood below, a gorilla fell from the platform and crashed on the concrete in front of me. I was afraid of the gorilla and hoped he wouldn't notice me, but then I saw that he was hurt, and I felt sorry for him. I didn't want the gorilla to die, because I loved him very much. In my dream, I cried.

CHAPTER 7

An Unexpected Brother

Sitting at Father's desk in Father's office in the West Wing, Neil McCarthy read the will. No one was left out. Every member of the family was provided for according to his station. Cecilia was the lioness. Her children were the cubs. I was the cat that walks by himself. Katie and John were sparrows. Only Cecilia got cash, and for years she would be in charge of everybody else's. No sparrow might fall, except it fell into her capable hand. Katie said: "That's just like Father!" She went home and cried. Louise, John's wife, informed Cecilia that Father had wanted John to have more. Cecilia knew what Father had wanted. She had helped him write the will. I was glad not to be a sparrow, but I didn't like having Cecilia in charge of my cash.

The scenes of my childhood were now Cecilia's domain. The houses were her houses, the trees were her trees, the flowers were her flowers, the bees were her bees. As she had done from the beginning, she treated me graciously like a visiting cousin. Without Father the core of the family was gone. I wanted something to fill the void. Whatever she might prove to be, Mary Moon had spent nine months in my mother's womb. Now, it seemed, there was no reason not to talk to her. Inquiring reporters could not wake Father from his final rest. Scandal hunters could no longer complicate his day. I called Mary at the studio.

"Mary *Moon.*"

"Hello, Mary. This is Richard de Mille."

"*Hell*-eo!"

"Mary, I'm interested in your mother, in her life and career."

"*Oooh!*"

"I'd like to talk with you about her. Can you have lunch with me?"

"That would be *lovely!*"

We walked to the Melrose Grotto, a murky dining room with padded white tablecloths and waitresses still hoping for a call from Central Casting.

"Your mother had an unusual life."

"Oh, she *did!*"

Mary told me what she knew about her mother's life. It had begun in northeast Scotland in the remote village of Strichen, which the natives call *Sthrikhen.* The family belonged to the Cameron clan. Sir Ewen Cameron of Lochiel, seventeenth chief of the clan, slew the last wolf in Scotland and built the old family castle, Achnacarry, which was burned by the Sassenachs in 1746 after the Battle of Culloden. *Sassenach* means Saxon. It's what Scots call the English. *Moon* unfortunately was English. When Mary was six months old, Walter Moon, her English father, cruelly and unjustly took her away from her Scottish mother. Mary grew up in Yorkshire with her father's family. They didn't care to talk about Lorna, but Lorna was Mary's heroine, and Mary's heart was in the Highlands. Ten years after Lorna died, Mary came from England to live where Lorna had lived, and work where Lorna had worked, and meet people who had known Lorna and would talk about her. At M-G-M Mary met the writer Frances Marion, one of Lorna's dearest friends. Most of Lorna's films had been written at M-G-M—like *Upstage* for Norma Shearer and *Mr. Wu* for Lon Chaney and *Love* for Greta Garbo—but her first job in Hollywood was writing for Mr. DeMille.

"Did she have other children?"

Yes! Mary's older brother, whom she had never seen. His name was Bill Hebditch and he lived in British Columbia. He was a rugged outdoor type who cut trees and raised cattle and built roads through the wilderness. Mary was eager to meet him but he stayed out in the country and Mary was a city girl. She knew just how the meeting would go. She had seen it already in *The Ten Com-mandments*:

MARY MOON (played by Olive Deering): I am Miriam, your sister.

BILL HEBDITCH (Charlton Heston): I am your brother Moses.

This was a bit of a shock. I had expected to be the brother, if there was to be one. Now we had big brother Bill looming on the northern border, like Paul Bunyan with his big blue ox.

"So she had two children."

"As far as I know, but she told Aunt Eva she had a third child in Hollywood. Do you know if it's true?"

I looked into the big brown eyes, set off by a little too much mascara, of Mary Moon, the stranger. How often do we have the chance to choose our relatives? Mary was cute, bright, amusing, full of perky British sayings—five feet tall, red hair, white skin, a figure to make a man look twice. She was a charming girl, or rather, a charming girlish woman, and I could make her my sister with a word, but if I said, "There was a third child," it could never be unsaid. Mary would be my sister for all time.

"There was a third child."

She gasped. "Boy or girl?"

"Boy."

The sun came out. "Do you know him?"

"Yes, I know him rather well."

"Can I *meet* him?"

"You've met him already."

"Good *Lord*! Where *is* he!"

"About three feet from where you are sitting."

Slowly, majestically the gates of Castle DeMille swung open to admit the little lost Scot, the lass from over the sea, the abducted infant, the motherless child, the prisoner of the Sassenachs, born to be rescued and included.

"Oh, *Richard*! *You* are my brother?"

"I am."

When Ann del Valle had signed on as public relations director for Cecil B. DeMille, Mary was already working for him. Years later, Ann remembered her.

> Mary was an island, sunny but remote. No one knew what was going on in her head. At the DeMille Unit, she sat all day in her little office clipping items from *Variety*, *Hollywood Reporter*, and newspapers in key cities. This was to tell Mr. DeMille what critics and his publicists were saying about him and his pictures. She didn't frequent the water cooler. She left her desk only to go to the bathroom, go to lunch, or stand in the hall and greet the Boss when he arrived in the morning. She did it every morning. During the day, she often managed to be in the hall or near a door when he was coming by. No one else did that. The rest of us stayed in our offices unless we had business with him. I didn't know why Mr. DeMille would keep someone on, year after year, just to clip the papers. Mary was bright and literate, much too good for that job. If I spoke to her, she answered with a sparkle. But when I offered her the chance to be my secretary in the Publicity Department, she didn't want to go. She didn't tell me she could write, or that she had been a newspaper reporter for ten years. She didn't talk about herself. She seemed completely content just clipping the papers in her office.
>
> Once toward the end, when Mr. DeMille went on that last trip down to New Orleans, when he was already very frail, Mary did an odd thing. She left work without a word. No one knew where she had gone. It turned out she had gone to the airport all on her own to see him off. Soon after he died, Mary came back from lunch one day joyous, outgoing, ecstatic. We had never seen her like that. "I've found my brother! I've found my brother!" she said. "Richard de Mille is my brother! Lorna Moon is his mother too!"

Margaret and I took Mary to dinner. The following week she came to our house. I told her more than once that William de Mille was my father, but she didn't want to believe it. Lorna had never worked for William. Mary had never met him. He was not the Mr. DeMille she had wanted to stay close to. Next day at the studio she told a friend in the steno pool that Mr. DeMille's son was her brother.

"So," she said, batting her eyes, "*I'm* related to Mr. *DeMille*!"

This mutant genealogical virus floated gently up through channels. Late in the afternoon it entered the ear of Y. Frank Freeman, head of Paramount studio, a personal friend of Father's. Mr. Freeman called Cecilia. From the age of fifteen, Cecilia had endured the rumor that Father's youngest adopted child was his natural son. Forbidden to tell the true story, she had suffered in silence. Without the needed nourishment of a tell-all book or a paternity suit, the rumor gradually withered and died. Now it was rising again from Father's grave—but now Cecilia was in charge and ready with a legal stake to drive through its lying heart. She called Neil McCarthy. Nobody answered at Neil's office. Nobody answered at his house on Sunset Boulevard. Cecilia slammed the receiver down. Joe made her a martini. Two hours later Neil still didn't answer. The telephone rang at our house.

"Richard. Cecilia. Did you talk to Mary Moon?"

"Yes."

"She's been running all over the studio telling people you're her brother and so she is related to Father. I'll sue anybody who says Father was your father."

"I didn't say it."

"Hedda Hopper knew all about you and never printed a word. We're just lucky Louella Parsons never got hold of the story. Mary's a nice woman, and I know why you wanted to talk to her, but you should have known better."

"Father introduced me to Mary a long time ago. He didn't say not to talk to her."

"Father made mistakes. Have any reporters called you?"

"No."

"What are you going to tell them?"

"William was my father."

"I'll sue anybody who says Father was your father."

Agnes wasn't at home. It took Cecilia a while to find her in Boston, where she was whipping the musical play *Juno* into shape for New York. At 2:30 a.m. Boston time the phone rang in Agnes's hotel room.

"Agnes. Cecilia. Have the newspapers called you?"

"*No!* What's *happened*?"

"Richard's been talking and the story is out about Lorna Moon."

"Lorna Moon?"

"Richard's mother."

"Oh, I'm sorry. I didn't know."

"It may be in tomorrow's papers. I didn't want it to hit you without warning."

"Well, that's very considerate, but why should it bother me?"

"Because your father was Richard's father."

"*Cecilia!* You *know* that's not true! Richard is *your* father's child!"

"He's *not*, and I can prove it."

"Oh, *Cecilia*! What are you saying! I can't . . . I don't know what to believe!"

"You can believe it, because it's true. Neil has the documents, and your father signed them. I'll sue anybody who says Father was Richard's father."

"Thank *God* my mother is dead! This would break her heart."

Three days later no reporters had called. Neil answered his phone at home. Cecilia told him the story was out and asked what to tell reporters. Neil said those old files had all been put in storage but he would write her a letter stating the facts as he recalled them. He sat down at his desk, took out pen and paper, and wrote a fluent, one-draft, splendidly convincing account to suit the needs of his client and cover the tracks of her lawyer.

NEIL STEERE McCARTHY

Dear Cecilia,

You are now the head of your family and I feel that I should inform you of some details concerning Richard that I handled and with which you may not be entirely familiar.

During the period covered by the incidents I am describing I saw William frequently and of course was well acquainted with him. William was during this time in a warm romance with Richard's mother to be. I remember that during this time I saw him with another woman and asked him chidingly if he was two timing Lorna. He answered "No, Neil—at least I am faithful in my infidelity."

Some months later William came to me and stated that he and Lorna were going to have a child and asked me to help him work out a plan where the child could be raised and William would make every provision for him.

He told your father of his desires and your father told your mother. Your father and mother had adopted two children at this time and William discussed with them their adopting his child. Your mother was agreeable as was your father but your father stated to Bill in one of our conversations that neither he or the mother should ever have any contact with the child to which Bill agreed.

Your mother was at the time active in the "Castelar Creche," a home for homeless babies. The mother had gone to San Francisco and was to have the baby there. When the baby arrived Mrs. McCarthy and I went to San Francisco and to the hospital where the baby and the mother were and there the mother gave us the child and we brought it to Los Angeles. We later took it to Castelar Creche and your mother took the child home from there. I later conducted the proceedings by which your father and mother adopted the baby under his present name.

We all thought we were protecting the baby and Bill and Lorna but some weeks later a mutual friend told Mrs. McCarthy that at a luncheon party Lorna had told the entire story to the guests at the table and that she and Bill were the parents. I still wonder how it escaped being in the papers at that time, particularly as Lorna was a very careless talker.

William was very appreciative of my help and not only paid my bill for services and expenses but gave me a beautifully fitted bag with sterling silver fittings. I still have the bag.

I felt you should have these details of the transactions.

Sincerely,
NEIL
Feb. 27, 1959

Neil's daughter Rosemary was seven years old the day her parents came home with me in the car.

You were brought to our house in the afternoon, and you spent the night in the guest room. We children weren't allowed to see you, and we thought that was pretty mean. We wanted to keep you, but the next day you were taken away. I've always thought of you as the brother I wasn't allowed to have. Later I saw an article in the paper with a picture of you.

WONDER BABY NOT WORRYING
Infant Left in Automobile
Finds Good Home
BY ALMA WHITAKER

He is a perfectly beautiful bountiful baby. And he doesn't know and doesn't care that he is really a tragic little abandoned baby.

His mother left him in Mrs. Neil McCarthy's automobile . . . with an unconvincing note about "not being able to make the fight." . . .

But for the moment he does not need our pity. . . . Mrs. Cecil de Mille wants him, and a mysterious rich San Francisco banker and his wife want him. . . .

NS was a tremendous liar. He could really dream up stuff. The story was that your mother must have been impressed by our family car, which was a Locomobile, a dark green convertible touring car. NS told us your father was a banker in San Francisco.

Neil S. McCarthy scored goals against George Patton on the polo field and litigated for Howard Hughes. He didn't let mallets or facts get in his way. His letter to Cecilia contradicts what he told his children, what he told reporters, what he told the court at my adoption, and what he instructed Mrs. McCarthy to tell Miss Pickrell at the Castelar Creche.

History: Baby McCarthy   Admission #105

Oct. 12, 1922—Mrs. N. S. McCarthy, 679 S. Ardmore, phoned that a baby had been left in Mr. McC's automobile downtown with a note pinned to it saying the father is dead and the mother is tired of making the fight. Date of birth unknown. Oct. 13, 1922—Mrs. McCarthy brought the baby. Weight 16 lbs. 2 ounces. Age 6–7 months. Name Pierre Labori. Child cries incessantly. Probably spoiled or frightened. Oct. 17, 1922—Mrs. de Mille at meeting of Board of Directors said she was thinking of adopting the baby. Nov. 6, 1922—Mrs. McCarthy and Mrs. de Mille called to say Mrs. de Mille had decided definitely to adopt the baby. Nov. 13, 1922—Dr. Carter asked Mrs. de Mille to take the baby today as Dr. Fish thought he had whooping cough. Mrs. de Mille came at 3PM and took the baby home with her. Dec. 22, 1922—Mrs. de Mille came and said Pierre is getting along wonderfully well. They have changed his name to Richard.

Having laundered lucky Pierre for thirty days at the foundling home, the conspirators whisked him away to a new life in a new family under a new name. During thirty years of digging up the past I sometimes woke in a sweat believing I was a Frenchman named Pierre, but to my relief the State of California has no record of Labori, *père* or *fils*. One day thumbing through an old encyclopedia, I chanced upon the fact that when Neil McCarthy was a boy dreaming of a legal career, Captain Alfred Dreyfus of the French General Staff was convicted of treason in an anti-Semitic trial made famous around the world by Emile Zola. Dreyfus and Zola were then brilliantly vindicated by the eminent French legal scholar Fernand Labori. When the renowned Labori died in 1917 Neil McCarthy, twenty-nine, was practicing law in Los Angeles. Five years later he picked the name of that illustrious lawyer as a suitable alias for the son of another scholarly writer and reformer, his own secret paternity client William C. de Mille. To make the game less obvious, he changed Fernand to Pierre.

And what about the baby found in the touring car? During the summer before I was born, while Neil was concocting a story to cover his client's inconvenient issue, Hollywood was all agog over Charlie Chaplin's first feature film, a smashing success titled *The Kid*. In this movie a young woman of the theater bears the child of a man she is not married to and in desperation leaves the infant with a note in a rich woman's limousine. The limousine turned into Neil McCarthy's touring car. The rich woman became Constance de Mille. The baby grew up to be Richard de Mille, not to mention Jackie Coogan.

Wonder Baby was not Neil's only laundered orphan. When Cecilia de Mille was six, her parents brightened her Christmas with an unexpected brother, fifteen-month-old John. When the boy was three, they decided it was time to adopt him legally. Though John had been living at home with the de Milles since December 1914, Neil McCarthy told the court he had been in the custody of the Children's Home Society since October 1915, abandoned by his parents, "Gus Gonzales and Ada Gonzales, his wife," both of whom had disappeared. According to Neil, before skipping town "Gus" and "Ada" had named the baby "Ralph," but the State of California knows nothing of "Ralph Gonzales." Since there was no plan to reveal John's origins to him, the true identity of his parents is today unknown, buried too early and too deep ever to be dug up. The unsolved mystery of his birth is one of the things that made John's life unhappy.

Not everything Neil wrote in his letter to Cecilia is a story he made up. Some of it is fact. Lorna did have William's baby, which she gave to the McCarthys to convey to Mrs. Cecil de Mille. On the other hand, Lorna was not a careless talker. The luncheon party is Neil's invention. His surprise that William's name didn't get into the papers is a fake. Lorna never exposed William. She did confess to her sister Eva far away in Canada that she had borne another baby, but she said it was a girl and allowed Eva to assume that the father was Cecil B. DeMille, Lorna's first Hollywood employer. Most of those who suspected something thought Cecil was my father, including both of William's wives and his daughters and stepdaughter. Just who the mother might have been, none of them could guess. Sixty years later Agnes recalled her dismay on learning the truth.

What hurt me so, Richard, when I heard about you was that my father never had time for us girls. The whole conversation with Cecilia was a total shock. I always thought you were Cecil's son. Everybody did. First, he had a reputation for having mistresses. Second, you were the dead spit of my father when he was a young man, the same long skeleton, the same long head, the set of the jaw, the forehead, the eyes. It was a ridiculous likeness.

Agnes looked at me and saw a replica of her *father*, so she believed I was her *uncle's* child. Katie and Natalie, two teenagers who weren't starving for William's love, came to a more logical conclusion. Katie said:

Nat and I got it right years and years ago. We were sitting in Father's study whiling away a boring Sunday afternoon looking at the childhood photos, his and Uncle William's, and suddenly we were both struck by a resemblance we just could *not* dismiss as nothing but a coincidence. Right there and then we dissected that rather improbable story they had handed us when you came into the family. We kept our deduction under our hats, but now it has proved us worthy to wear the mantle of Sherlock Holmes. I hope you are impressed.

The year before Father died Margaret George de Mille, Agnes's younger sister, had come to Hollywood with her husband, Albert Kaplan. Cecilia sent them to our house for dinner. Presumably she thought I should be closer to my sister, even if my sister still believed she was my cousin. It was the first occasion of that kind. I hadn't seen Margaret or Agnes for years. My own Margaret had never met them. It was a pleasant evening. Albert was congenial. Cousin Margaret was still a dazzler, almost as good-looking as when she had played the lead in *Green Grow the Lilacs* opposite Franchot Tone on the New York stage. I remembered her from my college days, laughing, joking, shining, pulsing in her little black dress. Now she was a businesswoman, stylish, composed, on top of things, Maggie de Mille, the Manhattan fashion editor. I treated her like the glamorous urbanite she was, and she treated me like a country boy. She let it be known that Ike and Mamie were her personal friends, to say nothing of Jack Javits. I told her I didn't care for Senator Javits, because I was a conservative. "Oh, Richard!" she said. "You're much too intelligent for that!" I said perhaps she had never met a conservative intellectual. The phrase struck her as absurd. Intelligent people were liberals. Albert spilled his claret on the Frank Lloyd Wright dining table and was much embarrassed. After the cleanup, everyone seemed to be having a good time.

The following year they came again, but now baby brother was out of the bag. The old wounds had torn open. Father William, who had left his daughters for another woman just when they needed him, who had given their childhood home exclusively to Agnes, now flung in Margaret's face the son he had always wanted, the boy he must have been talking to when he would greet three-year-old Margaret with "Hello, Old Man!" The betrayed daughter was wound tight, but she wasn't going to show it. Joe Harper had instructed me to take them to the Cave Des Roys, a club on La Cienega, where dinner would be on him. After a drink at our house we were gliding down Wilshire Boulevard in a jolly mood, when from the driver's seat I ventured a reference to "our father." Behind me Cousin Margaret snapped:

"I think that's for *me* to say, Richard, not for *you!*"

Well, they were our guests. The beef Stroganoff was superb. A splendid fellow with antique keys jangling on a chain brought the cabernet. The conversation was lively. But Cousin Margaret didn't say another word about our father, and it was the last time I saw her.

"Margaret told me about you," Frances Beranger said, "and the news astonished me, but she said, 'Well, I think it's *great!*' Margaret was amused at Agnes's reaction. Agnes was horrified. She cried. Margaret asked her, '*Why?* It won't change your life.' "

But it changed all our lives. If my sisters didn't want me as a brother, I didn't want them as cousins. Twenty years later I tried again with Agnes. She remembered asking Margaret what they should do about getting in touch with me.

"Margaret said that if you wanted to be in touch with us, you knew where we were. So I just left it that way. We didn't know how to begin, Richard. I was shy. You were shy."

It had been a stalemate of hurt feelings, which no one had the courage to break, least of all the supposedly amused, unruffled Margaret. When at last I was no longer too shy to speak to reluctant sisters, it was too late to speak to Margaret. She had died the year before.

CHAPTER 8

Nobody's Baby

My sister Mary Leonore Moon was born in 1914 not in Scotland, not in Yorkshire, not even in the United Kingdom, but on the plains of Manitoba four hundred miles northwest of Minneapolis. Walter Moon, her English father, was an accountant for a Winnipeg building supply company. Lorna Moon, her Scottish mother, worked for the *Winnipeg Telegram* and the *Saturday Post*. The couple lived on Maryland Street in a nice part of town. Lorna amused herself by acting in local theater. She played the lead in Wilson Barrett's 1895 play, *The Sign of the Cross*. In the movie version, which would be produced in 1932 by Cecil B. DeMille, Marcus Superbus (Fredric March), Prefect of Rome, implores Mercia (Elissa Landi), a virtuous Christian maid, to save herself from martyrdom by renouncing her outlaw religion and moving in with him. Instead the saintly girl invites him to climb out of the Empress Poppaea's (Claudette Colbert's) bed and go with her to face holy death in the arena. Marcus Superbus, right hand of Nero (Charles Laughton), the second most powerful man in Rome, a patrician blade to whom every door and every other bed is open, says: Yes! Come to think of it, Mercia dear, I *will* be glad to be eaten by lions, not because I believe in your foreign god, which of course I don't, but because I believe in *you*. Only in a Victorian play (or movie) could such a thing happen. One night the dialogue was too much for Lorna and her leading man. They broke into broad Scots: Will ye nae come wi me, laddie, te gie the puir hungry lions their supper? The audience roared, the curtain banged down, the Jacobites were fired. Lorna also played the lead in a Scottish comedy, *Bunty Pulls the Strings*. When a baby began to show, Walter took it in good humor, calling Lorna "Bunchie."

Mary was born in the house on Maryland Street. A woman was hired to tend her, but at night she cried. Walter said the child was crying for its mother. Lorna said a little girl cries for her father. Walter said a working man needs proper sleep. Lorna said an accountant sits in a chair all day. A reporter is out in the snow getting the story. Walter said Lorna took no interest in her baby. Lorna said she had spent nine months giving him a daughter and he should appreciate it. After six months of wrangling, Walter appealed to his brother Frank in England. Frank and Nellie had no children. Frank said they would be willing to take baby Mary if Walter would support her. Nurse and baby went off together to East Keswick, Yorkshire, and peace reigned once more on Maryland Street.

Mary blamed Walter for the whole thing. She called him Walter the Monster. Walter didn't want a baby. Walter sent Lorna's baby to England. When Lorna came home from the office, her darling baby was gone. There was nothing she could do. I said a mother who loved her child would go to England and get her back. She wouldn't go on living with a man who had stolen her baby. Mary wouldn't hear of it. Lorna was her idol. Lorna could do no wrong. She was an artist. She wrote books. Her name was on the silver screen. She had famous lovers. She lived her life the way she wanted.

Without a baby, I said. Mary called me a nitwit.

In 1917 Walter and Lorna moved to Minneapolis, where she worked for the *Minneapolis Journal* and he was an accountant and managed the apartment house they lived in. In February 1920 Cecil B. DeMille's *Male and Female* played at the New Lyric Theater. Lorna went to see it because it was "founded on" *The Admirable Crichton*, an early *Upstairs Downstairs* by the noted Scottish playwright Sir James M. Barrie. Crichton, the butler, is admirable both as servant in the mansion and as master of men and women on a desert island. The title had to be changed, of course, so moviegoers wouldn't expect a story about a naval hero. Lorna wrote the director a letter making fun of the liberties he had taken with a famous play. He answered: If you think you can do better, come to Hollywood and try. Late in the year she packed her bags and went off to Hollywood to improve its standards. Walter was upset, but experience had taught him not to try to stop her. He wished her every success and said that if things didn't work out, she could always come home. She kissed him and told him he was a dear.

Needing a change of scene, Walter returned to Yorkshire to visit Frank and Nellie and see how his little girl was coming along. They didn't take to each other. Walter felt odd about making friends with a child he had sent away. Mary, six years old, wouldn't sit on the lap of a large, cold stranger. She stayed close to Uncle Frank, who didn't pretend to be anyone's father.

Walter sent money for Mary's upkeep, but Nellie told Frank it wasn't nearly enough. Besides, people were asking questions. Frank said a child couldn't help what its parents had done and people ought to keep their noses out of other people's business. Mary crept out of the house without being seen. In the fields around East Keswick she gathered the flowers in Shakespeare's plays and kept a lookout for Robin Hood coming to carry Maid Mary Moon off to Sherwood Forest. The family carried her off to Leeds, an industrial city with a university.

I came running home from school and told my aunt and uncle about the coming wonders of television. They laughed at me. When we toured Scotland, I looked up at Stirling Castle, fortress of Mary Queen of Scots, so high and grand upon its rock, and asked them what had happened there. The silly, brainless Moons said, "Nothing." Just most of Scottish history, that's all! In 1066, when the Moons were the de Mohuns, they crossed the Channel with Willy the Norman to civilize the Saxons with pillage, torture, fire, and sword, and they hadn't learned anything since.

In 1926, when Mary was twelve, Lorna Moon's first book was published. *Doorways in Drumorty* was a collection of short stories about village life in northeast Scotland. *The Times Literary Supplement* said it was "very effective," but Uncle Frank and Aunt Nellie didn't read the *TLS*, and the book escaped Mary's attention. She did read *Lorna Doone*, a romance about a girl living in the seventeenth century. Lorna Doone was born heir to vast property and high station but as a child was carried off by distant relatives and made to forget her true family and her noble mother. In Lorna Doone's captivity Mary recognized her own.

When Mary was fifteen, Lorna Moon's novel *Dark Star* was a best-seller on both sides of the Atlantic. Arnold Bennett, author of *The Old Wives' Tale*, praised its narrative flow and original style. V. S. Pritchett, a short-story writer, soon to be a prominent critic, summarized the plot:

> *Dark Star* . . . is the story of [Nancy] . . . a lively and sensitive girl, born under the "dark star" of bastardy, and obsessed with . . . proving that she is the daughter of the aristocratic Fasseferns and not of a groom. Nancy grows up under the guardianship of a bloodless clergyman and his wife . . . and after she has lost the love of a young musician (who throws her over when she is no longer of use to him as an inspiration) she ends her life violently in the traditional Fassefern manner.

Beyond this somber, romantic theme, reviewer Pritchett called the book "remarkable for its spirited malice and sardonic humor." Divot Meg, the village trollop, is keeper of the White Ship, a rough hotel for wayfarers. Meg has more children than circumstances warrant. Village gossips scowl or grin over their surmise that likely travelers contribute to her profit, fun, and family, whilst her hapless husband, robbed of his tongue by tobacco in a short-stemmed pipe, rages in silence in his bed of pain. Carnival performers on the road from fair to fair stop at the White Ship, notably "Ramos, the world famous pincushion king."

> You could stick a pin in any part of him and never draw a drop of blood. . . . Divot Meg had a life-sized poster of him with pins sticking out of every muscle like the spines on a porcupine. It was pasted on her bedroom wall. She was so

proud of it and showed it so often that rumor said Ramos was the father of her little Jimmy. But when the school children took little Jimmy and stuck pins in him he bled like sixty, so they had no proof of the relationship.

Mr. Pritchett mentioned the vividness of the climactic murder scene. One night Snowey, a cocaine slut, drifts in off the high road and speaks to Divot Meg's husband as if she already knows him. Meg recognizes her as Bella, long-lost mother of the heroine, Nancy, who is now a respectable young lady. Resenting her daughter's rise in the world, spiteful Bella boasts to Meg that she will settle Nancy's pride by telling her that her father was not the laird of Fassefern but the groom in the stable, though in truth she doesn't know which man it was. To protect the innocent girl, Divot Meg kindly pulls off drunken Bella's wet shoes, helps her into a nice warm bath, brings her a hot toddy, and has a long sympathetic conversation with her, which ends with Bella dead in bed showing no signs of suffocation at the hands of her capable hostess. The doctor says death was caused by an overdose. The mute husband, filled with hate for his lusty wife, writes a note accusing her of the crime. The killing unfolds in exquisite detail. Suspense mounts from line to line. The reader roots for the careful, altruistic killer.

A librarian in Leeds showed the book to Mary. She read it eagerly. Again, she found herself in the story—a lively and sensitive girl oppressed by gloomy guardians, worried about her origin and her destiny. Of course, she wouldn't leap off a cliff to prove her respectability, much less to flatter a selfish man. Exceptional women like Lorna Moon and her daughter Mary belonged to an aristocracy of talent, made their own reputations, and had their pick of men.

The same year Uncle Frank fell ill. Mary "was passed around the family like a bomb with a lighted fuse." For a while she lived with Walter's mother, after whom she had been named. To prepare for college and stay out of busy people's way she boarded at Leeds Girls' High School, in a Jane Eyre Gothic mansion, where she endured algebra, geometry, and cricket and enjoyed elocution, poetry, and sewing. With credit in French and history and distinction in English literature she qualified for university at Manchester, Sheffield, Birmingham, Liverpool, and Leeds. Walter Moon had graduated from Leeds University, and Mary hoped to do no less.

A newspaper story said Lorna Moon, author of *Dark Star*, was gravely ill in Hollywood, but Mary knew that Lorna Doone had lain for days at the verge of death and then risen up and flourished. In May, there was a notice.

AUTHORESS DIES
Lorna Moon, novelist of Northeast Scotland and
scenario writer in Hollywood . . .

Mary's world turned dark around her. The mother she had been stolen from, the woman who would have kissed her, nursed her, tended her in a nest of love, the artist who would have taught her everything she needed to know, the heroine she would follow to the ends of the earth, had now been taken away forever. Aunt Nellie looked grim. Uncle Frank said he was very sorry. Mary couldn't answer him.

Soon she had a visitor, a tall, handsome, delicate blond young man with an American accent. His name was Everett Marcy. He had been with Lorna during her last illness and had promised to carry her ashes home to Strichen.

"Scatter them to the four winds from the Hill of Mormond— that's what she told me. And that's what we did."

Everett described Lorna's parents. Her father had been crushed by grief. Her mother had remarked: "Now, Mr. Marcy, isn't that just like her, not to want a proper funeral!" But Everett had been firm with them. Everything must be done just as Lorna wanted it. On a sunny afternoon he and Lorna's father climbed the hill together. The old man was recovering from an operation, but he carried the little casket and at the top scattered the ashes into the gorse and heather with great sweeps of his arm like a farmer sowing grain. Everett stayed for a week with Lorna's sister Sadie and her husband and two girls in their house at the foot of the slope, the only house in the village built with a veranda, in the South African style.

Pulling a flask from his hip pocket, Everett offered it to Mary. She declined. He took a swig and drew a packet from his coat.

"Lorna wanted you to have this."

In the packet Mary found a jade necklace and three brooches. She held the necklace in her hands and felt her mother's heartbeat in the smooth cold stone. In her hands the jade grew warm. She wore it a lot, Everett said. It went so well with her auburn hair. Mary realized with joy that this beautiful young man was not merely Lorna's friend. He had been her lover. He said he was a writer and he had been helping Lorna work on her new novel. He said he had learned a lot from Lorna. She was a wonderful writer. Mary was thinking what she would wear to go away to America with Lorna's beautiful lover, but he was standing up and saying he had to catch his train. He was just glad he had found her at home. She watched his cab pick up speed and disappear round the curve.

After Uncle Frank died, Aunt Nellie got into drunken rages. She stowed Mary's baby pictures out of sight in the garage and when they moldered she threw them in the trash. She gave Mary's dog away—"the only creature in the world that loved me"—and without notice to anyone he was put to death in the pound. Though Mary had qualified to go to university, Aunt Nellie said there was no money to send her. In America Walter Moon was doing famously in business, owned his house without a mortgage, and had no other children, but he never thought to ask about college for a daughter who hadn't taken to him, a daughter he hadn't asked for in the first place, a daughter whose mother had left him flat after seven years. Mary expected nothing better from a man who would send his own baby into exile. She certainly wasn't going to beg for help from such a man. She went to secretarial school, where she wrote Gregg at ninety words a minute. Lorna Moon had started out as a newspaperwoman. Mary Moon at eighteen was the youngest reporter on the staff of the *Leeds Guardian*.

One of her assignments was writing about tourist attractions in England, Wales, and Scotland, but with all her traveling she somehow never managed to pass through Strichen, Aberdeenshire. Though she would journey six thousand miles in search of her dead mother, she didn't visit the place of her mother's birth, local fame, and final rest. She never stood on Bridge Street looking up at the White Horse, recording in her notebook its 162 feet of white quartz laid out on the hillside in 1779 by order of Captain Fraser, son of Lord Strichen. She didn't walk from Aunt Sadie's house up through the Martin Wood, past the bed of shining quartz, round the ruined Hunter's Lodge, to stand gazing at the North Sea, thinking of her long-lost but otherwise faultless mother, whose ashes tinted the purple heather growing on the crest of Mormond. The reason is simple. No letter had come from Strichen welcoming Mary into the family, no Christmas greeting from young cousins, no recognition at all. Everett had told her grandparents that he would visit her in Leeds, but apparently they didn't care to meet their firstborn granddaughter. Mary wouldn't go where she wasn't wanted.

At twenty Mary received proceeds from the sale of Lorna's house in Hollywood. At twenty-two, now a woman with a small fortune in the bank, she married Martin, a bank clerk, also twenty-two and a "beauteous blond" like Everett Marcy. Mary's hair was naturally a modest Gloria Swanson brown, but after she saw *Bombshell* it turned Jean Harlow platinum. The glamour twins set up housekeeping in a flat in Leeds, but in spite of his good looks Martin was no bargain. He neglected to go to work, borrowed money from his wife, stayed out till all hours, came home smelling of Shalimar, said he had been with the boys, was shocked when Mary doubted him.

My marriage was a hideous blend of Andy Capp cartoon, Hitchcock's *Suspicion*, and Tom Courtenay's *Billy Liar*. You can find my husband in any abnormal psychology book, word for word, antic for antic, a man who didn't want to work, didn't live by the rules, and could never love anyone. I think he married me for my money.

Mary toured France and Switzerland writing travel articles for the *Yorkshire Evening News*. In her absence Martin consoled himself with Sonia Dresdel, star of the Harrogate Repertory Company. Mary didn't quarrel with Sonia.

We were quite good friends. I still see her on TV in *The Fallen Idol.* Anyway, Martin wasn't worth it. The last scene of *Billy Liar* is played in the Leeds Great Northern Station. I am the blonde who goes away on the train. The summer I left Martin, my stepmother came from Michigan on vacation to what she called "Yurrup" and took me back with her to meet my father. She called him "Moonie." "Moonie will love you," she said.

After Lorna left him to go to Hollywood, Walter had lived alone for a while. Then he moved to Manistique, a small town on Lake Michigan with lumber, paper, stone, and tool industries, where he was at first an accountant and eventually treasurer of Inland Lime and Stone, a subsidiary of Inland Steel. One day in 1925 while buying a cigar, he saw the merchant's daughter, Helene Marie La Foille, fourteen years younger than he, one of ten Catholic children, proprietress at seventeen of the Helene La Foille Beauty Salon—another dynamic, independent woman. Walter couldn't resist them. The following year Lorna sent him a copy of *Doorways in Drumorty* inscribed: "To Walt, For Auld lang syne, my dear." He saw she was never coming back. He talked to Helen (being English, he called Helene Helen) about getting married. At eighty Helene remembered the proposal.

I told him he had to go out and see Lorna. I said: "I'm not going to marry you till I find out how you kids feel about each other now." I didn't want any leftovers. You know how it is. You get tired of them. I wrote a book myself one time, about a Chinese that was murdered where I used to work, and Moonie said: "Not you *too!*" And he said: "Cut that *out!*" So I never wrote again. But I kept my business. He said he didn't want to be known as "Mr. Helene La Foille," but I was always financially independent. When Moonie went out to see Lorna, she asked him all about me. We were quite curious about each other. Moonie said: "The two of you would have made a great pair, believe me."

Lorna wasn't at M-G-M. The doctor had ordered six months' rest. A taxi took Walter up a narrow winding road to her house in the Hollywood hills. A Chinese servant let him in. Lorna lay on her bed in green satin pajamas. Behind her on the wall hung a large crucifix from which a sorrowful Savior looked down in compassion on her sickness and her sins. This was a surprise to Walter. As far as he knew, Lorna had never been religious. He was shocked to see how pale and thin she was, wasted to a stick, not the vibrant little armful she had been in the forests of Alberta. Her nose was shorter and the bump was gone, the one she had gotten in childhood when she believed she could fly and tried to fly down a staircase. In northeast Scotland a broken nose was trusted to heal itself. Lorna was proud of her new nose and showed it in both profiles. Walter had liked the old one, which he had foolishly supposed would make her a little more manageable, less likely to fly the coop. Wong, the servant, brought them tea.

They talked about Minneapolis, Winnipeg, even Alberta. Those days would never come again. Lorna still had her Scottish burr, though her voice was not as strong as it ought to be, but it was still deep. He told her about Helen. She said Helen sounded "pearfect," and he better marry her quick before some handsome traveling salesman could run off with her. That was the old Lorna. Suddenly she was tired and had to rest. She scribbled a note that would get him in to see the sights at the studio. She said the doctor wouldn't let her kiss old friends goodbye no matter how handsome they were. Her eyes were brown and green and gold. He couldn't look into them for long. At M-G-M Lon Chaney was too busy to see visitors, until Walter sent in word that "Mister Lorna Moon" had come. The man of a thousand faces rushed out with hand extended. "Lorna made me a star!" he said.

When Walter returned to Manistique, Helene wanted to know every detail. Walter told her most of it, the Chinese servant, the green pajamas, what Lon Chaney had said to him. She kept asking questions. Lorna was so pale, he said, wasted to a stick. Only her eyes were the same. Helene said: We don't have to get married right away. Three years later they were married in a small chapel on Mackinac Island. It was Memorial Day, May 1930, twenty-nine days after Lorna died. They lived in a house on Walnut Street.

They didn't have any children. Helene put Walter's pictures of Lorna—the old nose, the new nose, the frontier skirt, the Egyptian coiffure—into the family album along with pictures of Walter and dozens of La Foilles.

In 1939 Walter was elected president of the Rotary Club, and Helene took a vacation by herself in "Yurrup." She visited Nellie Moon, met Walter's darling daughter Mary, and brought her back to Michigan to save her from the threat of war and the ruins of a marriage. When the *Empress of Britain* docked at Quebec, Walter was waiting by the gangway to reclaim his footloose wife and face the daughter he hadn't wanted to raise. At twenty-five she would be just the age Lorna had been when he first set eyes on her in the western wilderness. Helene saw right away there was going to be trouble.

Oh, Mary was a doll when she lived with me. We had an awfully good time. But she and Moonie were no good together. They were cold toward each other, very much English. Mary would go around the house with her hair bleach-set, and Moonie would have a fit. "My wife never looks like *that!*" he'd say. She liked stirring him up. It made trouble between me and Moonie, but I didn't care. I adored her anyway. Well, why wouldn't I? I didn't have any children of my own.

Journalism was not a leading occupation in Manistique. Art, education, and social news proceeded from two movie theaters, a school library, and a blueberry festival. Family life on Walnut Street was "Archie Bunker and Gracie Allen, if Archie had gone to college." Mary had to get back to civilization. Hitler's bombers were over London. No fairy godmother had come to take her out to Hollywood. She found a job in Toronto on the *Globe and Mail*.

"Tronner" was bigger than Leeds, but it wasn't civilization. The only place to get a good meal was in the Imperial Dining Room of the York Hotel. No decent woman could travel alone without inviting brutal treatment from early Stone Age peasants. An educated woman had no one to talk to. Then the editor of the paper asked Mary out to his summer place, where she met Harry Parfit, a young publisher up from New York. Harry was a charmer, a

Richard Mead De Mill, the great-great-uncle after whom RdeM was named, one lawyer who wouldn't take the Devil as a client

Cecil de Mille, lost in story

Henry C. de Mille, who told stories to lead the people toward a better world

Beatrice Samuel de Mille, actress, wife, nurturing mother, schoolmistress, playwright's agent. On the back of this picture she wrote: "For my precious little Cecil from his 'Little Whole World,' Easter 1887"

Cecil ready to take on the world

"Let not your angry passions rise." Schoolboy
Cecil reminds himself to control his temper

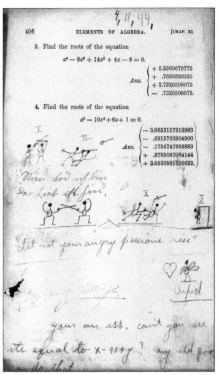

*Constance Adams de Mille, actress, a gentle lady
with an hourglass figure*

*Cecil De Mille in a play by his father
and Belasco*

Cecil B. DeMille, movie pioneer in Hollywood

Cecilia de Mille with John, the little
brother she got for Christmas 1914

Katie as RdeM first saw her, before she became
a glorious princess

Cecilia de Mille,
"Baby Bonzo," longing
to grow up

All eyes on Father at the breakfast table. Mother, John, Katie, and Cecilia

Katie at nineteen, extra player in Madam Satan. *Father is saying: "When you jump out of the burning dirigible, don't forget your parachute"*

Cecilia Hoyt de Mille, fearless rider down the dunes

*Cecilia getting control of her life,
Katie and John still unsure*

Cecilia de Mille, rising star on the Los Angeles social scene

RdeM held by Nurse Copsen, two months before he was "Wonder Baby," one month before he was "Pierre"

Katherine de Mille, actress. RdeM didn't want her to marry anybody

Richard de Mille, out of the laundry at nine months, held by Mother Constance

RdeM, age seven, the cat that walks by himself

RdeM, age eleven, bound for Hawaii on the Malolo *with Mother, Father, and staff to make* Four Frightened People

RdeM and Father boarding a train for Salt Lake City in 1937 to preview The Buccaneer

Margaret Agnes Belgrano, cousin of Manuel Belgrano, a founding father of Argentina; daughter of Frank Belgrano, "Mister Transamerica"; actress, dancer, wife, mother, at her wedding to RdeM

Cecil B. de Mille in his last year, with grandson Cecil in his first, 1958

William, "the intellectual of the family," ready for school in Germany

William Churchill de Mille at eight, a very thoughtful boy

Our Lady of Definite Opinions, Agnes George de Mille at eighty-five, dancer, choreographer, historian, biographer

William and Clara together at last, 1928

*Clara's daughter, Frances Beranger,
"Fran-sis" to RdeM, playing leads
in repertory, 1935*

gentleman, a prince, who treated Mary with courtliness, flattering admiration, and irresistible lust. He made her feel like somebody's baby, Sinderella at the ball, lost baggage found again, a deliciously illicit, beloved little hussy. And he wasn't married. For two years they met whenever he came north. One wonderful week in Manhattan they stayed at the Brevoort Hotel, dining out, seeing the shows, strolling on Washington Square, exhausting each other in their room, meeting Harry's family. The Parfits were hospitable. They treated Mary graciously. They didn't ask her anything about her family background.

One morning when Harry was just about to go overseas, the lovers woke at Niagara Falls, in the General Brock Hotel. Mary said:

"By the way, what is your religion?" Harry said he was a Jew. Mary said:

"Oh, what a *relief*! If you'd been a Catholic, my family wouldn't have *stood* for it!"

"Do you want to get married?" he said. Dear Harry, decent Harry, always ready to do the right thing. Or was it something more than that?

"I *am* married!" she said. "And I intend to stay that way, so I can never make such an awful mistake again!"

Harry did care for Mary. He respected her. She was sweet, pretty, bright, and well educated. She was dynamite in bed. But it wasn't for life. Harry knew that. His family knew that. What Mary knew, he couldn't say. She didn't reveal important thoughts, only cute entertaining ones. Maybe she was looking for love. Maybe she didn't know what she was looking for. It was the only time they talked about marriage. After settling Hitler's hash, Harry found the right girl, fathered handsome children, and acquired famous authors. He rose to prominence in the publishing field. He and Mary always wrote, and his children knew her name. That was Dad's flaming youth. The way he acts now, you'd never guess.

Mary showed me a picture of Harry and his lovely family. She was happy for him. She never blamed him for not pleading with her to get a divorce.

"This is Harry Parfit," she said, "one of my old flames—as indeed who isn't!"

At the *Globe and Mail* Mary read a glowing review of a new

Canadian novel said to be well plotted, colorful, and amusing. Young Rosie Dupris hungers for approval from ladies in the better part of town and struggles in vain to impose respectability on her happy-go-lucky family. In the end she learns that snobs are no better than folk like her. Author Eva Bruce lived with her husband Robert on Galiano Island, between Victoria and Vancouver. Her next book would be about life in the railroad camps, as she had seen it in her youth. What struck Mary most was the author's name, Eva Bruce, which Mary had heard for the first time from Walter. Eva Bruce was Lorna's younger sister.

Mary was thrilled to find a second novelist in the family, this one alive and well in British Columbia. When vacation rolled around she went west in search of her literary aunt. Canada is very big. Most of Mary's vacation was used up on the train, but she had a few days in "Van," a clean, orderly city between high mountains and blue sea, with splendid English gardens and a first-rate zoo. Uncle Robert was not a writer, he kept a store on Galiano Island, but his "Auntie Belle" had been Isabel Ecclestone Mackay, a well-known Canadian poetess of the 1920s and a friend of Rupert Brooke's. Sunday, all the Bruces came from Galiano Island to visit Mary at her hotel in "Van"—Uncle Robert, Aunt Eva, and their son and daughter, Don and Dorine. Uncle Robert sat smiling at his wife of thirty years, as she made the room ring with lively Scottish discourse. Listening to her Buchan burr thick as winter oatmeal, Mary heard her own mother speaking in the voice that should have warmed the heart of a little girl, but Aunt Eva had a daughter of her own. Dorine, nearly Mary's age, was a sturdy, likable young woman. Donald, a year younger, was a tall good-looking fellow, who spoke about Technocracy, a visionary scheme in which scientists and technicians would shape and govern a brave new world. Because of the war Don was working as a steel fitter in the shipyards, but his ambition was to write the great Canadian novel. Mary had tried to write a novel. It was hard to bring the characters to life, to show what they were feeling. At the moment, Mary was feeling drawn to her cousin Don.

"When we left," Dorine recalled, "Don somehow stayed on. He didn't come home until morning. Nobody said anything about it." Presumably the bachelor writers spent the night comparing plots, getting to know Technocracy, and reading the poems of Auntie Belle, but there was no time left for them to meet again. Two years later Don married Bertie, a schoolteacher, librarian, and occasional essayist, older than he, down to earth, not a visionary.

Back in Toronto a notice came from England. Martin had filed for divorce on grounds of desertion. Mary didn't care about Martin. He had only wanted her money. Walter the Monster had torn her from her loving mother's breast. Aunt Nellie had thrown her pictures out and sent her dog away to die. Uncle Frank had died. Anyone Mary trusted would abandon her. She had constant headaches, frequent dizziness, fainting spells. She worried about a brain tumor, felt tired all the time, couldn't keep her mind on her work, couldn't stop crying, left her job, reluctantly took refuge in her father's house.

Thirty-two years later, in April 1977, I saw the following exchange in William F. Buckley's *National Review*:

Dear Mr. Buckley:
   I have read two of your recent books, alas.
   Airborne is totally without merit, except for its title which, although clever, is a misnomer, since a substantial part of the trip was under power, with barrels of fuel lashed on deck, no less. The book has no substance, no message, no entertainment, no value. Your publisher should be more discriminating.
   Saving the Queen is a good story, but you have abominable taste and insensitivity.
   These two books are no recommendation for your *National Review* or any other of your publications.

Sincerely yours,
Louis E. Prickman, M.D.
Mayo Clinic
Rochester, Minn.

Dear Doc:
Please call me Bill. Can I call you by your nickname?
Cordially,

WFB

Thinking that was pretty funny, I sent a copy to sister Mary. She answered in a pique because "that smart aleck Buckley" had insulted "darling Dr. Prickman, to whom I owe my life and whatever sanity I have scraped together."

I spent my first day at the Mayo Clinic dredging up the hideous tale of how I was murdered by the Moons. Then, with my aching head tucked underneath my arm, I walked the diagnostic tower to be X-rayed from head to knees, pummelled, peered at, probed, and bled. On the fifth day I found myself facing half a dozen doctors sitting in a row. I ventured a small joke about the trial of Joan of Arc. It was a mistake. Three of those cats were shrinks. They told me they were not my judges, they were there to help me.

Dr. Prickman said there was nothing physically wrong with me, but apparently my life was so unbearable to me that I would take time out from it by falling in a faint. I want to tell you it's scary to be walking down a Toronto street, and the next thing you know you're staring up at strangers.

"If you don't like Canada," Dr. Prickman said, "why not pick another place? Where have you always wanted to go?" California, I said. I told him that I sometimes feel like screaming.

"Well then, scream," he said. "If you don't begin to express your feelings, one day you will come to a fork in the road. One arm on the sign will say, Insanity, the other will say, Suicide. Turn back, little lady, right now." He wrote me a prescription: "One hearty scream whenever the patient deems it necessary." I obeyed him to the letter, and except for flu going round the office I haven't been sick a day since. God bless Dr. Prickman, and may William Buckley's hair come out of curl on television!

When Mary wrote that letter, she had been a member of our family for eighteen years, and this was the first word she had said about psychiatry. Though Dr. Prickman had clearly failed to deepen or sensitize the superficial, tasteless William Buckley, it was reassuring to know that with one simple prescription he had unbottled the torment of Mary Moon, the baby nobody wanted, and sent her down the road to mental health in California. On second thought, when had I ever seen Mary's emotional cork come out? Calling me a nitwit wasn't the primal scream. When Mary wasn't reading a book or sitting quietly in a corner listening to the grown-ups, she was a little ray of sunshine, merry and bright, full of jokes, laughing, telling stories.

"The world," said cheery Mary Moon, "is a tragedy to those who feel, a comedy to those who think."

CHAPTER 9

Daddy and Tiger

The minute Mary saw the HOLLYWOODLAND sign, she knew she had come home—palm trees and snowy peaks, Coconut Grove and orange groves, lacquered nails in wet cement at Grauman's Chinese Theater, one-story pink stucco bungalow apartments in need of some repair. Wartime was winding down. The best years of our lives were coming. On the major lots the big reels were turning. Staffs of thousands thought they would never stop. Mary went straight to M-G-M, told them she was Lorna's daughter, and was hired for the International Publicity Department. Not that they remembered Lorna, who had gone out with silent films, but they knew an English schoolgirl when they heard one. International assistant Moon would know her Piccadilly from her peccadillo. Here at last she found the festival in the desert, the oasis in the wilderness of despair, new excitement every day, big names, colossal productions, shocking rumors, delicious gossip, a paycheck every Wednesday for marching in the last row of the parade, for cheering from the sidelines, for typing clean originals and four carbon copies of the great romance.

Frances Marion was delighted to meet Lorna's daughter after so many years. She spoke warmly about her dear departed friend, the sad loss of such a promising talent and the great career that

would have followed. She gave Mary her own personal copy of
Dark Star, Number Five in the limited signed edition of one hundred, this one also signed by Mary Pickford. Mary treasured the
volume and showed it to her women friends. Older women liked
to mother Mary. Her friend Margaruite, in the real estate business,
gave her a place to hang her stocking every Christmas Eve. Her
friend Niki, a film editor, took her in on Christmas Day. Men liked
Mary too, and they also took her in.

Rod Bugiardo helped to manage his father's restaurant, Casanova's on the Strip, where the stars came to dine. Mary loved going
there. One night she sat with Conrad Veidt, who played the magnificent evil magician in Sabu's *Thief of Bagdad*, and Martyn Green,
star of D'Oyly Carte's *Mikado*, whom she had known in England.
It was like old times. A fan who didn't have a clue who these two
celebrities were came up and asked them for their autographs. The
two performers solemnly wrote each other's names. It was hilarious.

Back at her apartment Rod said Mary was the sweetest girl he
had ever known. She called him a Latin lover and told him her
mother, Lorna Moon, had been a quarter French (how Mary got
this notion, I have no idea) and she herself was three-quarters
French, because the Moons had come across the Channel with
Willy the Norman. Rod said: Baby, I believe it! Then he didn't
call. A friend told her he had married a waitress at Casanova's.
Mary tried not to think about it. One night someone knocked at
the door. Mary opened the peephole, and who should be standing
there but the Latin lover himself, looking so miserable and
ashamed that she let him in. He said he owed her an explanation,
but first he needed a drink. She said she needed one too. He said
he had never loved Lisetta, but when she got pregnant his father
had forced him to marry her. The whole thing was a tragedy. Mary
was the one he loved. He couldn't stand not seeing her. He hoped
she could forgive him for doing such a stupid thing. She told him
to go away and leave her alone. He understood. He didn't blame
her. He knew it was just as hard on her as it was on him. He had
to kiss her one more time, just to say goodbye.

Kisses were love. They filled her with love. She didn't want to
wake up from love. He told her she was the sweetest girl he had

ever known. He said he was glad she was French, because French
women understood these things. Around one o'clock he said that
of all the girls he had ever known she was the one who deserved
the best. He said he had to go home now, because Lisetta would
probably be throwing up in the morning. Alone in the dark Mary
tossed and turned. She took a pill to make her sleep. It didn't
help. She took another. She didn't want to wake up alone. The
doctor at County Hospital said she had a strong constitution.

How much of this story did Mary tell her newfound brother and
sister-in-law? She told us the hilarious part, about Conrad Veidt
and Martyn Green and the autographs. The rest we learned long
after, from her women friends. Helen Lampson, an older woman,
was a studio animator. Father gave her an award for solving a technical problem on *The Ten Commandments*. Fellow workers thought
Helen was sucking up to the Boss and stopped talking to her.
Helen remembered how Mary stood by her, what a loyal friend
she was.

We had lunch every day in the Paramount commissary. Mary
gave me courage and helped me through the freeze. We became close friends. Most Sundays we spent together, going
to concerts, theater, or movies, or sitting in front of the television sewing. We were forever altering outfits movie stars
had sold to secondhand stores. Little by little she told me
the sad story of her life. She had always been searching for
some wonderful person who would make her happy. Ordinary
men didn't understand her or appreciate her. She couldn't
give up her vision of a prince on a white horse who would
really love her.

Girlfriends kept setting her up with well-meaning insurance
men and sincere accountants. Mary tolerated them, and they
didn't call again. She was waiting for Laurence Olivier holding a
glass slipper. She got Fred Wimpel, a Paramount musician. The
best-directed movie kiss might not carry you away without Fred's
liquid violin swelling on the soundtrack. But poor Fred was going
through a terrible divorce. What he really needed now was understanding and affection. Mary was the perfect girl to comfort a suf-

fering artist. At his hillside hacienda overlooking the reservoir, Fred gave fabulous parties. One unforgettable night Martyn Green and Groucho Marx and Stanley Holloway harmonized *Tit Willow*. It was a riot. Then Mary telephoned and a woman's voice said: Fred can't come to the phone right now. Is there any message? No, Mary said, no message.

Jack Palter wrote scripts for all the major studios. He told Mary she had talent and they could work together, but he liked to work in Paris. Paris is my kind of town, she said. Jack went on ahead to get them an apartment. Mary's French was pretty rusty and she studied every day at lunch in the commissary. She told Helen Lampson she would soon be off to Paris. Weeks went by, and Jack could never find the right apartment. Mary stopped talking about him. Her make-believe Romeos saw her talent in her boobs and didn't look any further. She was afraid to ask for more. She didn't want to offend the latest randy toad, who just might be the Prince in disguise.

Helen Lampson's daughter was twenty years younger than Mary.

You surprised me when you told me how much older she was. She had such a cute little figure, I thought of her as a Barbie doll. She used to come over all the time just to visit us. She was terribly lonely. There were times when she would cry and say nobody cared for her and she wished she could die. She said she had tried marriage once and that was enough, but she was desperate to get married. For months she dated a real jerk, a car salesman. He drove a white convertible Cadillac and always had a smile on his face. And a mustache. I think she went on picking men who only wanted to use her because she thought she didn't deserve anything better.

If your own father didn't love you, why should any other man? Following her mother's trail back toward the golden age, Mary got a job in the Paramount steno pool. One day she was sent to work in the DeMille bungalow.

"Lorna Moon's *daughter?*" Father's eyes lit up. "Bring her in to see me."

When Father looked at Mary, he didn't see an employee, he saw the daughter of his brother's secret mistress, the unsuspecting sister of his brother's unacknowledged son, who was now his own son, a pleasant damsel in distress whom he could help without telling anyone the reason. Neither the dramatist nor the conspirator nor the Good Samaritan in him could resist such a Machiavellian mix-up. He sheltered Mary and kept her warm in a trivial job where she wasted the few years that were left of her youth shrinking from opportunity, to bask in the passing smiles of an imaginary father.

After DeMille Productions closed down, Mary must have had thirty jobs in and around entertainment. Evenings and weekends she typed scripts at the homes of writers and producers—"unfortunately chaperoned by their attractive wives." But Hollywood was crumbling. Movie jobs were hard to find and they didn't last. Mary couldn't bear ordinary jobs, dull jobs without excitement, glamour, or romance, jobs Lorna Moon would never have accepted. She liked working for Edward James, called "the Little Prince," who was writing his memoirs but never got through Chapter One, because he couldn't find the perfect room to write in. A rich homosexual eccentric, Edward James entered history as a patron of Dali and Magritte and a crucial patron of Balanchine. Novelist Henry James, he said, was his distant cousin, Edward the Seventh his unofficial grandpa. All of it could have been true, but none of it was. Mary believed the Prince's tales and was thrilled to stay with him for late suppers and royal gossip. His imitation of Wally Simpson scolding poor Cousin Edward (the Eighth) was a perfect scream.

Newspapers in Los Angeles didn't have a good spot for an English feature writer who had altered her driver's license to take ten years off her age. Slick-paper editors made rosy promises and then were out of town. Encouraged by her friend Margaruite, Mary studied real estate, passed the exam, and got her license. But the market was in a slump. Her one transaction was to invest her own savings in a vacation lot at Lake Arrowhead, where the values were bound to triple in five years. A UCLA adviser told her she could get a B.A. in seven years of night classes. Mary wrote to England for her high school credits. At the Scottish games in Santa Monica she wore the Cameron plaid and searched for kin among the tartans.

She took up psychical research. A photograph of a soul leaving a dying body taught her that death is not the end. At a miracle service she was lifted to her feet by Kathryn Kuhlman's ringing words: "*Faith* . . . is the *power* . . . by which the thing *desired* . . . becomes the thing *possessed*!"

"KO'd by the Holy Spirit," Mary fell in a faint and was born again. None of it filled the hollow in her orphan heart.

Margaret and I had moved to Santa Barbara, where I taught psychology at the university. Mary came to stay with us at Christmas. She brought a letter from brother Bill in the frozen north.

Hi Sis. Another year gone by. Beryl went out to cut our tree. The old bones creak a little more. 5 AM to 5 PM seems a lot longer than it used to. Have a few late born calves coming out of the woods. Each one has its own expression. Some are curly faced with big surprised looking eyes. I get a chuckle every time I see a new one. Guess they all look alike to some people. Last few months been working at the lumber mill repairing the machinery. Quite a change from logging in the woods. Don't know if you heard that our Auntie Annie Lyall died. She was 86. We had been to Calgary to see her in September. Hadn't seen her since I was a kid. She sure took a dim view of what our mother did. She told me that when Mother left, she wanted to adopt me. I was four years old and my Dad had to board me out when he went off on jobs. When are you going to come up here and see some of your hillbilly relations? It's a lot later than you think. Love from your brother Bill XXX

Bill and Beryl Hebditch had a farm at Ashton Creek in eastern British Columbia, 160 acres with a well, a barn, and a log cabin bought with a veteran's loan. They kept chickens, cows, and sheep and planted fruits, vegetables, and grain, mostly for their own use. To bring in cash Bill drove heavy equipment, slashing up the mountain to seven thousand feet for a power line or plowing snow off forest roads for the logging trucks. Beryl worked in the box mill making four-pound fruit baskets—"with a tin around the edge. You had a machine that you clamped the pin on with your foot." At home they did the chores before sunup and after dark. When it came time for Mom and Pop and the two boys to take a bath, water was hand-pumped from the well, heated on the wood stove, and poured into a square tub set on the kitchen floor. This was in the 1950s, not before the Civil War. Bill felled and hauled trees and put together a little sawmill where he and Beryl cut ties to sell to the railroad and boards for a new house on the farm. Bill piped water from the creek, but light still came from kerosene lamps and the toilet was still a two-holer down the garden path. Now it was 1970 and forty years had passed since Bill had learned from a lawyer's letter that he had a sister, but all he had ever seen of her was snapshots in tight sweaters.

Mary fluttered her mascara. "Don't you think we all ought to go up there and meet the rest of our family while there is still time?"

In August, four city people to whom all calves might look alike, Richard, Margaret, Mary, and thirteen-year-old Cecil, arrived at the Empress Hotel, an elegant nineteenth-century monument in the English garden city of Victoria at the southern tip of Vancouver Island, where carriage horses trotted through the parks. The country people would drive west in their camper three hundred miles to meet us. Don Bruce, still saving society through Technocracy, would cross the strait from Vancouver on the ferry. Eva Bruce, almost eighty, wasn't well enough to come down on the train, so we would drive north to see her. Bill didn't want to go north with us, but he was eager to meet his brother and sister.

Despite having entered the world through the same tight tube, Bill and I had gone very different ways and were leery of each other—the older and the younger, the chain saw and the silver spoon, the woodsman with his fourth-grade education, the professor with his Ph.D., Bill Bunyan roaring up the mountain, crashing through the forest on his mighty diesel, Dr. de Mille buzzing down the freeway in his Fiat. The showdown came at sunset outside McKenzie's Grill on the Victoria waterfront. Stalking tensely toward the other, each was surprised to see a five-foot-six tourist wearing a hopeful smile. Before saying goodbye forever, our tiny truant mother had thoughtfully made the country mouse the same size as the town mouse. The closer we came, the less dangerous each seemed to be. As though we had done it a thousand times, we put our arms around each other, and I knew he was my brother Bill.

Beryl (pronounced "Burl" in the country) was a rugged frontier wife, a woman you could count on to dig your spuds, hoe your corn, bear your boys, and help you build a house, not a flicker of pretense or an ounce of whimsy in her anywhere. At dinner Bill told us about when the water line froze up. Couldn't keep it open. Had to lay six hundred feet of new pipe, insulate it with hay bales left over from the harvest, thaw the rest with boiling water pumped from a can, give the one-inch line a ninety-foot enema with the half-inch hose. He grinned. "Running water at last! No more dust-bathing with the chickens!"

Mary said it was heroic. Bill asked her:

"When are you coming out to visit us on the farm?" Mary said: *"Oooh!"* Beryl said:

"She can help with the milking, eh?" Mary blanched. Margaret whispered:

"She doesn't own a pair of flat shoes."

Next day Cousin Don joined us for high tea at the Empress Hotel. Bertie, his wife of twenty-five years, didn't come along. The tall, slender, hard steel fitter who would someday write the great Canadian novel was now the large, soft editor of the *BC Motorist*, a magazine for British Columbia tourists. He sat smiling like a Buddha. He took snapshots of the brothers standing in front of a potted palm with their sister's soft, white, smooth, bare shoulders wedged ecstatically between them. He talked quietly with her in a corner. She told him the job situation was desperate in Los Angeles. He asked if she would still like to write travel articles. In *Canada?* she gasped. He said his assistant had quit and he needed a girl Friday. What about the other days? said naughty Mary Moon.

Eva Bruce lived in the town of Campbell River, 150 miles north of Victoria. Daughter Dorine lived next door and kept an eye on her. Eva was surprised to learn that Annie Lyall, her oldest sister, had lived so long back there in Alberta and only now was dead. The two sisters hadn't spoken since 1935.

"Mrs. Lyall meant less than nothing to me," Eva said.

Perhaps it wasn't a close-knit family. What the two had quarreled about no one seemed to know, but Don later told Mary that when his mother was young she called herself "a witch on wheels," and he was not one to contradict his mother.

In her little two-room house Aunt Eva had few possessions. After husband Robert went to a nursing home, she gave her clothes and books away to strangers and mislaid the records of a lifetime. Sitting on her creaky bed, she poked about in a dusty box for souvenirs she didn't find. Only memories were left, colored by old wishes. The six of us went out for lunch, grilled salmon by the Campbell River, then sat in Eva's garden getting acquainted. Bill and Beryl, we explained, couldn't come today because they had to see some people in Victoria. Eva was very disappointed. She spoke in her Buchan burr about "puir luttl Billy" abandoned in 1912.

"He was the *sweetest* young un! After Lorna left, I took care of him for a year, and he was *really* cared for! But his father didn't want me to see them anymore. He wanted the child to forget his mother." Eva shed a tear at the misfortune of her little nephew and because he wouldn't come to see her. Margaret and I were sad to see Aunt Eva so forlorn, a frail old woman neglected by an ungrateful nephew.

I wrote to my hard-hearted brother reminding him that our aged aunt had been a mother to him when he needed one. Beryl set me straight. Will Hebditch, Bill's father, had been working miles from home. When he returned after a week, his wife was gone and his little boy had been left with neighbors. Though Eva and Robert lived nearby, Bill didn't remember her ever taking care of him, or seeing them at all. "They were his only other relatives there," Beryl said, "and they didn't bother with him all the time he was growing up."

A picture of Bill eight years old shows a grim little fellow making the best of things, refusing to complain. In eighty years he didn't say an unkind word about our mother, or a kind word either. He did remember she had hurt him when she cleaned his fingernails. Did you ever hear from her after she left home? I asked. "One phone call," he said.

The deserted father and son passed a year or two alone, then lived with Mrs. Ransom, a large, capable farm widow with children of her own. Whatever mothering Bill got, he got from Mrs. Ransom. He didn't speak about her either, but he would speak about his father.

Dad told me he had seven years' apprenticeship to his father in the watchmaking trade. Until I was about 15 our house was always ticking, clocks and watches all over the place in various states of repair. I asked Dad why he gave it up. He said he never liked the work but it brought a welcome dollar. In England in those days, if Great-granddad hoed turnips you were expected to do the same. My Dad loved the country. He spent his spare time as a lad going out to farms. Before he got married he was a traveling watchmaker going all over England and Scotland repairing clocks and watches. In 1910 the British papers were pushing emigration. Come to the land of opportunity, file on 160 acres of virgin soil for $10. Sounds marvelous I admit. But a gentleman farmer in leggings and tweed jacket with his cow man in tow is a far cry from clearing 160 acres of timber and brush with an axe and a shovel. As a frontier farmer my Dad was out of his depth. Still, never at any time did he say he regretted giving up his old life and coming out to Canada.

Mary's ten-year-old car was totaled by a drunk driver, and she had to come by Greyhound at Christmas. In February the Sylmar temblor knocked the freeway down and shook up her resolve. In April her friend Niki died. In May she landed a "horrible" job scheduling concerts for a Greek pianist. In August her friend Margaruite was buried before anyone remembered to tell Mary she was ill. In November Mary wrote from a tenth-floor apartment in Vancouver's posh West End.

My balcony looks out on Galiano Island, a lovely beach at English Bay, and shining gypsum mountains. By day it's

Santa Monica Bay, by night it's a metropolitan city with big department stores, Rexall Drugs, Trader Vic's, Colonel Sanders, Forest Lawn, underground newspapers, Satanic murders, a black woman who dances nude with a boa constrictor, just like Los Angeles. I brought Graymalkin and Riley Finick with me on the plane, but cats aren't allowed and I had to smuggle them in. Now they can never go outside till we come back to southern California.

At the *BC Motorist* I'm a junior executive with lots of responsibility for administration and planning. My new boss, the lovely and talented Don Bruce, works seven days a week, and I'm here to lighten the load—editing, writing, proofreading, rewriting news releases, attending conventions, liaison with the Mounties. I'm back in journalism, which I should *never* have left! I could walk to work, but DB picks me up on his way to the office and brings me home at night. I think it's his sneaky way of getting me to work on time.

In her desk Mary found a notebook. She called out to the office staff: "I've found Donald's little black book!"

Staff fell on the floor laughing. All the pages were blank. Prim and proper Editor says I'm turning his life into a nightmare. He's sending me to Honolulu. He says it's to make a speech about BC to travel agents, but it's really to get me out of the office.

Articles by Mary Moon began to appear in the *Motorist*. One of them bumped the Editor out of first place.

DB says I'm after his job and he's afraid that's not all. I told him he should live in a more exciting city with a warmer climate, but he's scared of the USA. He says Vancouver is exciting enough, especially with me here to fill his days with terror. He was appalled when I told him that the mystery writer Georges Simenon claimed to have enjoyed 10,000 different women.

Thanks for the lovely, *lovely* invitation to come at Christmas. Back to civilization again! Sure beats sitting in my apartment watching Santa on TV.

For seven years Mary lived in her Vancouver apartment, a few blocks from Don and Bertie's apartment. She saw Don almost every day but she never met his wife. Bertie didn't come to the office. Don didn't invite Mary to his home. Sometimes he talked about Bertie. She had been born in Fernie, a mining town in eastern British Columbia, known as the "King of Coal." Her father, Major Robert Black, died at Vimy Ridge. Her childhood was pure misery, but she rose above it—university honors in English, teaching certificate, chairmanship of the Vancouver Aquarium Education Committee. Still, there were times when she wouldn't see anybody. Right now he couldn't talk to her about things going wrong at the office, or she would burst into tears. His mother was going off the deep end. It was getting him down. Mary said, it's a good thing we have each other to talk to.

Dorine had a good opinion of her sister-in-law:

Bertie was a good wife for Don and helped him in many ways. Never complained about the pittance they had to live on when he was so involved in Technocracy. It took the two of them four years to get up enough courage to get married. Mother was furious when they wrote and told her they had done it. I'll never forget the day the letter came. Mother ran to a friend's house shouting, "I've lost my son, I've lost my son!" They thought Don had died.

Mary wrote an article about "Ogopogo, the Bashful Beastie of Lake Okanagan," British Columbia's answer to the Loch Ness Monster. The Indians called him God of the Water and carried a chicken in the canoe to toss to him while they paddled hard for shore. White men had seen him too, and Mary related their adventures in the *BC Motorist*. To each observer he looked different. Ogopogo of Okanagan was seventy-five feet long, a great black reptilian mass. No, he was blubbery, dull, and gray. Not at all! He was shiny green. His head was like a snake, a horse, a sheep, a dragon, a swan. His legs were short but his tale was long. He wouldn't hold still for photographs. The article was a smash hit in the Okanagan Valley, where Mary was wined and dined and asked to speak to the Chamber of Commerce. She loved every minute of it. She wrote texts for two photographic travel books, which sold a hundred thousand copies. Her picture was printed in the Vancouver *West Ender.* "Mary Moon has achieved international recognition by being listed in the *World's Who's Who of Women.*" Her real career had begun at last.

Mary told Don it was high time they made plans to head south. She gave him "California lessons" to get him ready for life in the semi-tropics. He would retire with a pension and begin his novel. She would freelance or at worst get a PR job. Already she was working seven days a week saving money to make the move. Don listened with a smile. He had been to Los Angeles, a dark Satanic milieu populated by poor devils wheezing in the smog. He knew Bertie wouldn't like it. He said: "Your beloved Los Angeles never put you into the World's Woo! Woo! of Women. It's better to be a big frog in a little pond." Mary said:

"Your little pond is a puddle, and there's nobody here but you and me. If you drop dead tomorrow, I won't even go to your funeral. I'll be too busy packing." He called her Miss Ingratitude of 1974. She told him he was just another pretty face.

Don was Mary's guide, protector, confidant, and entertainer. At the door of her office he barked: "Come, Watson, come! The game's afoot!" When a vice president wanted to fire Moon and hire a salesman, Don said: "We have got a foeman who is worthy of our steel!" To the publisher he said: "If Moon goes, I go too." Moon stayed.

Beyond a million laughs with Don, she had no social life at all. She swam in the apartment pool four times a week and didn't make a single friend. She covered the wall of her apartment with framed color photographs of glory days at Paramount, the old DeMille Unit gang, and a portrait of Don, her friend in exile, her lovely boss, her fellow writer and romantic. She read the Los Angeles Sunday *Times* and wrote to friends who were far away: "I know and love every inch of that city, which brought me almost the only happiness I have ever known." In Mary's song of happiness, bluebirds like Bugiardo, Wimpel, and Palter went unsung.

Fed up with politics at the *Motorist*, Don landed a better job as executive editor for the Western Postal Region. Before they could fire her, Mary resigned in sympathy and started a book on Ogopogo. Querying eighty publishers in three countries, she found one in Vancouver. During the research and writing, Don supported her in secret. He told her that as long as he was around she wouldn't have to worry about groceries or rent. They met at lunch to discuss her project. Sometimes Mary cooked for him at home. Don's advice was invaluable. His prim and proper pose presented a delightful challenge to an affectionate, lonely woman who fancied herself a quarter French and felt a delicious bond with Dorothy Wordsworth, who had been "an item" with her brother William. Clowning together in the park, they photographed each other sporting deerstalker hats and peering at clues on maple leaves through a magnifying glass. Writing to a woman friend, Mary called Don "the man in my life." She didn't like sharing him with a wife, even an invisible one. When he came back from a month's vacation spent in Europe with Bertie, Mary wrote as if he had been traveling alone.

Missed him dreadfully every day. I think I've found the Father I've always wanted. When I'm miserable he says, "Tell Daddy all about it." When I'm not getting anywhere, he says, "Just keep soldiering on. You simply cannot fail at *everything, all* the time." When I said, "I can't give speeches," Donald said, "Of *course*, you can. Go out there and knock 'em *dead*, Tiger!"

Mary was a capable writer. Her book *Ogopogo* was a solid professional job, reporting a popular mystery from different points of view. It satisfied skeptics and believers and was well received by scientists as well as laymen. Reviews appeared in more than fifty newspapers, magazines, and journals. She worked hard at promotion, and sales were very good. A follow-on article was published in *Smithsonian* magazine and reprinted in a historical anthology, the only chapter by a nonacademic writer.

Mary loved seeing her book in the shops and finding it in the library. Proudly she announced: "The Moon in the card catalogue is no longer my mother!" In March 1978 she appeared coast-to-coast on Canadian and American TV standing on the shore of Lake Okanagan "In Search of . . . Ogopogo." While the credits were rolling, I called her on the phone.

R: It's very exciting to be related to a famous person!
M: We try to keep humble.

She sent a tabloid clipping:

UNWANTED CHILDREN
WHO GREW UP TO BE GREAT

Unwanted, neglected, or mistreated children who overcame obstacles to become giants in science, literature, art, and government: Leonardo da Vinci, Elizabeth I, Sir Isaac Newton, Lord Byron, James A. Michener.

At the bottom she wrote: "So *there*, Lorna!"

The newborn celebrity didn't rest on her laurels but scoured western Canada for a hot exclusive. In April she began a new project, rewriting the adventures of one Bobby Sutton, "a retired safecracker and jewel thief, on the lam from U.S. justice, who lives quietly with his family in Vancouver when he isn't risking life and liberty in Bolivia cooking up shady deals with Nazi fugitive Klaus Barbie, the Butcher of Lyon." In 1978 this was a promising topic, since it would be five years before the French would get their hands on the elusive Barbie and haul him back to France for trial. There was also a CIA connection, and Mary was bombarding the stonewallers in Washington with Freedom of Information Act demands.

From April to mid-August we didn't hear a word from the journalistic dynamo. Then she sent a brief note: "Working on the absolutely frightening Nazi book. No money until it gets published, alas. November *Fate* will have an Ogopogo story by me." Everything seemed to be okay, until a letter came from Dorine.

Dear Cousin Richard,
I just wanted to let you know that Don passed away July 31.
It was a terrible shock to us. He was only 64, in the prime of
life and at the peak of his career. It was cancer. Two weeks
after he entered the hospital he was dead.

I wrote sympathetically to Mary. Her answer revealed what her
previous note had hidden.

You were right to think I was too upset to tell anyone about
Donald. I couldn't go to the funeral. I still can't cope with the
situation. The worst thing is that the one who used to comfort
me isn't here to pull me through the worst heartbreak of my
whole life. Before my darling Donald died, he said I should
go back to Los Angeles, but I don't know if I can do it
without his help. I have supported myself since I was
eighteen, but now my age is against me. For the first time in
my life I am frightened.

I wrote urging her to finish the Nazi book and come back as
quickly as she could. She asked to postpone our Christmas until
summer. There was one bit of good news. The *Smithsonian* would
publish her article. All in all, she was taking it well.

On Friday, 13 October, the apartment manager called. Mary had
listed me as next of kin. The body had been removed, but someone had to pay the rent and dispose of the personal possessions. I
flew to Vancouver. Bill and Beryl came from the farm. We loaded
useful items into their van, went to the bank and to a lawyer, and
settled with the manager. The date and cause of death weren't
known. The coroner wouldn't report for several weeks. Bill was
suspicious. I was not. Mary had worked long and hard. Finally she
had tasted success. She had ability, ambition, and three thousand
dollars in the bank. She had promised to come south. Bill was
stoically downcast. Living out there in the forest, he knew the
ways of beasts and men. Beasts were easier to figure. Mary had
sent him many letters, photos, and press clippings. He had grown
very fond of her, his starry-eyed little sister. Once they had met
for dinner at Lake Okanagan, but she would never come out to

the farm to see how country people lived. He was sure they would have found a few things to talk about. "Country people are smarter than city people think," he said.

Bill didn't want to drive in the Vancouver traffic, so I drove his truck. I told him about double-clutching four-by-fours in the army. He was impressed. He begged me to come for a visit. I could drive the tractor, pick raspberries, milk the cow. I said I would pick raspberries, once things calmed down. "Why didn't she *call* us!" he said.

I spoke with Bobby Sutton, safecracker, jewel thief, author on the lam. He had dialed his ghostwriter every day for three weeks. Finally a man picked up the phone and said he was with the coroner's office. Bobby suspected the CIA. They were protecting Barbie. Mary was asking too many questions. The spooks could make an execution look like a suicide.

After working three days in Mary's apartment with the balcony door open and a big fan running, I came home with records, letters, mementos, and manuscripts. Soon a small but weighty package was delivered to our house bearing a five-dollar duty stamp. I wrote to U.S. Customs that, while my late sister had been popular on two continents and had appeared on coast-to-coast TV, I didn't think her ashes would bring a price from collectors. Customs rescinded the duty. Weeks passed before I was rid of the acrid smell of formaldehyde and the vision of blood and hair on the bathroom floor. Brewing coffee in the morning kept bringing them back. Some subtle trick of chemistry.

Just before landing in Vancouver and going to Mary's apartment I had been reading about the Buddhist saint Milarepa, who went back after many years to his village in Tibet and found his mother's house fallen into ruin. In a heap of rags and earth overgrown with weeds he discovered her long-dead body. Overcome with grief and the futility of earthly life, he lay in meditation for seven nights and days with his head resting on his mother's bones, then rose in tranquillity and carried them away to be ground into powder, mixed with clay, and molded into *tsha-tshas*, which are little memorial figures. Mary's little memorials were in print.

For twenty years I had thought of Lorna as Mary's mother, whom she adored and would someday write an adoring book about—Lorna Moon, Woman of Mystery, focus of Hollywood intrigue, best-selling novelist, gallant survivor against the odds, doomed artist, tragic heroine. Now the story belonged to me, and Lorna was my mother. I had some questions to ask her. Why did you abandon Bill and Mary and me? Were all three of us unwelcome? Did you care about any of us? The first thing I had to know was how my mother's second child had died. The record of Mary's final year was in her notes and letters and her appointment book.

Wednesday, 4 January. Mary was in Hollywood seeing a few friends and looking for a job that would pay the rent, so she could do some freelancing and wait for Don to retire and come south. She called Don at his office in Vancouver.

Saturday, 7 January. Mary was in Vancouver writing letters promoting *Ogopogo* and asking magazines for writing assignments. She was expecting Don at three.

During January she conferred with Bobby Sutton, watched her friend Elke Sommer in a movie on TV, booked her Los Angeles Christmas flight a year in advance, lunched alone at a hotel to celebrate "Robbie Burns's Birthday," saw Don Sunday morning, the 22nd. In February she corresponded with the *National Enquirer*, conferred with Bobby Sutton, had solitary lunches out, laughed at *Fawlty Towers* on TV. Don was away from the office for days, and she couldn't call him.

March was an exciting month. Don came two Sundays in a row and read the early Barbie chapters. Mary watched *herself* on TV, and got a fan call from her brother. Easter weekend, all alone except for Riley Finick, she watched *The Ten Commandments*, relived the glory days once more, heard the thrilling voices of charming, famous actors who had spoken to her kindly, saw the fiery hand of God write the holy words on stone, animated by Helen Lampson, her friend, remembered how safe and warm she had felt in the bungalow, protected by the tribal chief, the great showman, the boss benign. Monday Don had the day off, and she couldn't call him.

Saturday, 1 April, Don came to the apartment, and again the following Saturday and Sunday. Always Don understood her, believed in her, respected her, made her feel worthy of success, confident, unafraid. When they were together she could almost see the happy ending. In the last reel, baby comes home, the lost love is found, the desired is possessed, the unwanted child is comforted, cherished, admired, kissed, caressed. Monday night she watched the Oscars. Tuesday she worked with Bobby Sutton. Wednesday she came down with the flu and had it for three weeks. Riley Finick was restless. He still missed Graymalkin, gone now for two years. In May he wouldn't eat. The vet came and charged forty dollars. Riley bit and scratched and wouldn't take his medicine. Don was out of town for a week. While he was gone, Riley died.

In June the weather was glorious, ninety degrees on many days. Don came early Sunday morning. Mary swam every day and treated herself to *salade niçoise* at the Café de Paris. She rewrote the Bolivian prison sequence. Wednesday, 21 June, Don came by at 6 p.m., an unusual time for him. He said he wasn't feeling well. Dr. Tollman had ordered him into the clinic for tests. Every day Mary called, but there was nothing definite. Friday, 7 July, she went into Elle on Seymour Street and bought an expensive but modest-looking tie for Don's birthday. Sunday the 9th she wrote in her appointment book in shorthand: "No DB." Shorthand was for things she couldn't say out loud.

Friday, 14 July, Don went to General Hospital for an operation. During the first week he improved, during the second week he didn't. On Thursday, 27 July, Mary went to Dr. Bell and told him she couldn't sleep. Instead of the sleeping pills she expected, he prescribed a drug she had never heard of. At home she put the bottle away for when it might be needed. Friday she called the hospital. Mr. Bruce was sleeping. She left a message. He didn't call back. Saturday she was afraid to call. The Sea Parade was on TV. She had covered it for Don, when he was her editor. She met Bobby Sutton at 2 p.m. William Holden and Richard Widmark fought the Civil War on TV. Sunday she worked on her manuscript and waited for Don's call. She watched Bing Crosby and Grace Kelly. Monday she called the hospital. The nurse said Mr. Bruce had died early in the morning.

Mary dressed and went out to the library. The pharmaceutical compendium listed the drug Dr. Bell had prescribed, Maprotiline, an antihistamine used to reduce the anxiety of depression. She made extensive notes:

Maintenance dose, ⅒ gram, should not exceed ⅓ gram. May cause ataxia (unsteady walking). Doctor should prescribe the smallest possible amount. A 22-year-old woman died 5 days after swallowing 3 grams. A 58-year-old woman recovered completely after ingesting 5 grams. In combination with alcohol has been fatal in the range of 2 to 10 grams.

On the way home she bought a birthday card for her nephew Cecil and a bottle of amontillado.

Tuesday she gave ten chapters to Bobby Sutton. *The Russians Are Coming!* was on TV. The paper said the funeral would be Thursday at 2:30. Bertie would be there. She knew what Bertie was going through. Now they would never meet. Wednesday she worked on Chapters 11 and 12. *The Conversation* was on TV. Thursday she went to Dr Bell. The pills are helping, she told him. He renewed the prescription. At home she counted the pills. Two more appointments and she would have 12 grams, 36 times the maximum dose. Noting the second appointment in pencil—for the future; ink was for the past—she wrote what she would say to the doctor: "We're doing fine."

She wasn't planning to kill herself. She was planning to be ready if the blackness came down again, as it had when Rod Bugiardo went home to Lisetta. She didn't know if it would come, but if it did she didn't want to wake up to a doctor saying she had a strong constitution, to facing each new day with a smile, when nobody cared for her, when she was more alone than she had ever been. She watched TV every day, swam in the pool, worked on the book, wrote many letters, sent a birthday present for Cecil, sent it early to make sure he would get it in any case, gave clothes to the Salvation Army, mailed books back to their owners, applied for Social Security in Canada and the United States.

The first two weeks in September it rained almost every day. Mary delivered Bobby Sutton's last two chapters to him. She counted the pills, made calculations, and went to Dr. Bell. He gave her a flu shot to keep her well. Saturday there was a thunderstorm in the afternoon, but Sunday the sun came out. It was a beautiful day. Standing on the balcony she could see English Bay shining bright and clear. Beyond lay Galiano, where Don had lived when they had met in 1942 and spent the night together, when they were young and full of dreams, and desires.

Sunday the 17th, she listened to *Tosca*. TV promised Ingrid Bergman and Cary Grant in *Indiscreet*, a delightful comedy to banish your sorrows and dry your tears, but the program was changed. They ran *Billy Liar* instead, and it all came back—the dog that loved her, the aunt that didn't, saying goodbye to disappointment in the Leeds Great Northern Station, going away forever.

Nine days later the phone rang. No one answered. Mail collected in the box. The rent came due and was not paid. Twenty-five days later tenants began to complain. The manager entered the apartment. He rushed to open the balcony door. The TV set and the lights were on. The tenant lay where she had fallen, on the bathroom floor.

The coroner's man gathered up the empty prescription bottles but wasn't interested in the empty amontillado bottle or the deceased's appointment book opened to a new page where the writing turned from ink to pencil, for the future. The phone rang. He picked it up. He said the tenant wasn't there. He said he was with the coroner's office.

In a filing cabinet the next of kin found a tie from Elle on Seymour Street waiting for a miracle, and a birthday card showing two affectionate lions, with the message: "Your love makes my world go round." An empty cat carrier was hidden in the closet. One of many framed pictures had been turned to the wall. Turning it back, the visitor saw his Canadian cousin Donald alive and well and in good spirits, smiling like a birthday boy, like the daddy you've always wanted, someone you can count on to be there when you need him, to love you just the way you are, to believe you deserve the best, to send you out to knock 'em dead, to keep you soldiering on, to share your joy as you become what you were always meant to be, while there is still time.

CHAPTER 10

Old Pictures

Raspberries don't really want to be picked. Bill and Beryl laughed at my half pint. Each of them had picked a quart. On the way back from picking we stopped to admire Bill's root house, homemade timber and concrete set into the north side of a hill, roof covered with earth, forty degrees cooler inside. "Make a good bomb shelter," he said. "Cost me twelve hundred dollars to store ten dollars' worth of potatoes. I should be in the government."

They were living in a new house, the third one they had built, this time with the help of a cabinetmaker. It had plenty of room for visitors—five bedrooms, two baths (both indoors), central heating, double glazing, electricity and gas, workroom, living room, kitchen, and breakfast room. Even Mary would have liked it. Our country breakfast skimped along on raspberries, eggs, bacon, oatmeal, fried potatoes, toast, jam, and pickles. Enough to hold everybody till lunch.

Bill took me up "the mowntun" in the four-wheel-drive to visit calves with curly faces, then "ho-am" again to set a trap for the chicken hawk. After we watered the vegetable patch and shelled peas on the porch, we took the Buick to get gas. I drove, pumped the gas, and cleaned bugs off the windshield. Bill told Harry at the station he had hired a chauffeur. As the sun slowly set over a brace of Molson beers, we compared our daily rounds—making hay, mending fences, freezing the best parts of a moose, helping eighty-year-old neighbors put down their water lines, publishing articles on fake science, speaking at conventions on academic fraud, visiting George Sand's biographer on the rue des Saints-Pères. "We live in different worlds," Bill said. "But you're a good chauffeur, and you'll get better at the picking."

After supper Bill and I sat on the settee and looked through the family album. In the woods south of Entwistle, Alberta, wiry old Will Hebditch and ample Mrs. Ransom stood in front of their log cabin. Sturdy logger and farmer Bill pulled one end of a tree saw while his father pushed the other. Volunteer Bill in his army tam came home on furlough to get married. Beryl Dorothy Violet Fry laughed in her wedding dress, a tall, strong, rangy girl with a narrow English face. Crouching beside a forest trail, she turned trout in a frying pan. She stood in a sunny doorway holding a baby.

Altogether they were married twelve days short of fifty years. Bill was the only man in her life. The first time he saw her, he was sixteen, she was three. She and her parents and brothers had just come from Gloucestershire to settle on a farm near the Hebditch homestead. He watched her grow up for fifteen years, and the older she got, the less he could see in other girls. Beryl remembered the courting.

"While we were engaged, he built me a house on my parents' land. Sawed his own lumber at the mill and hauled it down and put it up. That was a nice house. Warm as toast, I'll tell you." (Not counting the outhouse at twenty below.) "Bill's father sang at the wedding. He had a beautiful voice. He was good at reciting poetry, and so was Bill." Two months after the wedding the Edmonton Regiment shipped out. Next to her new house, nineteen-year-old Mrs. Hebditch built herself a woodshed out of slabs (sides of logs) left over from Bill's sawing. She packed her water from the well, cooked and heated with a wood stove, bore a strapping boy, and sent snapshots to his daddy. Far away in England, Sergeant Bill spent the war boiling stew in big pots for hungry fighting men. He crafted love letters to his wife out of poems learned in boyhood from his father.

After five years in the army Bill came home with $148 and two service ribbons. He arrived in the nick of time, because Beryl and her family, not knowing when he would return, had loaded everything they owned into a boxcar bound for opportunity in the west. They came to rest in the Windermere Valley, just across the line in British Columbia. Bill and Beryl had plenty of money, since Beryl had sold her house for $500.

We bought an old house in Athalmer, moved it, and fixed it up. Downstairs we opened a restaurant. Bill and I built the counter together. He made all the tables and stools. I covered the stools with leatherette. There was four small tables along one wall with hinges on, so you could hook 'em up and clean underneath 'em. We could seat twenty-four. Farmers and loggers came from all around. We were the only restaurant there except for the hotel. The sign outside said "Bill's Coffee Shop." Another sign was for Black Cat cigarettes.

R: What hours were you open?
B: Seven to eleven.
R: Seven in the morning to eleven at night?
B: That's right.
R: Did you have electricity?
B: No. We had gasoline lamps, an icebox, and two wood
    stoves.
R: Who did the cooking?
B: Bill did some and I did some. Everything was on rationing.
    We had an awful time keeping up with the sugar and lard.
R: What did you have on the menu?
B: We had a lot of breakfasts, bacon and eggs, ham and eggs,
    coffee, muffins, pies, buns. I made the pies, Bill made the
    buns, and we shared the doughnuts, which we sold in the
    shop. We could have sold dozens more if we hadn't've
    been rationed. The mailman came by every day, and we
    always had a hot meal for him, roast beef and such, and for
    anybody else who wanted it at that time, 'cause you
    couldn't keep stuff warm like you do today.
R: How long did you have the restaurant?
B: A little over two years. We did very well, but Bill had

enough of five years cooking in the army, and when I got
toxima the doctor told me to stay off my feet. Bill got a
job falling timber up on Steamboat Mountain, about thirty
miles out. So we lived up there two years. I taught the
kids on correspondence. In 1952 a minister named Reverend Job told us about Ashton Creek.

R: Reverend Job?

B: Yes.

R: What was the best time in your life?

B: The day I got married! And all the years we shared together after the war. It was rugged but we were happy.
You couldn't find a better man than Bill Hebditch, I'll tell
you. If it wasn't for cancer, we'd-a had our golden wedding
anniversary. But you couldn't wish for that when he was in
pain. He didn't say it hurt, but you knew when you was
with him. It's hard to be left on your own when you've
had a good man.

In the Hebditch family album were three photographs of Lorna
taken in the studio of Andrew Gray of Strichen, Aberdeenshire.
The first, October 1907, shows a flourishing young woman sitting
in a long white dress, holding a sprig of studio leaves, looking up
from a large book lying open on a table. One can see she is a
reader. Thick, dark hair tents the brow. The eyes are calm, dark,
inquiring, the face long but rounded, the lips full, quizzical, and
inviting. Two months later we see her standing beside a dashing
city gent who is wearing a top hat, leather gloves, long black coat,
and pointed waxed mustache. In this dapper fellow you would
never recognize Mrs. Ransom's dusty rumpled weather-beaten
woodsman standing thirty-five years later in front of a log cabin.
Watchmaker Hebditch's slender five feet eight towers above his
tiny wife, smartly hatted with ostrich plume, bedecked with er-
mine scarf, one leather-gloved hand firmly grasping her newly acquired escort by the elbow.

The third picture shows a baby where the big book was before,
sitting on the table in a wide-skirted dress of white cotton organdy
adorned with ribbon and puffed sleeves. The plump young mother
stands close by in heavy dark taffeta with deep tucks in the

sleeves, a white dickey with small tucks and a high ruched collar. Her long hair, gracefully pinned up, shines with youth and health. She looks down at the child with interest, holding him firmly but not too tight, as he clutches her necklace for safety and watches the camera with suspicion. In spite of his skirt and puffed sleeves, one-year-old Bill Hebditch looks just like his dapper dad, not a bit like Lorna. None of her children looked like her.

Seventy-two years later this mother and child reappeared in the Aberdeen monthly *Leopard Magazine* to illustrate an article on the long-forgotten Buchan authoress Lorna Moon, whose lately redis-covered books were being reissued by a local publisher. The pho-tograph had been borrowed from the writer's cousin, William Center, ninety-five. William's mother and Lorna's were sisters, and their families had lived together during four years of his childhood. The oldest living veteran of the Gordon Highlanders, Cousin William had fought the Hun in Flanders, put down rebels in India, and bested the Boer in Africa. He couldn't recall whether the baby had been a boy or a girl, but he spoke of his cousin (in the Buchan dialect) with affection:

"She was a very nice quine [girl]—and 'affa cliver, though she wis jist at the common school." The last time he saw her, March 1904, they were both eighteen. The soldier boy had come to the village to take leave of his relatives before sailing away with the regiment. His Aunt Maggie, Lorna's mother, whom he described as "a queer lady," showed little interest in her departing nephew, but as he set foot in the road again the nice quine came after him regretting that he couldn't stay longer and, he remembered, "she gied me half a croon," a generous gift.

The district of Buchan, where Lorna was born, forms the north-east corner of northeast Scotland. At the northeast tip of the district stands the port of Fraserburgh (pronounced Fraserburra), boldly facing the North Sea, grave of many a fisherman, beyond which lie Norway, Sweden, Lapland, and the Arctic. The town was founded by royal charter in the sixteenth century on the lands of Sir Alexander Fraser. The crofters (farmers) of Buchan brought their grain and cattle into Fraserburgh for shipping. The fisher-men's wives walked the roads carrying the catch down into the district to sell to villagers and crofters. Historian David Fraser, kinsman of Sir Alexander, describes Buchan as one of the ancient earldoms, the granary of Scotland, renowned for corn (grain) and cattle, a rolling land of stone walls and squat stone-built farms, of trees stunted by wind under wide skies. In the names of its people and places ring the ancestral sounds of Celtic, Pictish, Saxon, and Norse. Despite Lorna's personal descent from Highland chiefs, notably Sir Ewen Cameron of Lochiel, the Buchan folk are Lowlanders, said to be more Norse than Celtic, bearing many one-syllable names—Cill, Coutts, Crab, Gatt, Gauld, Gill, Gow, Robb, Rae, Sim, Sleigh, Tate, Watt, Low—and not nearly so many Macraes, Mackays, Macduffs, Macphersons, and MacDonalds as one finds in the Highlands and islands to the West.

Traveling inland from Fraserburgh one soon catches sight of Mormond (Gaelic *mormonadh*, or big hill) rising seven miles southwest, sheltering Strichen in its lee from the North Sea blast. The population of Strichen Parish when Lorna was a girl was not much different from today, some 800 in the village, 1500 on the farms. Standing atop Mormond and looking down into the village, one's view traverses three main streets: North Street at the foot of the slope, High Street through the center, and Water Street along the far side following the river curve of the North Ugie Water. Cutting across these three from Mormond to the river, Bridge Street takes one over the Brig and out onto the high road, which runs north to Fraserburgh and south to Aberdeen. High Street, about a mile long, takes the measure of the village. At its midpoint rises Town Hall spire, at its western turning the spire of a church. Lorna was born at 33 North Street, grew up on Bridge Street, wrote letters home to 13 High Street, and can be seen in portraits at the Anderson and Woodman Library on Water Street.

The name Strichen, once Strath-Uigin, means the Valley of the Ugie. Ugie means Little Water, or small river. Many of the houses are built of granite blocks quarried nearby. A hundred years ago many of the roofs were thatched. Water came from wells and streams. The peat bog furnished fuel; big houses had several flues. The soil is rocky and mostly poor. Farmers labored from predawn dark until late at night, getting little from much toil. Villagers raised tatties, kale, and turnips in their gardens and kept rabbits and chickens. Most of them went to one of the churches. Lorna's mother always went, to make a good appearance on the Sabbath day and sing the hymns and say her Episcopal prayers. Lorna's father stayed away. His youngest granddaughter, Evelyn Scott, spoke fondly of him, in her lilting contralto and delicate Scottish burr.

> He was a vociferous atheist and, give him his due, just as much on his deathbed as before. There were no appeals for mercy. He just bore it out. He told Robbie Cassie [the village undertaker] there would be no prayers, but he left money for them all to have a good meal afterwards. He spoke to me a lot about his atheism. He derived great amusement from the Christian zeal which drove the ardent churchgoers of Strichen during a row between the kirks when I was a girl to smear each other's door handles with shit—"all to the glory of God!" he said. He would address comments to God. In bad weather he would sometimes look up at the sky and shout: "*Hey*, you up there! We've had *enough* of this, you know!"

Lorna dedicated *Doorways in Drumorty* to her father—"To My Dad, This, His Wee Nottie's First Book"—and she wrote about him in letters to her editor. About her mother, she said little. In the Bobbs-Merrill Author Questionnaire she gave her parents' first names correctly—Charles and Margaret—but then she wrote that she herself was "Lorna Leonore Flora MacDonald Wilson Cameron-Cameron," third daughter (she was the second) of "Charles Ewen Donald Cameron, Laird of Fassefern," and his noble cousin, "Margaret Helen Cameron of Erracht." These resounding Highlanders piping from glen to glen were creatures of Lorna's imagination (and later of Mary's). Lorna's mother's family name was not Cameron but Benzies. Her father was not Charles Cameron but Charles Low, "Da Low" to grandchildren who grew up in the village. His second daughter, born 16 June 1886, was not christened "Lorna" but Helen Nora Wilson Low. Everyone called her Nora. "Lorna" wasn't born until Nora was twenty-six and on her way to a new life in Winnipeg with Walter Moon. As a girl she had been an avid reader of *Lorna Doone*—

the sweet, the pure, the playful one, the fairest creature on
God's earth and the most enchanting, [a] lady of high birth
and mind . . . the grace of [whose] coming was like the appearance of the first wind-flower . . . it was a thing of terror
to behold such beauty

—and after years of wishing to grow up as bewitching as the noble
Lorna Doone, Nora couldn't refuse Walter's convenient offer of
his rhyming name, or the provocative echo, "Lorna Moon."

Though not by any means a laird of loch or castle, Charles Low
occupied a station of respect in the world of work as a master
plasterer and construction contractor well liked by his fellows and
his workmen. In his laboring days he took jobs where they were
offered, many of them far away—Canada 1882, the World's Fair
in Chicago 1893, the diamond fields of South Africa after the Boer
War, San Francisco after the quake. Sometimes he made a lot of
money, sometimes he made little. Married to Maggie at twenty-
one, he sent her as much as he could, as often as he could. Maggie
stayed in the village, bearing, feeding, clothing, housing, and when
he didn't send enough supporting their five children—Annie,
young Charlie, Nora, Eva, and Sadie. She was a good-looking
woman, though a little grim. A traveling salesman asked her,
"When your husband is away, who winds up the clock on a Saturday night?" Known for being straitlaced, the handsome, haughty
Mrs. Low treated all such questions with contempt. Setting her
lips in a straight line, she waited for her husband. Still, she would
have been disappointed if no man had asked. After being away
three years, Charles came home from South Africa. His third
daughter, Eva, was thirteen.

Dad had spoken out against the Boer War, saying it was a
war of greed and aggression. People called him a traitor and
wouldn't give him any more contracts even if his bids were
far below the ones accepted. So after the war he went to
South Africa, not only to make money but also to make his
point about the war. When he came back, he arrived in the
evening. We children were sent to bed, but I couldn't go to
sleep. I wanted to have another look at my father. I slipped

downstairs quiet as a mouse. The light was out, but the fire was flickering. There was complete silence. At first I thought they had come upstairs to bed, but then I saw them. Mother was in the armchair bending forward. In the lap of her black dress a heap of gold sovereigns twinkled in the firelight. Father's empty money belt was lying on the floor. Its studs made sparks of brightness. Father was sitting on the footstool looking up at Mother. He didn't have his shirt on, and he had the whitest skin. I'd never known his skin was so white. Something was going on between them that I didn't understand. I was afraid to stay longer, and crept back up the stairs to bed. I never told my sisters what I had seen. I felt it would be blasphemous, like shouting in church.

Maggie died at eighty-two in 1945, Charles at ninety, seven years later. All their descendants left the village. Granddaughter Jean Scott went to lecture at the University of Strasbourg. Granddaughter Evelyn settled in a western county on the northern shore. Few in the village remembered the Lows. The books of Lorna Moon disappeared. The author's name was forgotten. Then in 1980, it became a household word again. How did it happen?

When Charles Low was in his eighties and his health was failing, he gave his copies of the two books to his friend Robert Bandeen, the village librarian. Bandeen kept them for thirty years, then showed them to his friend David Toulmin, a writer of rural tales. Toulmin read them with growing excitement, judging them to be works of art and authentic descriptions of Buchan life in an earlier time. He persuaded a publisher friend to reissue them. Articles soon appeared in *The Leopard*, and Scottish television produced a documentary on the rediscovered northeast author.

All this happened without my knowing anything about it. Still believing I was the only one on earth interested in my secret mother, I wrote to a friend in Oxford, who tracked down a young sociologist living at New Deer, a village seven miles from Strichen, and willing to do research in Buchan. My man in Buchan dug out dusty records, tramped about in graveyards, interviewed gossips and survivors, and discovered Cousin Evelyn working in tinted glass and watercolors between Cawdor Castle stained with Duncan's royal blood and Findhorn Gardens known for growing forty-pound New Age cabbages with the help of eco-fairies.

Cousin Evelyn and David Toulmin had already gotten into a row in the *Leopard Magazine* and in the TV documentary over Toulmin's assertion that Charles Low had angrily condemned Lorna's books for insulting him and provoking a scandal. According to Toulmin, the trouble began in 1926, when *Doorways in Drumorty* reached the village. Certain folk who had watched little Nora Low grow up from infancy to womanhood felt exposed and shamed by "Lorna Moon's" boldly frank portrayals of village life, in which they recognized themselves. Not even her father had escaped. One of the stories, Toulmin said, told how an irresponsible plasterer lived the high life in America while his wife and child at home fought a losing battle against poverty and sickness. In guilty outrage, Toulmin supposed, Charles Low gave the books away. His contempt for his daughter knew no bounds. One day as he was repairing the doorstep of his house, some villagers came walking along High Street, and one of them said in a bantering tone:

> "Man, Charlie, that's an affa fancy trochie [little trough or box] ye hae fer yer cement. It's ower gweed [over good] for that job. Ye'll niver get it clean again. Faur [where] did ye get that grand troch?" Charlie stood up with trowel in hand and stared at his inquisitors. "Man," says he, "that's the trochie they sent Nora's ashes hame in frae America."

"Absolute rubbish!" Evelyn retorted. "My grandfather was extremely proud of Nora and her work. Indeed, she was the light of his life. His feelings toward her verged on adulation." His eldest daughter, Annie Lyall, agreed: "Father was very proud of Nora's writing."

Everett Marcy had found Charles Low crushed by grief at his daughter's death, and so had a young schoolteacher who was renting a room from the Lows.

> I was coming back to Strichen on a Monday morning at some Godless hour, and there in front of me was a placard saying "Death of a noted Northeast Authoress." I couldn't think

who that might be, but when I got back to my digs, I knew instantly who it was, because Mrs. Low was looking extremely grim, and Charlie was practically in tears. All they could do was push the *Press & Journal* at me and say, "There is Nora's obituary."

Robert Bandeen, the Strichen librarian, flatly denied that Charles Low had condemned the books. Toulmin's tale of the negligent plasterer neatly reverses the meaning of Lorna's story, "The Funeral," in which an absent father, unjustly accused by village gossips of being irresponsible, succeeds at last in sending money, just in time to pay for his child's funeral. Impressed by the splendor of the funeral, his critics then declare that they have always known he sent his money home and is a worthy fellow little deserving such misfortune. The story was Lorna's defense of hardworking fathers against spiteful hypocrites. It could not have offended Charles Low.

Nora's casket was never used for rough work of any kind but kept spotless for fifty years, first by her parents, then by their housekeeper. Today anyone may see it in the Strichen library, unmarked and unblemished, without a scratch inside or out, as it was on that spring day when Charles Low carried it up the Hill of Mormond.

Yet Toulmin was an honest man who wanted to tell the true story of a "divinely gifted" writer he had rescued from oblivion, and reputable villagers had remembered old Charlie's saying precisely what the casket rumor reported. For me it was a puzzle, which took some time to sort out. The answer was in long-past threats of libel suits from angry villagers stung by Lorna's lash, and in the character of Charles Low, who, Evelyn admitted, was a bit of a puzzle himself:

"He was much brighter than most of the other people in the village, and he would say things to provoke them. They never knew whether he was serious or not."

Nephew William Center, for one, couldn't make sense of his uncle. "I niver kent richt fit wis adee wi' him," Cousin William said.

CHAPTER 11

Ten Downing Street

In June 1984 Margaret and I traced Charles Low's sorrowful progress from the Neuk (the nook, the corner), a house hidden in the trees on Burnshangie Road north of the village, where Everett Marcy had stayed a week with Aunt Sadie and her family when Cousin Evelyn was ten, past the remnants of the Martin Wood, up the slope of Mormond Hill, round the nose of the White Horse stretched out on his right side sprouting tufts of grass, between clumps of yellow gorse and heather not yet blooming, to the ruin on the crest, where we strained to read the words cut into the stone in 1779: "In this hunter's lodge Robb Gibb commands"— meaning that Captain Fraser and his fellow huntsmen were bound by "Robb Gibb's Contract" of loyalty and love. Master of Horse to James V of Scotland, whose daughter was Mary Queen of Scots, Robb Gibb was asked by the King why he served him. "For stark love and kindness," he replied. Far below us lay the village, a tidy gray huddle of stone houses, much as it had been a hundred years before, when Nora Low was born. "Another mile o' misery," Cousin Evelyn called it.

We walked the mile from end to end. At Market Terrace and High Street, on the northeast corner, stood the two-story house whose doorstep Charles Low had been repairing when some solid village folk who thought of him as a local "worthy" (colorful character) came strolling by and in that jocular tone used for subtle ridicule derided him about his fancy mortar box. Though "a wee mannie" no taller than his wife, Da Low was not a man who would submit to disrespect. Who were these feckless philistines to question his equipment? Which of them had read *Mendel's Principles of Heredity* or Darwin's *Origin of Species*? Who among them had advised James Ramsay MacDonald, Labour's first Prime Minister? Had any of them seen the future shining in Chicago, rebuilt San Francisco after the quake, told the English to their face in a South African pub they should hang their heads in shame for taking other people's land? The most these village blockheads had the wit to do was vilify a poor dead lass's truthful books. Cocky Low, as he was called, gave back better than he got, thus starting the grim rumor about his daughter's casket, which some, like David Toulmin, would take at face value half a century later. "No, *no!*" others said to my man in Buchan. "*That* wasn't it. He *mixed* his daughter's ashes *into* the mortar to *use* on the doorstep, so he could *tread* on them every *day!*"

Strichen comment was often sharp. At seventy-seven the former schoolteacher who had rented a room from the Lows still recoiled from her memories of that "*terrible* place! Well, it was called *Stricken.*" But from another point of view there was plenty to chaff old Charlie about. Hadn't he sided with the Boers! Wasn't he soft on the Kaiser! True, he had worked in munitions during the Great War, but with all his pacifist havering any patriot could see his heart was never in it. For years he was the only socialist in the village, and he would go *on* about it. One word would set him off. He would argue with anybody. He would argue with God! He'd dress up in his Sunday suit with a carnation in his lapel to go out and buy a postage stamp. He and his whole family had put on airs in their day that were ridiculous for a man who worked with his hands and took great pride in being the local spokesman for the Labour Party.

The house on the corner had four bedrooms, two for Mr. and Mrs. Low, two for well-mannered lodgers like the policeman who snored all night keeping the young schoolteacher awake, or the dentist from Aberdeen, who pulled teeth in his quarters. Next door was the one-story house where Mrs. Low had had her tearoom and sold her cakes and candy, and ice cream in the summertime, watching every penny—"the only person I've ever known who sold eggs by weight," the young schoolteacher said. Behind, inside a low stone wall that flanked Market Terrace, lay the long narrow garden where Mrs. Low had grown her greens and kept her roasters and laying hens. "A virtuoso poultry woman," Cousin Evelyn called her.

> She used the deep litter system long before anyone else. The hens were kept in a henhouse with nesting boxes and perches and enjoyed a fenced run in which Grannie Low scattered peat dross, which she later removed to fertilize the garden. She would go out on the road with a little sickle to cut grass for the hens. She grew kale and hung it up, so they would get exercise jumping up to eat it.

At the far end, against the back wall, stood "Ten Downing Street." We found it in the first place by asking a boy on a bicycle: "Do you happen to know the way to Ten Downing Street?" The lad pointed instantly. Anyone in the village could have told us where it was. "Ten Downing Street" was a one-room cottage in the corner of the garden. I peeked in and saw ducks and rabbits. Sixty years earlier, this crumbling barnyard hut had been a refuge for Charles Low, his neat, trim little fort, where he went to read his books and argue with his newspapers or write letters to Ramsay MacDonald or to Robert Boothby, Buchan's Member of Parliament. Boothby is known in America for having suffered thirty-seven desperate amorous years in the cruel but charming clutch of Lady Dorothy Cavendish, gracious, ruthless wife of Prime Minister Harold Macmillan, but in Buchan for thirty-four years Boothby was known as the farmer and fisherman's friend in the halls of government power. Though a Tory and close ally of Winston Churchill, whom he served as Parliamentary Private Secretary, Conservative Boothby took a shine to socialist Charles Low and came to chat with him in the cottage. While giving campaign speeches, Boothby would interrupt himself to say that his friend Charles Low, sitting there in the audience, might correct him if he was in error. Because of these high and cordial political connections, Da Low's cottage came to be known as Labour Party Headquarters in Strichen, where once a letter discussing great matters had come from Prime Minister Ramsay MacDonald, 10, Downing Street, London, addressed to "Mr. Charles Low, 10, Downing Street, Strichen."

Some of Da's less prominent friends came to the cottage to discuss bowling on the green in summer, curling on the ice in winter, and good bets on the stock exchange any time of year. Da Low was an intuitive, philophonical investor. He advised his friend Mary Urquhart, whose husband Geordie ran horse buses between Strichen and Banff and was a masterly hurler of the 38-pound curling stone, to buy shares in a mining company called Eileen Alannah. "It was a pretty bad investment," Cousin Evelyn said. "Da Low used to read the prices in the paper and say: 'Oh *dear*! Mary's Eileen Alannah is going *down*!' I think he bought it because he liked the sound of the name."

Though he could have had a bedroom all to himself in the house, Da Low slept in the cottage. "He said it wasn't hygienic sleeping in the house with lodgers," Cousin Maggie Whyte recalled, "but I don't think he liked the main house. He felt confined, so close to his wife."

"Oh, it was purely *that*!" Cousin Evelyn laughed. "He couldn't bear living at close quarters with her! He got my father to build him his own little retreat at the bottom of the garden, with a bed and a little desk. He came up only for his meals. Grannie Low was a very good cook, in the Scottish style, but they were quite ill suited to each other. It was a deplorable marriage."

Grannie Low was a well-favored woman. Even at sixty-six she impressed the young schoolteacher as much with her good looks as by her fine housekeeping:

> She had run the hotel before. At the house she took in female English teachers from the Strichen School. My digs were twenty-six shillings per week. That was rather lush. I got a bed-sitting room with lavatory but no bathroom. The place was scoured clean in every corner. The food was appetizing and ample. Other teachers came to eat in the dining room next door and sometimes schoolchildren came.

> Mrs. Low was a real stunner, beautiful, majestic. She had

white hair that rippled black, an aquiline profile, jet earrings and black satin when she was dressed up—God, she was imposing! But she was cold as ice. I remember her coming in with a pail o' tatties, and Charlie said, "Oh, Maggie! You used to have such bonnie arms!" He must have been very fond of her at one time.

Born in 1863, two years younger than her husband, Grannie Low had been the eldest daughter of a farmer, George Gordon Benzies, and his wife Mary Robb, a domestic servant. George's father had been a blacksmith, James Benzies, who married Elizabeth Mantoch. Mary Robb's parents were Archibald, a farm worker, and Anne Willox Jafferay Robb. I list these names and occupations to show the dearth of clans and castles in the Benzies family and the lack of Cameron lairds. For thirty years before he took Mary Robb to wife and settled down at fifty-six to try his luck at farming, George Gordon Benzies was a soldier. Retired from the service after the Indian Mutiny of 1857, he was given "a rather poor croft at the side of Mormond Hill, consisting," Cousin Evelyn said, "mainly of heather and bog." While his bride, twenty years younger, bore and raised four girls, George, without any sons to help, cleared and worked the land, often longing for the days when regimental HQ would send supplies if one ran short and relief when spirits flagged. George was not a cheerful man. One day, Cousin Evelyn said, he had had enough. "He leaned over the side of a burnie [Scots for a small stream] and made a very neat job of slashing his wrists."

On that barren, rocky farm, in that gloomy family, hard upon the "mile o' misery," Grannie Low grew up. As a girl, she learned the skills of the expert housewife, but she didn't take to school. She did write letters to her friends and to family members, like the following, written when she was seventy-six to her eldest grandson. In the last paragraph she mourns the death in an auto wreck of her youngest daughter, Sadie, mother of Jean and Evelyn, who didn't flee the village like the other Low girls but stayed behind, a great comfort to her aging parents.

you will excuse me writing with Pencle but I have not been well this last day or too my old hand is shakie holding the

pen. I been making jam we had a terrable crop of berries had
to give stons away [a stone is 14 pounds].

Daw has a fine garden and taties I never tested better. a
Strichen man who is a sculptor is making Daw,s head and its
very like him. we will send you a P.C. [picture postcard] of
it once its finished

Mrs Uqhart has a great los in Geordie I think we have all
got set back of late its hard to live without the ones who are
gone Sadie was just our right hand Daw and me miss hir
terrable but must carrie on well may God bless and keep you
your loving grannie

"Grannie Low, I think, never read a book," Cousin Evelyn said,
"and she resented anyone's reading. Da Low spent his time reading. In his little house he would recite poetry at the top of his
voice—A jug of wine, a loaf of bread, 'The Shooting of Dan
McGrew.' People passing in the street would hear him. He loved
words and he loved music. He woke up in the morning singing
like an angel. He would have liked to be an opera singer."

Da Low's letters were like this one written to the same grandson, Annie Lyall's only child, a schoolteacher in Canada, just before the start of World War II:

I was very pleased to get your letter and to know that you
remember your visit to Scotland [as a small child, many years
before]. I of course will never forget it, for you gave me the
scare of my life. You stopped me at a shop window and told
me to take my time and see what I was going to buy for you.
We entered the shop, I in fear and trembling. I had visions
of railway engines, rocking horses and other costly toys. It
was a great relief to me when after looking at everything you
settled on a penny whistle. Well much water has run under
the bridge since then. Father time has dealt very kindly with
me, in spite of my four score years I am hale and hearty, my
hearing is slightly bad, otherwise I am wonderful. The silly
old world is in a queer state. When will the nations of earth
realise the utter futility of the popular argument that to preserve the peace, you must prepare for war. This race in ar-
maments will end in war just as sure as night follows day. It

will be the old, old story. The drums will beat and the pipes will play, and the poor dupes who go to their death will be told that king and country need them. Your mother will be pleased to hear that Jean Scott has been awarded first class honors at Aberdeen University, we are all very proud of her, she is certainly gifted with brains. My best and warmest wishes. I am your loving Grandfather

Granddaughter Evelyn would be a painter and teacher of painting, but that did not impress Da Low nearly as much as her sister's writing. "Da Low did love Jean," she said. "He thought she was wonderful because she was good with words. I can remember shouting, 'All you have to do to please this bloody family is write a *book*!' "

The source of Charles Low's literary bent is not apparent in his lineage. No doubt the same could be said of Homer. His grandfather, George Low, was born in 1802 into a Fraserburgh family of slaters. Attaching slices of stone to sloping roofs was slater George's living and his downfall. He died at fifty-four, after lying twenty-one weeks in unrelieved agony with a broken back, having lost his footing on a steep and slippery roof. George's grandson, little Charlie, whom he never saw, grew up with George's widow, Elenora. An old picture shows them together, baby Charlie sitting on his grannie's lap looking out in astonishment at the world. She is dressed all in black except for a white mutch (a close, frilled lace cap) and looks to be a kindly woman with a lurking sense of humor but firm in her resolve, not ready to put up with any sort of nonsense, a governess who will require obedience to rules and will instill good character in a bright and spirited boy who is fond of his grannie. One day, when little Charlie has a family of his own, he will take this old picture to Andrew Gray of Strichen to be duplicated, so that his four daughters can each have a picture of Dad when he was a baby and of his beloved Grannie Elenora —whose name he has fondly given to his second daughter, Helen Nora Wilson Low. All well and good, you say, but why leave out Charlie's parents? Who were his father and mother? Now here you put your finger on Da Low's predicament, whereby hangs a doleful tale of a lass from the low countree and a lord of high degree and a wee drop o' disillusion on the wrong side o' the blanket.

Like his political hero, James Ramsay MacDonald, Charles Low to his lasting shame knew his birth to be a result of illicit lust unredeemed by any tardy wedding between a proud and dutiful groom and a blushing big-bellied bride. James and Charles were the sons of unmarried servant girls. James's mother was Anne Ramsay, servant on a farm where his father, John MacDonald, worked as a ploughman. Charles's mother was Mary Ann Low, only daughter of slater George and Grannie Elenora, who got into trouble while working as a housemaid down on Deeside. Deeside lay along the banks of the river Dee west of Aberdeen (mouth, *aber*, of the Dee) and east of Balmoral, home in the Highlands to Her Gracious Majesty Queen Victoria. Wealthy, prominent personages resided in Deeside mansions tended by armies of stable boys, gamekeepers, hunt masters, coachmen and serving girls, footmen and washerwomen, butlers, cooks, and scullery maids, with plenty of room for mischief upstairs, downstairs, in between the hedgerows, rolling in the hayloft or in His Lairdship's chamber. Learning that the culprit would neither marry nor support her, poor embarrassed Mary Ann traveled south to London carrying her disgrace and in the fullness of her time delivered a bouncing baby boy. Finding work in the City, she brought the baby to Fraserburgh to live with his grannie, who was glad to have him to comfort her in widowhood.

James MacDonald Ramsay (as the defect of paternity obliged the parish authorities to enter his name in the Register) likewise was raised by a resolute grandmother, Bella Ramsay, a seamstress. They lived under a thatched roof in a tiny two-room house in Lossiemouth, a fishing village on the northern shore west of Buchan. Bella Ramsay was poorer than Elenora Low but more ambitious for her grandson and better informed about schools. James spent more years than Charles studying in schools and wouldn't earn his living by manual labor. Once out of school, the two were self-made men and self-taught political philosophers. James, of course, rose to be Prime Minister of Britain, while Charles made his political mark by organizing meetings of Fabians, Social Democrats, and Independent Labour partisans, not to mention scoffers, on the Strichen market stance.

All their lives Charles and James endured the stigma of illegitimate birth. In 1914, Ramsay MacDonald, MP for Leicester, made an antiwar speech in the House of Commons and was forced to step down as leader of the Labour Party. Seeking to expel him from Parliament altogether, his enemies ferreted out and published the shocking birth certificate of "James MacDonald Ramsay," whom they accused of running for office under a false name and pretending to be a respectable gentleman. "No wonder the Moray Golf Club requests him to resign," they said. This sudden, rude exposure brought the accused, as he wrote in his diary, "the most terrible mental pain," which Charles Low suffered with him, fearing the scandal would destroy a great man's power to do good. "He told me his idol had feet of clay," Cousin Evelyn said.

Both men were called traitors for speaking out against war. Both felt a burning interest in science. Both hoped that a better world would come out of socialism. One should not suppose that British socialism in the nineteenth century aspired to the heights later reached by Lenin's, Mao's, and Hitler's plans to replace human culture with the Empire of the Ants. Socialist good intentions in Britain were to lighten the burden of the poor and get better treatment for employees. The theme was not heaven on earth, leaping forward into perfection, or purifying the race, but simple compassion and all-round fairness. As a youth Ramsay MacDonald was inspired by Henry George, whose *Progress and Poverty* impelled him to announce, "The land must be nationalised," but in maturity he held moderate views, like Charles Low's.

When Da Low was eighty-eight, a newspaper reporter came to Ten Downing Street to interview the "Premier of Mormond Braes." Nearing the end of his life, the old warrior voiced dismay at the turn the labor movement had taken. He said:

> I am humiliated by the attitude of the workers. They have got what was fought for and now reward their success with idle, lazy ways. They do not seem to be the men we fought for.

In the peace and quiet of his overgrown garden, in his now historic little house, no one rose to take offense at Cocky Low's iconoclasm—not like the old days, when Henry Scott had had to haul his contentious future father-in-law out of a South African

pub to save him from the drunken wrath of greedy British impe-
rialists proud of their recent conquest of other people's land.

Adorning Da Low's cottage were busts and paintings of
nineteenth-century socialist crusaders. The newspaper illustration
shows him holding a painting of Ramsay MacDonald, who, the
caption says, was "one of his closest friends." This is journalistic
flattery and exaggeration. Five years older than Ramsay MacDonald, Da Low was already building houses in Canada when the
future Prime Minister was still a pupil-teacher drilling Latin and
Greek verbs into the heads of younger Scottish schoolboys. Later,
for all their common purposes and beliefs, Da Low would have
had few chances to consort with a politician rising to prominence
in England. Still, he must have felt closer to his political hero and
fellow illegitimate than to certain jocular, derisive, solid village folk
he had known and argued with and provoked for years.

At the time of the interview, Grannie Low had been dead five
years and Da Low was no longer hale and hearty. Without a wife
to badger him, he slept in the main house, downstairs in the parlor,
where Margaret McLeman, his housekeeper and friend of many
years, tended him and kept the fire going. After his death the
house was sold and other villagers lived in it. A traveler from a
warmer clime, a grandson Da Low never saw and didn't know he
had, came looking for the past, knocked on the door at 13 High
Street, and was taken into the parlor, but the grate had grown cold
and there was no sign of the local spokesman for the Labour Party.
I think of him there in his last days, the partisan of principle, the
old campaigner for a better world, gazing into the embers, remembering his childhood, his apprenticeship in Fraserburgh, father-
hood on North Street, adventuring across the sea, coming home
to four little girls, not one like another, to a vigorous young wife
managing five children, to Mrs. Low proprietress, lips set in a
straight line, enforcing proper rules at the Temperance Hotel, to
Maggie in the tearoom dazzling the diners with her silver hair:

> a splendid woman, a difficult woman, but most women are
> difficult. Not my Annie of course or our beloved Sadie. So
> many times we climbed the hill to sit in the eye of the White
> Horse and I would tell them stories. Young Charlie wouldn't

sit still. He was kinda saft [rather stupid], but his mother worshipped him. Kept his picture in the kitchen looking foolish in a kilt. Always getting into trouble, climbing in and out of windows, getting into brawls. Left South Africa in a hurry when they said he killed a kaffir [nigger]. Charlie said it wasn't true but he was off to New Zealand in the morning. Wrote to his mother every Christmas. In the end she didn't know it, out of her mind, poor lass, with the pernicious anaemia. Thought she was to have a baby, the only thing that had ever kept her down before. Margaret McLeman was an angel looking after her. Nora was the brilliant one. The way she had with words! Sailed away at twenty-four and didn't come back until the American brought her ashes home to us. Only her books and pictures now, and the little casket resting there on the table. Four pictures in the frame I had carved to hold them, lovely in the bloom of health, cut down and cast into the fire without warning. Eighty years like yesterday. But we have to carry on.

CHAPTER 12

Putting on Airs

They had an air about them, those girls. They sailed through. They could do anything." Cousin Evelyn knew why.

It was no secret in the village that Da Low's mother had had no husband, but it was a mystery who his father was. Villagers said he had blue blood in him, and Da Low didn't contradict them. His unusual qualities of intelligence and refinement and his formal manner appeared to confirm the rumor. Many believed that his father had been the Deeside laird in whose house his mother had been working. My mother and aunts all grew up in the complete conviction that they were of noble blood, on whichever side of the blanket, and this belief made them bold in anything they set out to do, an attitude of *droit du seigneur* which was generally accepted with deference in the village.

Da Low's wife had no such claim to descent from aristocrats, but she did enjoy the feeling of being a cut above common folk by virtue of her marriage to blue blood. "She'd a likit to be upper class," said Cousin William. She raised her daughters to act like ladies and hoped they would marry even better than she had.

True, her husband was distinguished and well spoken, but he was still a laboring man, and the Lows of Strichen had married without a pound in the bank or a door to call their own. Maggie Low believed that to marry well a young lady shouldn't waste her time reading books. What she needed was household skills, social arts, and stylish clothing. Villagers called the four Low girls "the big one, the little one, the bonnie one, and the queer one." Annie, the oldest, was the big one, Sadie was the little one, Eva was the bonnie one, and Nora was the queer one. Eva remembered how different Nora was from the rest.

Annie and Sadie had blue eyes and were fairly buxom like me. Nora was dark-eyed and petite, a changeling left in the cradle by fairies. She had her own way of doing things. Annie and Sadie and I sat down meekly at the piano to have our music lessons. Nora demanded the violin. When we went to the dressmaker's house to have new outfits measured and sewn according to Mother's prescriptions, Nora insisted on choosing her own patterns and materials, often reducing the poor dressmaker to tears. I fought fiercely with Annie and Sadie, sometimes hating them for hours. Nora didn't get into quarrels. She seemed to be off in a world by herself. She was five years older than I, and I did look up to her, especially after she began to write. I think Nora was Father's favorite. He called her his "Wee Nottie."

Mistress Low and her well-dressed girls paraded the length of High Street in stately single file, Sundays hurrying to church, weekdays coming from the market, lacking only a village crier to clear the way for them. Such deliberately haughty displays buoyed the Low girls' high opinion of their social standing and comforted their mother if she happened to think back on certain details of her courtship and wedding that were best forgotten. Collecting bits and pieces of the story through the years, Cousin Evelyn put it all together for herself.

Like thousands of other poor boys in Scotland, Da Low made up his mind to emigrate to Canada, where there would be

work for him, but just before he was to sail he met a girl in
Strichen, Maggie Benzies. She was an outstanding beauty,
and she bowled him over. Nevertheless, he caught his ship
and arrived in Montreal with £5 in his pocket. The first night,
he told me, someone stole his coat, and he almost died of the
cold. He got work repairing a church by telling them he was
a Catholic. A year later a letter came informing him that he
had a daughter and her name was Sarah Anne. This was a
great shock to him, the first he knew that he had got his girl
in Strichen into trouble. It took him months to save the
money to return to Scotland and legitimize the child. If he
hadn't known what it meant to be brought up a bastard, I
don't think he would have done it, but he couldn't inflict
bastardy on his daughter. He tried marriage for two years,
then fled the country again. He lived abroad on a pittance
and sent home all the money he could. Every few years he
came back, and always begot another child. Though they had
little in common, she was still irresistible. I asked him, "How
did you live in Canada? Did you have other women?" But he
said no, and I don't think he did. He went abroad simply to
find work and keep away from his wife.

The marriage of a poor farm girl, determined to rise in the
world, to a rumored aristocrat and self-made man of ideas was
torment for both of them, but each in his own way took pleasure
in their girls. Besides dressing her daughters well, Maggie taught
them to make their beds and clean their rooms and scrub their
faces and busk their hair and cook and sew and feed the hens and
not look back at boys or men who stared at them in the street.
She sent them to school every day with their stomachs full even
when there was nothing in the house to eat but porridge. In better
times she treated them to fine Scottish cooking and homemade
candy and ice cream. Taking an egg from under a hen, she would
write a girl's name on it and give the child the chick that hatched
to love and call by name. Despite all this care and attention, she
was cold and sometimes cruel.

"I don't remember any caresses from Mother," Eva said. "I remember severe beatings, no doubt well deserved, because, as she

often told me, I was 'stubborn as a mule.' " Cousin Evelyn never forgot how sister Jean had lost her doll.

Jean had a ragged cloth doll named Ada, which was her only comfort. She had brought it with her when we came from South Africa. It was very dirty and getting dirtier every day. One day Grannie Low said, "I'm *fed* up with the sight of that dirty *doll*!" She took it from Jean and threw it onto the fire. Ada burned to a cinder while Jean screamed and screamed.

"Mrs. Low was a cruel old besom [broom]," said the young schoolteacher.

Da Low left the child care and discipline mainly to his wife. After all, he was seldom at home, and she was always there. Though he was sometimes cold to his wife and often made fun of her limitations, to his daughters he was charming, warm, and entertaining. He sang to them and told them stories and helped them put on plays. Just after World War I, Strichen villagers held a parade. Annie, a matron of thirty-six, was visiting from Canada. Riding a festooned bicycle and wearing a pair of snowy white wings, she won first prize as "An Angel of Peace." Underneath the picture in her family album, Annie wrote: "Wings made by my dear Dad."

Nora was a special case (as Lorna told it in a letter):

Dad and I were very thick, as the saying goes. My mother took full charge of bringing up my sisters, but she let my Dad try out all his theories of child raising on me. I suppose she thought nothing he could do could make me worse than I already was. Dad's theories of sandaled feet, all clothes hung from the shoulder, and no mystery about sex gave me a perfect start in life with good straight toes, an unpinched waist, and unashamed knowledge of reproduction. He read me Mendel's Law of Hybrids, which he illustrated with a cage full of white rats. Dad's rats were, like him, perfect ladies and gentlemen and never did anything but rub whiskers while I was observing them. What I learned about sex from Dad's rats was that the female first got fat and then the male gave her babies by rubbing his whiskers on her. There was a woman in the village, a genteel spinster named Miss Clark, who kept a boardinghouse for "selected gentlemen," most of whom happened to have mustaches. The poor woman was afflicted with asthma, and her mouth was always covered with a respirator [a gauze filter]. Now I understood why. She didn't want a baby. But, I thought, why doesn't she select gentlemen who don't have mustaches? My mother gave a marriage benefit (called in America a shower) for the church organist. I was permitted to "pass the buns" (the cookies). The bride-to-be was radiant in a new silk dress, which excited the envy of the other women, one of whom said: "Wait till you have a few bairns hanging on to your tails. Ye'll no be wearing silken gowns *then*, I'll warrant." To which the giggling girl replied: "Oh, but I'm not going to have *children*!" I stopped short and said gravely: "Then you must wear a respirator, like Miss Clark's." Silence filled the room. Dad called me out and asked: "What did you mean about the respirator, lassie?" "So she won't get a baby, Dad. I've seen the rats doing it. Miss Clark is scared to get a baby from the boarders' whiskers. But she needn't worry. She isn't fat enough. *I'm* not fat enough even." You can imagine my dad's terror and dismay. All his work in biological education shot to hell, and his fourteen-year-old daughter still at the mercy of randy men.

Lorna wrote of her father with love. About her mother she said little. She didn't take sides between them as a child or later. Once during a family chill, Cousin William Center said to his cousin Nora:

"I dinna know if it's your father or your mother to blame." Nora answered:

"Ah well, there's nae een o' them to blame."

When Charles Low came home one year and poured gold sovereigns into her lap, Maggie had the means at last to purchase a three-story building on Bridge Street, where she could do what she did best. Soon the Temperance Hotel became known as a good place for commercial travelers passing through the parish. The rules were strict but the rooms were spotless. The cooking was outstanding. And Mrs. Low had pretty daughters that were not afraid to smile at a young man of business who would mind his manners.

Only one of Maggie's girls married a man she approved of. Annie, who until that time had been the most practical of the lot, married a sickly bank teller, and they upped and offed to Canada, where after wasting Annie's best years he ran away with another woman. Nora eloped with a Yorkshireman, who like a muckle gowk gave up a good trade in clocks and watches and a fine brick house to scratch in the dirt around a grimy log cabin in Alberta. Eva, always difficult, was sent on doctor's orders to quiet her nerves in Canada, where she threw her luck away on a Hudson Bay Store man who sold dry goods from a tent at the end of a railroad. She never had a penny. And they were bonnie and well brought up! Not one of them used her looks or learning to get a man of wealth or position. Sadie, dear lass, settled in Strichen and made the best marriage of the lot, in Maggie Low's opinion. Sadie's daughter Evelyn disagreed.

Grannie Low worshipped my father. She wouldn't buy clothes without his approval. She'd cook "a delicious hare soup" for him and watch for his arrival. "Henry's coming!" she would say, and dip her comb in soapy water and comb her hair before he came in.

Henry Scott, a mason and builder, was a successful business-man. After the Boers were beaten, he went down to South Africa, where he prospered in the mine fields and met a fellow builder named Charles Low. At twenty-one Sadie Low was mooning over a young rake seven years at university without a thing to show for it. Her mother told her it was time for her to get a husband. Mr. Scott, a man of substance, had asked her father for her hand. He would support her in a proper manner. Growing impatient with the young rake and eager to be supported in a proper manner, Sadie took ship for South Africa to marry Henry Scott. Evelyn said it turned out badly.

Jean was born the following year in Johannesburg. I came two years later. Liking neither the country nor her husband, my mother returned to her parents, bringing Jean and me. When my father realized that she wasn't coming back, he too returned to Scotland. She resisted all his attempts to part her from her parents, so he built a house in Strichen, where Jean and I grew up. My mother was desperately unhappy and longed to leave my father, but she was too attached to a life of luxury, with fine clothes, an elegant house, a housemaid, and a gardener. She detested her children and would touch us only to hit us. If it hadn't been for my father's love, I don't know how we could have survived. But he went on binges, and we were frightened of him. We were frightened of them both. When our mother was killed in the car smash, we thanked God for releasing us. Jean was eighteen, I was sixteen.

After Da Low died, Evelyn was determined to clear up the mystery of the Low blue blood. She went to Robert Bandeen, the registrar of Strichen, and asked to see the record of her grandfather's birth. Vital records were closely guarded, but Evelyn was a close relation. Bandeen opened the register. Evelyn read that her great-grandmother had been Mary Ann Low, which she already knew, but to her surprise her great-grandfather was designated not as the Deeside laird in whose house Mary Ann had been a chambermaid but as the laird's butler. The key to the famous mystery, discovered after ninety years, was that the butler did it! "I thought it was very amusing," she said, "but for my dear grandfather his illegitimate birth was a hurt he never got over."

Robert Bandeen was Da Low's friend and would have shown him the register if he had wanted to see it, but Da Low didn't want to see it or be reminded of it. He preferred the splendid rumor to the dismal document, the noble rascal to the common scoundrel. Besides, how could one be sure? The laird would never claim the child even if it was his. He would ride by with head held high and not look down at a young woman standing in the courtyard with hopeful smile and swelling belly. And there was satisfaction in the rumor. The Lows' obscure but seldom-questioned kinship to nobility was a pebble in the boot of every solid village snob who laughed at men that read books and sued when their daughters wrote the truth about how village hypocrites lived their spiteful lives. Charles Low would never be the one to remove that pebble.

Mary Ann Low and her fatherless child are reborn in the pages of Lorna Moon's *Dark Star*, where Mary Ann is Bella, the unlucky chambermaid, whose daughter, Nancy, aches to learn from fragments of village gossip the truth of her origin. Was her father the lowly groom who walks the stallion from farm to farm or the delicate young laird, Ramsey Gordon of Fassefern? Like Charles Low and Lorna Moon, Nancy chooses the nobleman.

CHAPTER 13

A Person of the Better Class

To complete their list of his grandchildren and great-grandchildren, Da Low's solicitors wrote to his eldest daughter, Annie Low Lyall, in Calgary, Alberta. She was happy to reply:

> Talk of turning in one's grave! Father's ashes must be stirring! He didn't know of Nora's extra-marital doings. He was proud of her writing, and it didn't seem kind to tell him things about her that would hurt him. If you think you should include her out-of-wedlock children, there is another one I know of, a daughter she had to Cecil B. DeMille in Hollywood. I don't know if the girl knows who her mother was. All of my grandchildren were born in Alberta, but Ingrid is now in Montreal.

Annie Low was born in Strichen on the ninth of January 1883, but her father couldn't get back for the wedding until June. Having spent her first six months as an out-of-wedlock child, she spent her next eighty-five years cultivating a good reputation among people of quality. She did well in Episcopal School and was commended for diligence at Strichen Higher Grade School. As District Vice-Templar of the Juvenile Good Templars she led the children in Saturday concerts. After a course from Normal Correspondence College, she passed the King's Scholarship Examination to become a teacher. Among the mementos she left at the end of her long life was a set of books called *Little Masterpieces*. The honorific inscription says:

> Given to Annie Low
> on her 21st birthday
> by McAndrew Anderson
> son of the Lord Mayor
> of Aberdeen Scotland.

Just what young McAndrew had in mind or whether his father had deputized him to go about the countryside rewarding village maidens isn't entirely clear, for close inspection of the handwriting reveals that Annie wrote the inscription. One gathers that the Lord Mayor's son didn't press his advantage, seeing that in the following year Jim Lyall, twenty-two, son of less prominent folk, came from the nearby village of Turriff to work at the bank in Strichen, and Annie bent her appraising eye on him.

Jim Lyall was tall, thin, and reflective, a striking contrast to plump, practical Annie, but he had curly brown hair, a broad, well-trimmed mustache, good manners, and a responsible position. The next year they married, and after a respectable interval Annie bore a son, whom she named Charlie after her dad. In 1910, when Charlie was three, the young Lyalls sailed for Montreal seeking more room for their elbows, a higher social hill to stand on, and more coin for their purse. The Lows were sad to see them go. It seemed most of Scotland was going out to Canada. Soon Nora and Will Hebditch left their home in Yorkshire, taking little Bill. Eva followed two years later. Only Sadie remained at home, a lonely lassie with no big sisters, roaming the oddly quiet rooms of the Temperance Hotel.

Jim Lyall went to work at a bank in eastern Canada. Nora and her little boy came to stay with Jim and Annie while pioneer Will was out west looking over his wilderness and picking a good spot for a cabin. Annie was puzzled by Nora's strange indifference to her child.

He was a charming little lad, but she paid no attention to him. If he wanted anything he appealed to me. He liked my cooking very much. I can still hear him saying, "Fine pogie [trout], Auntie Annie!" One day Nora said to me, "It's easy for you to be a good housewife. You are in love with your husband." One can have some sympathy for the mess she got herself into, but to just go off like that and leave a little boy! The DeMille child was taken from her by its father, who said she wasn't a fit person to raise it. Hollywood's version of the pot calling the kettle black!

By 1913 the Lyalls had worked their way across Canada to Vancouver on the western shore. Eva remembered visiting them during the Great War.

One evening we all went to church. The congregation said a prayer for the fighting men. Jim Lyall had a twin brother who was fighting in France. Suddenly I noticed Jim staring straight ahead. All the color had gone out of his face. Annie and I took him outside and asked him what was wrong. Instead of saying he felt sick, he said, "My brother is lying in a ditch and he's calling for water. It's dark but lights are flashing." We tried to reassure him, but later we learned that his brother had been killed that very day. In Scotland it's called second sight.

The Lyall twins had been known as the strong one and the weak one. Jim was the weak one. He had trouble with his lungs, and the doctor in Vancouver said he needed a drier climate. He found a job in Calgary, where Annie would live the rest of her life and where she would climb the social heights at the Alpine Club. Climbers of Mount Everest and the Matterhorn came to climb the Canadian Rockies at the Alpine Club of Canada, founded in 1906 at Banff and modeled on the Alpine Club in England. Annie Lyall was the first summer hostess at the club after Mrs. Arthur Wheeler, wife of the founder. She said it was the job she had been born for. At the club she was famous for her fine cuisine, her spotless rooms, her cheery greeting, her hilarious jokes and stories. No calamity, members said, would dismay Mrs. Lyall. If a climber tore his only pair of Harris tweeds sliding down a mountain, Mrs. Lyall would patch them good as new by morning. Though a bear might raid the pantry, diners would sit down on time. In the winter of '32 Annie was a guest of honor at the Dolomite Club Dinner. Letters and cards flew thick and fast between Annie and club members who had gone home to England. Lady Rosemary Hills invited her to come and stay in Eton. In London, Mrs. Wedgwood gave a party in her honor. At the famous pottery Annie decorated a vase, which she kept on display in her china cabinet with the large slate-blue tea set edged in sugar icing, given her by her dear friend Katherine Wedgwood.

After twenty wonderful summers at the Alpine Club, Annie retired but didn't slow down. At the Provincial School of Agriculture she taught home economics to women from the farms. As president of the Handicraft Guild, she lectured on types and uses of wood. She built furniture for her house. To eke out her small pension, she sold handbags which she made from woolen cloth she wove on her loom at home. She cultivated a lovely garden which she opened to meetings of the Weavers Guild, of which she was a founder. A columnist in Calgary called her a cultural leader and said there really ought to be an Annie Lyall Boulevard. Two unfortunate episodes threatened to spoil this admirable picture. The first was when Annie's husband asked for a divorce.

Some of Jim Lyall's sunniest memories were of standing on quiet banks casting flies with young Charlie out over peaceful streams. He liked to put on tennis whites and rally with his son. Otherwise, Jim's life was going nowhere. He worried about his health. He got on poorly with his wife. A man with gumption, Annie said, would rise in his profession. A man whose best friend is the bottle will end up in the gutter. But a man needs a dram to help him through the day. A man needs understanding. Eva Bruce, Annie's sister, came for a visit from Entwistle, where Bob Bruce had his dry-goods store. Eva quickly saw that Jim was starved for affection. The way Annie kept after him would drive a sensitive man to drink, let alone a man with second sight. Eva told Annie that her husband needed understanding. Annie said that if Eva's husband would get up earlier in the morning, Eva wouldn't have to dress like a cotter's widow cutting peats in a bog. Annie went off to work with a scowl, and Eva, the bonnie one, nine years younger, stayed behind and took the occasion to comfort her sensitive brother-in-law. When she returned to Entwistle she couldn't resist sending him a letter of fond remembrance. Annie found the letter, and the sisters never spoke again.

Annie made it clear to Jim in many little ways how much she despised his moral failure, his perfidy, his self-indulgence, and his lack of gumption. The bottle became his only friend, until he met another affectionate, understanding woman and asked for a divorce. Annie said it was out of the question. Divorce was a public disgrace, not something a Low would do. Jim left home and didn't write. Six months later a call came from Chester D. Gunn, Coroner, County of San Diego. James Lyall, of Calgary, had died by his own hand. What arrangements should be made? Annie told her son that her name was *not* to be connected in *any* way with a suicide; luckily the Coroner didn't know there was a wife. Charlie made arrangements for cremation and disposal at Goodbody's Ivy Chapel in San Diego. Newspapers in Calgary ran a simple notice, but the *San Diego Union* published the details. Yesterday James Lyall, retired banker, fifty-two, of 3690 Sixth Avenue, where he lived alone in the rear apartment, stood in front of a mirror in his bedroom, put the muzzle of a .22-caliber rifle to his heart, pressed the trigger with his thumb, and fell backwards onto the floor. The manager found the body. I would guess that as he waited for the pain of life to end, my Uncle James regretted things he had done, and not done, recalled a few bright moments, felt a chill, saw lights flashing once more in the darkness, and heard his brother calling out for water, the strong twin, the wrong twin cut down in the cruel war.

The second threat to the family reputation came when Annie's son married beneath him. Irene, as Annie would later call her, was, in Annie's description, a woman of low character, who trapped Charlie into marriage and then proceeded to entertain another man in her bed while Charlie was off working to support his wife and baby. Well, of course, he had to divorce her, and that *was* in the papers. After an imbecile judge saw fit to give custody to Irene, she neglected the child, leaving her alone for days while traveling with the boyfriend.

Annie felt much better when Charlie married Ida, a daughter

of missionaries. Ida was tough and practical, had managed the
lunch counter at Woolworth's, and could manage Charlie almost
as well as his mother. She gave Annie two grandchildren, a fine
boy they named Charles after his father and great-grandfather, and
a girl named Penny. But then Charlie's health declined, and he
and Ida sold their house and bought a diner in Stettler, a hundred
miles away, where Ida managed the diner. When the children were
seven and two, Charlie Lyall died of cancer, and eight years later
Ida went the same way. On her deathbed Ida revealed a family
secret to her son. His father had been married before, and young
Charles had an older sister, grown up and married and living in
Montreal. His sister's name was Ingrid. Penny, who was only ten,
was still too young to be told about their sister Ingrid.

At seventy-five Annie was too old to raise the children, but their
father's life insurance and a family friend they called Auntie Edna
would take care of them in Stettler. Because of the distance and
expense Annie seldom saw them, but one day two years later she
invited them all for dinner. Penny remembered the visit:

> Before we started for Calgary, Auntie Edna told me that I
> had an older sister and I would meet her at Grannie's house.
> That was quite a shock. Ingrid was a complete surprise, thirty
> years old, red hair, *very* tall. She didn't look like Charles or
> me. I sat on a stool and listened while the grown-ups talked.
> After that night I didn't see Ingrid again for thirteen years.

At seventeen Annie's grandson Charles entered the University
of Alberta, where he paid his way working for the faculty and
teaching other students. In summer he dodged polar bears and
chewed the fat with Eskimos while surveying the frozen north. He
got a degree in engineering, studied computer science, and wrote
science-fiction stories. He started his own consulting business—
from which he took time out to specify the word processor on
which this book was written. No one helped me half as much with
my computer setup as my newfound Cousin Charles. "That's what
family are for," he said. And no one had helped Cousin Charles
half as much as his Grannie.

She was the only one who told me I could make it to university, I *could* do science, I could write. Nobody else gave me that. I would rate her with the best of my professors, people who always had time to help you, always demanded the best from you, growled at you when they didn't get it, took great satisfaction in your competence and success. Grannie respected competence. She once said: "A competent plumber is better than an incompetent philosopher."

Penny was not impressed by Grannie's pithy sayings.

I always knew that Grannie preferred Charles to me. She was annoyed with me because I chose to marry young and raise a family rather than attend university. My first marriage was a disaster. It was over in two months, but it gave me my older son. Grannie never approved of my second husband. All she cared about him was that he came from farming people, drove a truck, and didn't go to college. She didn't seem to know or care that it takes a great man to accept another man's child, adopt him, and provide for him.

When it came to marrying into Annie's family, those blue-blooded aristocrats descended from a Deeside laird, an incompetent Rotarian would get the nod long before a competent truck driver. "He's nae gonna set the heather afire, is he!" Grannie said. Her Scottish burr waxed and waned as the occasion required. Most of the time she spoke like someone raised in London.

"She was very class-conscious," Cousin Charles observed.

She certainly considered herself to be of "the better class." I don't think she ever noticed that in Canada she was living in one of the most egalitarian societies ever created. Tea at Grannie's was always a full-dress affair, with the children spotless and on their best behavior. It's hard for me to remember her without recalling a lecture on manners and my proper place. I could sit down today for tea with Queen Elizabeth without making a single mistake.

During the Depression, when prices hit rock bottom, Annie bought an abandoned store and paid two (competent) carpenters $1.25 an hour to remodel it. She invited them (once) to dinner to celebrate the final nail completing her "Wee House." There she set up housekeeping with a pipe-smoking Russian dentist, Dr. Margot Heimburger. Annie did the cooking while Margot filled the cavities. They lit their Christmas tree with candles. During the warm season, they rose at dawn to work in the garden. "Grannie had a huge lot," Cousin Charles recalled,

> and it was impeccable, not a blade of *grass* out of place, a bed for each kind of flower, something always ready to show for the entire summer. Out in the garden they were a team, but in the house they kept their distance. Margot's chair was on one side of the fireplace and Grannie's was on the other. Neither of them would ever think of sitting in the other's chair. Grannie pointed to her chair and said, "That's my divinity chair." I didn't get it until I read *Hamlet*: "There's a divinity that shapes our ends." Grannie pointed Lorna's books out to me in the bookcase. She showed me Lorna's picture in a magazine. She said, "This is my *sister!*"

Though she didn't approve of Lorna's extramarital doings or her heartless rejection of a little boy, Annie Lyall did enjoy being related to a successful author. She wouldn't speak to her sister Eva but showed Eva's book to friends. She liked to say about her housemate: "Margot speaks five languages!" She talked about "hobnobbing with the Everest climbers and other famous mountaineers—a very special kind of people." To Annie, the important thing was to be well thought of.

Four years after his Grannie died, Charles invited his older sister Ingrid to his wedding. She came with her two children, 2500 miles from Montreal, to be with Charles and Penny for a second time. After the ceremony, they went to celebrate in the park. Ingrid had a glass of wine and blurted out a second family secret. She had written to Grannie after Ida died, offering to take her orphaned brother and sister into her home. Grannie refused and wouldn't tell her where the children were living. Charles didn't seem to be

surprised by any of this—Grannie sometimes confided in him—
but Penny was horrified. Grannie had deliberately taken her sister
away from her and given her nothing in return. Ingrid, who should
have been close to her, was now a stranger and might always be.

Before I heard this story or knew about Ingrid's offer to take
the children or realized what different views Charles and Penny
had of Grannie, I told Charles I wanted to get in touch with Ingrid.
He gave me her address but said he doubted I could learn anything from Ingrid, because she didn't know about our Scottish
family and didn't like to talk about the past. She certainly wouldn't
want to hear anything negative about Grannie. "Ingrid worships
Grannie," said my cousin Charles.

By this time Ingrid's children had grown up, and she and her
husband were living on an island in the South Pacific, where Ingrid
had worked in a bank, run a private post office, and written three
unpublished novels. I wrote introducing myself and saying I was
writing a book about her great-aunt Lorna Moon and other members of our family. The reply was prompt but frosty.

> You say you are writing about my grandmother's family. That
> is, of course, your privilege. I do not wish to be rude, but I
> am unable to answer most of your questions. After my mother
> divorced my father, when I was in the first grade, we became
> unpersons as far as my grandmother and her son were con-
> cerned. My mother rarely spoke of them. Even at sixty-three
> the only way I can deal with memories of my father and
> grandmother is to lock them in a black box and keep the lid
> firmly closed.

The precision and restraint of Cousin Ingrid's reply encouraged
me to write again. This time the answer came from Pandora, beset
by demons escaped from the black box.

> In your first letter, I wondered who Irene was. Now I believe
> you must be referring to my mother as "Irene." My mother's
> name was Marie. Why the Lyall family should call her
> "Irene" I do not know. My mother said she divorced my
> father because he was a womanizer. Women would come to

the door asking for him, not knowing he was married. The law being what it was, she couldn't have gotten a divorce unless he had been caught in bed with another woman by a third party. I know he never paid any child support, even when he owned a house in a good neighborhood. Mother said she tried time and time again to get him to obey the court order. This was during the Depression. We were living in one room and sleeping in the same bed. Mother was cleaning two-storey houses for a few cents an hour and lunch. The lunch was very important, because it meant she ate less of our food and there was more for me. Social workers came to see if we had too much food to qualify for relief. We didn't, and we qualified.

Mother said there was a custody battle, which went to the Supreme Court, during which time my grandmother was trying to have her declared unfit and unable to support me. She would find out where Mother was working and phone the owner so she would lose her job. After Mother got custody, we were of no further interest to my father or grandmother. I remember when my father taught me to tell time. I remember watching him the night he packed his bags and left without saying a word to me. After that night I never heard from him again, but once when I was about thirteen I saw a familiar-looking man across a hotel lobby where my mother and I were sitting. He left without giving any sign of recognition, and I asked my mother who he was. She said he was my father.

At twenty I was working in the Royal Bank in Calgary. Mother came to see me, greatly upset. She said my father had died six months before and no one had had the decency to tell her. I telephoned my grandmother, whom I had not seen in a dozen years, introduced myself, and asked if I could come and see her. In her house, I asked her as tactfully as I could why we had been excluded from my father's funeral. She said she didn't want Charles or Penny to know about me or my mother or that their father had been married before. Out of the blue she said I would never be a lady. I was stunned. At the risk of sounding conceited, I will say that

I was well spoken, well mannered, well behaved, well groomed, had an impeccable reputation, was well read beyond my years, appreciated music, was an opera buff, had studied singing and acted in school theatrics, and had skipped two grades in school. I was born in wedlock and—my grandmother would have to say—was well bred at least on my father's side. And yet I was not a lady and never would be. I had to wonder what she thought the qualities of a lady were. She had all the visible attributes of a Victorian lady, complete with the hypocrisy of the age. Appearance was everything. She collected friends in high places and managed to sprinkle an earl, a countess, a Wedgwood, or some other personage throughout her conversation. She presented the perfect picture of a white-haired, soft-spoken, plump, lavender-scented grandmother, which hid the soul of a shark.

Well, it seems that Ingrid didn't worship Grannie after all. I asked her to tell me more about her mother. Marie Henrietta Larson had been born in Stockholm, a daughter of a captain on the Cunard line and a lady doctor. The Larsons had a large city house in Stockholm and a farm nearby. Marie and her sister Ebba had been educated in a German convent, which was how well-bred young ladies broadened their outlook at the time.

Mother fondly described her first ball gown to me—green silk with dancing slippers hand-made to match. Why did she come to Canada? It could have been a restless spirit. It could have been the fact that her twin brother was drafted into the army and froze to death a few weeks later on the Swedish frontier. Mother crossed Canada on a train unable to speak a word of English. She spoke Swedish, Norwegian, German, and French. She joined Ebba, who was married and living on a farm near Rosebud, Alberta. Why didn't she return to Sweden? She met my father, who was teaching school in the area.

The Lyall family rumor that my mother "slept around" infuriates me. This piece of dirt has the smack of Grannie putting the shoe on the other foot. Mother met her second husband a year after the divorce, and there was never another

man in her life. She worked long, hard hours, kept herself
and me scrupulously clean, insisted on good manners, and
expected me to do my share of work around the house. She
set standards of behaviour and acted with a delicacy that were
an example to me, which I have tried to pass on to my children. She was a true lady, not the false coin offered by my
grandmother.

It's no mystery why the two of them didn't get along.
Mother couldn't abide pretentious people. Annie Lyall made
a career out of being a Scot, as if they were the chosen people. Mother said to me, "A Scot is just a shipwrecked Swede
too dumb to get home." She told me about one afternoon
when Annie was having some ladies to tea, and Mother and
I were there. I was three years old. One of the ladies asked
me to get her a drink of water, which I did. After the ladies
left, Annie realized that I was too short to reach the tap. She
asked me where I had got the water. I led them proudly to
the toilet. Annie nearly had a stroke. Mother thought it was
hilarious. She said the woman got what she deserved, because
she was too lazy to get up and get her own drink of water.
She said she should have had more sense than to send a
three-year-old. She said I had shown initiative by solving the
problem on my own.

Ingrid said she had gone back to see her grandmother several
times before leaving for Montreal. I asked why she would do that.
What was she looking for?

Many things, including love. When my parents were divorced, it wasn't my father I missed. I forgot him right away.
It was Grannie. I adored her. To me she was all wonderful
things, Santa Claus, the Tooth Fairy. I still remember the
happiness I felt when I was with her. I missed her terribly,
and I never forgot her. When I was about eight, Mother and
I used to visit friends who lived near Grannie's house. On
the first visit, I slipped away across a park and knocked on
Grannie's door. She opened it, and I said, "Hello, I'm In-

grid." What happened then I can't remember. I know I didn't go back there until I was grown up.

At twenty, I was all things young. Idealistic, naive, and as I learned foolish. I mistakenly believed that if I was a good person trying to do the right thing, I would win approval even from Annie Lyall. I didn't want to believe what Mother had said about her. I had always silently hoped that Mother was exaggerating because of her own pain. I could understand that my grandmother wouldn't want to impose a previous wife and child on the children of a second marriage, but the total denial of our existence was too much. It was as though we were unclean, something that had to be locked away in a room with bars, so no one would know the family shame. After I left Calgary, I wrote letters to my grandmother, hoping for some change. Eventually I understood that all my efforts at reconciliation had been futile.

My daughter read your letters and noticed something I had missed. My father was only twenty-two years old when I was born! My parents were only children themselves! Looking back at myself at that age, I was staggered. I owe you a debt of gratitude. I have to admit that I wanted to throw your first letter into the garbage, but having learned some wisdom over the years, I did nothing until I was calm. My first and second letters to you were very hard to write but acted as a catharsis of emotions and events I had never told anyone before— particularly Charles and Penny, who were innocent parties. Thank you for your letters, which have cleared up so much for me. Finally, I can forgive my father, and in forgiving find peace with his memory.

In Annie's family album are four photographs of Ingrid, pre-served from that happy time when Annie expected to take a hand in the rearing of a darling granddaughter, who would be a source of pride, not a token of public shame. The first picture shows a pretty, smiling little girl, fashionably dressed in wool beret with matching fur-trimmed coat, knit leggings, and black patent-leather sandals. In the second picture she stands clutching a toy dog. The third shows her in dark wool middy and skirt with satin stripes and tie, sitting close to her father. The fourth shows her standing in a vegetable patch between her father and a tall blond woman. In the album the woman is not identified, but on a list prepared for me by Cousin Charles she is called "Irene (Ingrid's mother)." I asked Charles how he thought Marie had become "Irene." Charles said he didn't know.

I asked Penny if she thought Grannie had given Marie a false name to cut her off further from the family. Penny said, "I think Grannie was a lot like that. And she *would* have her way. She was a *stubborn* woman!"

In a letter written shortly before she died, when her mind was wandering a bit, Annie wrote: "Just had a visit from my son Charles, who is now Dr. Lyall, teaching at Edmonton University." She was, of course, thinking of her *grandson* Charles and giving him an imaginary academic promotion. So doing, she fulfilled a dream of having a son who was still alive and standing on a social peak where people of quality could see him and remember the gracious, dedicated cultural leader, the lavender-scented Victorian lady, white-haired, soft-spoken, who had never been too busy to help her boy rise in the world, who taught him about his rightful place, trusted him with family secrets, always demanded the best from him, took great satisfaction in his competence and success.

"At Grannie's funeral," Charles said, "I was *astounded* by the number of seventy-, eighty-, and ninety-year-old people from the Alpine Club. She was very well thought of there."

CHAPTER 14

A Witch on Wheels

Annie's sister Eva was *not* very well thought of. Being "the bonnie one" didn't help. Unpredictable, rebellious, fearless in misconduct, she was the black ewe of the Lows of Strichen. Among the many keepsakes on display in Da Low's cottage—a fine portrait of Maggie Low, a picture of the Lyalls, Nora playing Parisian coquette in an ornamental frame, Sadie and Jean and Evelyn Scott, Nora's books in a place of honor—there was no trace of "Mrs. Bruce," not a picture, not a book, not a button or a scrap. Margaret McLeman, who kept house twenty years for the Lows, recalled that Eva long ago had paid a visit home, after which she seemed to be dropped from the family. No one ever said why. When Mrs. Low died, Da Low wrote the sad news to Annie, but Mrs. McLeman had to write to Eva.

Left behind at sixteen by her married sisters, Eva had gone wild. No one could reason with her. She was too old to whip or lock in her room. The doctor said she would do better if she could get away from home. When at twenty she took ship to follow Annie and Nora, her parents felt great relief, hoping she would come to her senses on the Canadian frontier. In a railroad construction camp Eva baked bread for the crews. Mounted Policemen taught her how to shoot. The few married women there taught her, she said, "how malevolent the female of the species could be." At twenty-two she married Bob Bruce, easygoing, nine years older. She had to propose to him, she said, because he was the only man west of Winnipeg who hadn't asked to marry her. They built a house in Entwistle ("*Ent*issle" to the locals), a few rough wooden buildings, one of which was Bob's store, on a street leading to the railroad track. In the forest eight miles south, already deserted by his wife, pioneer Will Hebditch was batching it in his lonely cabin with his motherless boy. The first year of her marriage, Eva bore a daughter, the second she bore a son. In old age she remembered happy times with the children:

> On some winter days it was too cold for them to play outside. We would play "visitors" in the house. Dorine would put on a hat of mine, Donald would put on something of Dad's. They would skip out at the back door to race around and knock at the front. I would greet them with surprise as "Mr. and Mrs. Thompson"—"How dya do, and isn't it terrible weather!" Then we would sit down to talk about "our children." They would tell me naughty things *their* children had done, some of which opened my eyes, I can tell you. It was hard not to laugh. I wish I had it all to do over again—the children, I mean. I was never happier.

After most of Entwistle burned down, Bob Bruce built a new store across the river in Evansburg, a one-phone coal-mining town. The Bruces bought a large old house overlooking the river. Dorine and Don walked up the hill to a two-room school. They skied, skated, played tennis, and cheered at baseball games and hockey matches. "It was a wonderful place to grow up in!" Dorine said.

In 1921, Eva's sister Nora, the fugitive Mrs. Will Hebditch, now known as "Lorna Moon" the Hollywood movie writer, published her first Drumorty tale in *Century Magazine*, on whose pages she consorted with the likes of Katherine Anne Porter, W. H. Hudson, and Romain Rolland. Presently she wrote to Eva that she had borne a daughter to a Hollywood director. Eva knew who that must be. Lorna had been working for Cecil B. DeMille. Eva asked for a picture of the baby. Lorna said she couldn't send a picture, because the baby had been "kidnapped by her father." Eva suspected "just one more of Nora's high-powered fabrications."

Inspired by her sister's independence and achievements, not to mention her glamorous Hollywood connections, Eva in her snowbound house set out on a rival literary career.

I published my first story in 1923 and was paid $35 for it. Having written it in one afternoon, I saw rosy prospects. A story a week, and the Bruces would be living in luxury. I didn't sell another for five years, this time to the Macfadden string for $125. In between I entered a contest to write advertisements for Coca-Cola. I had never tasted Coca-Cola, but I won $300. In 1932, the women's magazine *Chatelaine* bought my story "Pyjamas." The editor, Miss Sanders, thought it was a bit racy but later told me it had been the most popular story they had ever run. The next year she published my story "Making Over Mary."

In Eva's story "Pyjamas," a man who resembles "a thoughtful parrot meditating profanity" is married to a woman whose independent ways provoke neighboring housewives. Eva's "Making Over Mary"—"a rollicking tale of an old maid who unlaces her strait-laced niece"—is similar in tone to Lorna's "Wedding of the Wheat," a lighthearted romance published fifteen months earlier and called by Lorna "a piece of fluff, bad enough to be good enough for the *Cosmopolitan*." Following her sister's trail, Eva was determined not to be left behind again.

"Mother had spirit and courage," Dorine said.

I think she and Aunt Lorna were alike in many ways. Mother could charm the birds out of the trees, and she had a wonderful knack of making people want to do things for her. I remember doing the floors—Don did them too—when Mother went out for the afternoon. We were about eleven. At an early age I started doing all the cooking. Any time Mother was away, visiting Aunt Annie at the Alpine Club, spending the weekend in Edmonton, going home to Scotland, I was looking after Dad and the house.

Though Bob Bruce didn't realize the full extent of it, he and Eva had a modern marriage. She had seen her parents trapped in an old-fashioned marriage and would not submit to that. Easygoing Bob was devoted to the children and would never leave her any more than he would make her rich, but his idea of marital bliss could be put on the cover of *The Saturday Evening Post* without drawing a single complaint. A woman who wrote true confessions for the Macfadden string had to know what she was writing about. A passionate woman could go crazy living with such a man. At home she did what she had to do to keep her husband happy. She didn't burden him with the details of her outside activities.

"Don was Mother's favorite," Dorine said.

Late in life I learned that he was really my half-brother. His father had been our Episcopal minister in Entwistle. Not that religion came into it. Religion was seldom mentioned in our home. When Don finally let the secret out, I was shocked. But it did explain one thing. When Don was baptized he received a beautiful embossed goblet as a gift from the minister. I received the Holy Spirit. Don was eleven months younger than I, so Mother must have been fooling around when I was two months old! And there was a newspaper man who was her friend for years. I don't think Dad ever knew what was going on. He was blinded by love.

Eva's novel, *Call Her Rosie*, was a well-constructed yarn with colorful characters sharply distinguished. It featured a father and daughter who "smiled on each other like lovers" and a jealous mother who spoke to her daughter out of "hate piled up behind clenched teeth." The villain was conformity, something the author had never indulged in. Like Lorna Moon's *Dark Star*, published a dozen years before, Eva's *Call Her Rosie* came down hard on prudes and hypocrites. When *The New York Times* called *Rosie* "lively and satisfying," Eva's career was on its way.

In childhood Eva had listened in rapture to bedtime stories invented by her dad out of bits of Buchan lore. One was a tale of the White Horse and how it had been ridden boldly into battle by the laird of Strichen when he fought Napoleon. Now Eva was the storyteller, and at first her father praised her writing as he had praised Lorna's, but after her one visit home, he had nothing more to say, to her or about her. She didn't complain about his silence. On both sides the wound was hidden, but it never healed.

A doctor in Edmonton said Eva's womb had to come out. An operation like that could put an end to her troubles, but whatever the result the surgeon's bill would be a burden. Times were hard, the mine was closed, the postmaster was selling cough syrup and liniment on the side. The only merchant making a profit was the local moonshiner. Eva had to cut costs. She certainly wouldn't stick her family with an expensive funeral. She called the undertaker and offered him $39.50 "without the pipes and drums." Never having sold a funeral directly to the corpse before, the undertaker couldn't speak. "Or I could write ads," she said, "to liven up your trade." Finding his voice, he agreed. "And make me beautiful," she said.

Eva survived the operation but ever after walked with a cane. Still she walked proudly, with back straight and head held high. On good days her charm and wit won the hearts of neighbors and shopkeepers. On bad days she quarreled, fumed, and schemed. On no days did she write. Her novel about the railroad camps remained a work in progress, a book an angry father would never have to see. Asked about her career, she said, "My life would fill volumes, my works a couple of lines."

Why was Eva cast out? Shortly after the break with Annie, she had returned to Strichen to sit with her dad in Number Ten and ask him many questions just to hear the dear voice that had gladdened a childish heart singing *The Standard on the Braes o'Mar* or telling stories that took the day's unhappiness away. She strolled the bank of the North Ugie Water remembering clumsy, excited boys. She faced her mother as an equal. All of her mother's rooms were taken, so Eva stayed at the Neuk with Sadie and her family.

Sadie Scott kept fine linens and a polished sideboard but not a happy household. When she wasn't in a rage, she brooded in her room. As understanding as ever, Eva saw that Henry Scott needed cheering up. The way Sadie was carrying on, it was no wonder poor Henry drank. Though he was twenty years older than Sadie, he was still a vigorous man and needed what only a woman could give. If Mother's little girl wouldn't do what a grown woman does to keep her husband happy, she would have only herself to blame. Still bonnie at forty-four, Eva pulled her blouse tight, stared into Henry's eyes, and said how pleasant it would be on a summer's afternoon to venture out for a wee spin along the lanes and byways to see the old familiar crofts and spires once again. He could hardly believe she meant what he knew she meant. After twenty years with a wife who cared more for easy living than for the man who provided it, he felt little duty to resist. He said indeed it would be pleasant.

Daughter Evelyn, fifteen, came along for the ride. No use setting spiteful village tongues to wagging. Henry, a builder and property owner, drove a few miles down the road, stopped in front of a house, and told his daughter to wait in the car. He and Eva went inside and didn't come out for what seemed hours. Cousin Evelyn remembered going on several of those outings. When Eva got back to Canada, she sent her brother-in-law a letter of fond remembrance. Sadie found the letter and rushed with it to her parents. They were very upset. The following summer Sadie went on holiday to England to get away from bitterness and despair. Her life ended in the car crash. No one said that if Mrs. Bruce had stayed home in Canada, Sadie would be alive today. No one said that forgiving somebody won't bring anybody back. No one wanted to speak about Eva or to think about her—unless it might have been Henry Scott, in the two years before he married sturdy young Jean Mathieson (who gave him two new daughters, Anna and Nanna. Villagers said, "If they have another, it'll be called banana").

Whether Henry thought of Eva, it is clear she thought of him a few years later when she wrote her novel. In the story, an aging man unhappy in his marriage smiles like a lover on a young woman in the family. He drinks too much and his name is "Henry." Another aging man is cruelly disappointed by a young woman named "Jean Mathieson." A mother who doesn't read books hits her daughter. This epistle to the home folk was not written to win back the love of an angry father. It was a message of defiance, and it was the last. Burning her Ugie brigs behind her, Eva said goodbye forever to all who wouldn't love her just the way she was.

One who would love her was her daughter. Nearing the end of her own life, Dorine remembered her mother's storms and furies:

For no reason I could see she would be angry at Dad or me. Sometimes our life with her was hell. Because of the way she was, I hurt for many years. Now that I'm walking with my Lord I have forgiven her. I realize that she didn't know what she was doing. After she became senile, she would keep smiling at me and kissing my hand. I believe the Lord took away all her torment, so we could finally show our love for each other. My daughter Lynne, who is full of surprises, tells me she and her husband are going to Scotland. They're taking Mother's ashes back to Strichen, as she wanted.

Dorine woke at daybreak and wrote to me again:

Hello. The birds and I are up. I love to hear them having their morning chat. I looked around for something to do and found a letter from you. What luck! Yes, Lynne and Ralph did go to Scotland. Even using the maps you sent, they had a hard time finding Strichen, it was so small. They saw the Mormond Hill and walked up through the broom. At the top an icy wind was blowing. As they scattered Mother's ashes Ralph started to laugh. He said I don't know why we came up here! All the ashes are blowing back into the village! Isn't that just like Mother. Perverse to the last.

Death was not a doorway or a mystery to Eva but a simple fact of life, like desire, motherhood, and sickness. She took them all as they came, asking no favors, confessing no sins, making no apology. She said:

I can't understand why people want another life. It's the last thing I want. Wrap me in a winding sheet, put me in the fire, scatter the ashes to the four winds, and be done with it. However, I am assailed on all sides by Pentecostals, Mormons, and Jehovah's Witnesses trying to get me into heaven. I enjoy their company. They are so passionate. At the end, your Uncle Robert wanted me to talk to him about life after death. I never told him my real opinion. I told him we would be together. That made him happy.

Aunt Eva wanted me to understand her sisters:

In Strichen Annie was the village belle, a real Lily Langtry type, but she couldn't diet herself and soon lost all her appeal to men. She was furious about it. She hated to see pictures of her younger sisters. She envied Lorna's sylph-like form. After the way she treated her own husband, she had some nerve to criticize Lorna for the way she lived. Richard, neither you nor I can say what Lorna should have done. If our mother could have shown us any love—but then I think of that driving ambition that took Lorna from obscurity in a tiny village to fame in Hollywood. Her whole purpose in the village was to get away. Some would call her ruthless, but her career fills me with awe. I can't sit in judgement on her any more than on a bolt of lightning.

CHAPTER 15

Getting Away

As the Lows were a perennial mystery in Strichen, Nora was a puzzle to her sisters. She was the cat that walked by herself keeping her own counsel, dreaming of being a gypsy, a Moor, a great lady, a poetess. At nine she wrote eulogies for sparrows frozen by winter winds, discovered by a little girl on the ice of North Street. At twelve she was a princess confined in a "fretful" gray tower, peering out through narrow garret windows at her domain, plotting to get away before they could take her head off in the morning. At fourteen Nora lost herself in a famous novel about Lady Lorna Dugal, a seventeenth-century heroine better known as Lorna Doone.

Dark-haired, very wonderful, with a wealthy softness on her, Lorna Doone was a lady born, and thoroughly aware of it. Her father was the Earl of Dugal, her mother descended from the ancient princely chiefs of Lorne, but at seven she was kidnapped by her relatives the Doones, a band of murdering brigands who kept her captive in their mountain fortress. She went about the countryside in the saddle or on the shoulders of the largest, fiercest man among them. Though her eyes were soft and kindly there was in them some great power that made her captors call her "queen." Year by year her beauty grew until by its boldly proud

or gently modest glory she could do with most men aught she
set her mind upon. Still, she never spoke a word that gave more
pain than pleasure, but hearkened to each person's troubles,
comforting the afflicted with a look of pity. Again, she was excitable and passionately affectionate. The scent of the gorse on
the moor would drive her wild. And she was mysterious. No man
could fully know her. Nonetheless, when she spoke, she was
truthful and transparent. Her silvery voice was a beautiful
bell. Though she never saw the inside of a school, unaccountably
at twenty she wrote like a philosopher on deep and diverse
topics. Married at last to the brave young man who rescued
her from captivity, she gave him several children but was never
once seen taking care of them. Too fair and dainty for rough
work and not at all inclined to cook, nonetheless she loved to
linger in the warm and friendly kitchen, where she was surrounded by admiring household women, whose toil she brightened with her playful ways and flashing wit. Gifted with a leap
of thought too swift for them to follow, she was indeed too clever
for most men, including her husband. And she was hard to control.

Nora Low at sixteen slipped out into the dark to spend the night
with Callie Birn, a neighbor girl her mother didn't approve of.
Lorna Moon the novelist would propose to write a book titled
"This Mortal Sappho," but since Miss Moon apparently held the
wholesome nineteenth-century view that the lyrical Lesbian had
leapt to her death for love of a *man*, Nora's trysts with Callie must
have been warmed by girlish gossip. However innocent those
nights, she would regret them twenty years later.

At nineteen Nora was counting on a young man named Bob
Dingwall to rescue her from captivity. Annie remembered him
well. "He came often to the club when Jim and I were courting,
and for a time all seemed 'merry as a marriage bell.' Then to our
amazement he married a woman much older than himself, and
Nora was heart-broken."

Perhaps young Bob wanted a woman dedicated to hearth, home,
and husband, a wife who would tend the bairns and put the supper
on the table, not a poetess or a princess. One day a commercial
traveler came to Strichen. *Dark Star* would recall him thus:

The arrival of the new watchmaker had caused a great flutter by reason of the fact that he was single and had a business of his own. He was a little man, with a bantam-like briskness, but when he sang "Oh, let me like a soldier fall," you could well believe that he was over six feet. . . . At first it seemed that the oldest Webster girl would get him. She was pretty, or would have been if she had not sucked her thumb in her cradle.

But soon he caught sight of a red-haired elf flitting about the Temperance Hotel. Annie continued:

> Will Hebditch fell for Nora, and she accepted him just to show Bob Dingwall that he was forgotten. I'm sure she never really cared for Will in the right way, and when he took her into the wilderness it was the last straw. I think if she had married Bob, she would have had a normal life. But she would still have written, as she had that gift.

One may doubt sister Annie's comfortable assumption that native talent, driving ambition, and wild romantic illusions would fit right in with washing diapers, wiping noses, boiling kale, and plucking homegrown chickens.

It was summer 1907. Will and Nora strolled on Bridge Street from the hotel to the river, passing brightly painted doors, scarlet, purple, green, or blue, each bidding cheerful welcome to a gray and fretful house. They climbed the Hill of Mormond to the Hunter's Lodge and looked down at the village. Soft breezes wafted sweet perfumes of summer blossoms. They sat in the grass like other young couples and talked about the future. Will said he was on the road because he liked the country, the trees, the farms, the streams, the fish waiting to be caught by him. His southern way of speaking carried her off to distant places, to the world she wanted to see, beyond Buchan, beyond the sparkling granite of Aberdeen. She asked about his business. He said his business was going well, but he liked the summer traveling better than the Selby winter. She asked about his house. He said it was a fine brick house of two stories with bay windows. Watchmaking had provided a good living for his father and also for him, but he didn't want to end up teaching it to his son. He was looking for something more exciting. She said what excited her was the thought of working for a newspaper in Edinburgh or writing stories for magazines in London. He asked if it would be a crime to take her in his arms. Not if you do it gallantly, she said. You are so little, he observed, barely an armful. A wee lass, she answered him, is big enough for a wee mannie. He said: Your hair is beautiful in the sun. So I've been told, she said—and then, as his smile faded: But never by such a handsome, well-spoken gentleman. He wondered if it would be rude to kiss her. Some kisses are rude, some aren't, she said. Och, your mustache is tickly! I used to think babies came from the gentleman's mustache. She straightened it for him and twisted the ends. From that moment he was lost.

When October came Will said: It's time for me to be in Selby, but I'll come again next year and I'll hope to find you. She said: Is there a girl in Selby? The place is packed with 'em, he said, and they all want to get married. In the night the captive princess slipped down from the garret and tapped at the door of the roving knight. She put her finger to her lips and said they must speak softly. In his arms she told him how her dad had put on circuses of children, cracking a whip over their heads as they pranced about the green or perched on boxes roaring. She touched the corner of her eye, and it was a while before she recalled what she had come to do.

Will stayed on in Scotland, looking for new business as far away as Inverness, returning like the moth to the Temperance Hotel. In December Nora told him he was bound to be a father. He was startled but not dismayed. Only a fool would have to be told the penalty of gallantry. The penalty was marriage. Mother doesn't know, she said, but Dad says we must go without delay to Aberdeen, so the boy will be well born. How do you know it's a boy? he said. She stared at him with topaz eyes and said: You told me you wanted something more exciting for your son. He said: Nora, I have never in my life known anyone like you. She said: Is that a compliment? He said: Of course it is.

On Christmas Eve 1907, by warrant of Sheriff Substitute of Aberdeen, Kincardine, & Banff, Will Hebditch, twenty-nine, watchmaker of Selby, took to wife Helen Nora Wilson Low, spinster, twenty-one, of Strichen, by declaration in the presence of James Dalziel McIntosh, Charles Low's solicitor, who hurried down from Fraserburgh to see that nothing went awry that hadn't gone awry already. The season was wrong for a honeymoon, but the bride had to agree that 2 Stonleigh Green Lane *was* a fine brick house looking out on a very respectable street. Will had heavy furniture, a lumpy bed, and many clocks. Selby wasn't London, but it was useful for a writer to live among the English and hear them speaking Yorkshire and observe their un-Scottish ways. Yorkshire folk were kind to Scots who were small and had red hair and were in the family way. The women asked what name had been chosen for the little one, said how many they had at home, and gave advice on nursing. The men said very little and pretended not to see.

Eight months and nine days after the declaration, Nora delivered the lad born for something more exciting. She told Will she wanted a nurse, and he spared no expense. Mrs. Low came on the train in a new black dress to inspect her grandson. When he was a year old, Nora carried him back to Strichen, where he had his picture taken sitting on a table looking like his dad. On pleasant days in Selby, mother, nurse, and baby went out riding in the cart brought by the donkey man. Nurse said donkey was the better-looking. Nora laughed.

Just as she was getting used to Yorkshire, Will announced that he had bought 160 acres in Alberta for ten dollars. Nora was thunderstruck. Then she remembered his rhapsody on the Hill of Mormond—the trees, the farms, the streams, the fish—and called herself a great fool for not listening carefully while there was still time. Annie and Jim were living near Toronto, which was said to be a city, but who had heard of a city in Alberta? One thing Nora knew. She couldn't go back to Strichen. Mother would say: You made your bed, and now you have to lie in it. Dad would sadly shake his head. The Webster girl would laugh at her. Worst of all, Mrs. Robert Dingwall would be *kind*! Nora would rather die. She had been born facing the wind, and she would go forward.

Will was briskly making plans. They would take most of the furniture, some of the clocks, and all of the fishing rods. The furniture would be stored until they had a house. Where shall we be living in the meantime? Nora asked. I'll pitch a tent, he said, in a clearing by a stream. There'll be game in the woods and water for cooking. On the other hand, Nora thought, Alberta is most of the way to San Francisco. If the stream freezes over and the game runs out, one can just keep going.

At Entwistle on train days, men in dark suits and dusty boots trampled the grass of King Street, hurrying down to meet the train. Will Hebditch stood beside the track to greet his wife and son, who had been staying in the east with Annie and Jim Lyall. Will had taken a room for them near the general store. Nora said it was a shack. The next day he took his family in the wagon to the homestead. Some men were helping him build the cabin, but Will was living in the tent. He said Nora could see it all when the sun came up. Supper was cold but Billy said he liked it. Toilet facilities were crude. In the night Nora woke to hear women wailing in anguish and despair. She was terrified. Will said those were not women, those were coyotes. It was hard to go back to sleep. What am I *doing* here! she thought. Luckily Billy slept right through it. In the morning Nora sat on a fallen tree in a floppy hat, while Billy and his father tramped about the forest talking and laughing.

A month later the Hebditches moved into their cabin. On good days Nora called it Hebditch House or Castle Will, on bad days Tumbledown Manse. Life was work from dawn to midnight. Nora had never expected to be a pioneer woman chopping sticks for the stove, a former violinist hauling water from a stream, a poetess beating a farmer's trousers against a tree trunk to loosen mud caked on from rooting out spruce stumps with axe and shovel. She had to admit he worked like a slave, getting cuts and calluses on his slim watchmaker's hands, and refusing sympathy from an otherwise cold and resentful wife. It was a holiday for both to go in for provisions.

Entwistle at first sight had been the end of the world to Nora, two rows of dingy barns pretending to be houses. Now it was the link to the world she had left behind. At the general store a tall stranger was speaking Yorkshire. Even to Nora, it was a welcome sound. Will answered in the dialect, and the two compatriots quickly became friends. Walter Moon of East Keswick had been in Canada a year, surveying the land and selling supplies on the road. In spite of his bluff self-assurance, he was only twenty-two, four years younger than Nora. Rather good-looking, she thought, in a conceited sort of way. Will invited his new friend to visit them in the forest.

As a boy Walter Moon had worked on his grandfather's farm and knew enough about farming to see that Will knew little. He felt sorry for Will's wife. She was making the best of things, but anyone could see she wasn't happy. A woman like that didn't belong on a farm. She should be riding in a carriage.

When the money from selling the house in Selby was used up, Will hired out to other farmers. He was gone for days at a time working far away. Walter came by when he could, bringing news, provisions, and good cheer. Sometimes Will was there, sometimes Nora's sister Eva, sometimes only Nora and the child. She always had a smile for him, and soon Walter made a point of dropping in when he guessed she would be alone. Nora was glad to cook for him. They talked about his work. Walter said he knew bookkeeping and would like to run a business. There were opportunities in the city. What city would that be? she asked. Walter had Winnipeg in mind. That's awfully far away! she said. We should never see you. That is true, Walter admitted, but I've been thinking, Nora. You're not the kind of woman who should be living on a farm. Will works hard and does his best, but he'll never have much here. This is not good land, and he is not a farmer. You belong with a man who can take proper care of you.

Walter! she said. What are you saying! You want me to leave my *husband*? Indeed, I do! said Walter Moon. He took Mrs. William Hebditch in his eager arms and kissed her full, blushing lips, which parted in surprise and lingered in appreciation. There hadn't been much kissing in the Hebditch household since Will had bought his stumps and rocks.

Walter said: You can bring the boy. Oh *no*! she said. I could never do that. Billy is Will's *son*. He belongs with his father. He likes the forest and the farm. Giving Will a son is the one thing I have done for him and the only thing I can do. As you wish, said Walter. Perhaps it's better all round. I'm going to Winnipeg soon, and I want you to come with me. Kiss me again, she said. He did. Don't worry, she whispered, Billy won't wake up.

Oh, Nora! Walter cried. I love you, Nora, Walter sighed. She murmured: You *are* romantic, Walter. And you're quite a man. How many newspapers does Winnipeg have? Three, he said, and a chamber of commerce, it's a proper city. I will go with you, Nora said.

After Christmas Will went off to work near Edmonton. Nora kissed him on the cheek and told him very earnestly to take good care of himself. That was like the old Nora, and he made the journey in good spirits. Nora told sister Eva she was going away with Walter. She would write when they were settled, but Will mustn't know where they had gone. They had to wait for train day, which would give her time to pack. On the way to Entwistle they left Billy with Mrs. Ransom, who saw at a glance what they were up to. But, she thought, poor Will Hebditch might be better off without such a wife. She gave Walter a sour look and spoke solemnly with Nora. Don't worry, she said. Billy will be fine with me. I'll be glad to keep him for you. Nora told her worried son he must be a good boy and wait here for Daddy. When are you coming back? he said. She kissed him and hugged him and said: Daddy will come soon. Billy watched them drive away. Mrs. Ransom said: What did you have for breakfast, Billy?

Will came home to an empty house. A note on the table said: Will dear, I'm going and I'm not coming back. Billy is at Ransoms. Will was very angry, but if he had lost his wife, he was glad to keep his son. He raised the boy to be a good man, honorable, industrious, kind, loyal to the end. Many times in childhood Billy was lonely, cold, and hungry, but he didn't complain, about his dad or anything else. In eighty years he never forgot the woman he had called Mother, the first woman he had loved, though she didn't return his love. And he could never forgive her.

Walter said they would have to travel as Mr. and Mrs. Moon. You will be Nora Moon. He smiled. No, she said, that's not right. But, Nora, he said, it will be much easier if people think we are married. That's not what I mean, she said. *Nora* isn't right. I will be *Lorna*, Lorna Moon. Walter laughed. It sounds like Lorna *Doone*! So it *does*! said Lorna Moon.

CHAPTER 16

The Career Woman

In Winnipeg the nearlyweds rented a house on Maryland Street, rather a daring thing to do in 1913, but they seemed a pleasant young couple, and nobody suspected them of adultery, desertion, or imposture. Walter kept the books of Barker & Co., Tile & Brick. Lorna worked almost a week for the city editor of the *Winnipeg Telegram*. She filed a thrilling account of leaping sheets of flame roaring out of crumbling windows but forgot to ask about the dollar loss. Demoted to the women's page, she wrote about the volunteers of the Sunshine Society helping the old, the sick, the poor, the laborer whose $10 a week would not buy fresh eggs and milk for a little boy with tuberculosis.

Writing to Eva, Lorna described her life behind the headlines and wondered how Will and Billy were getting along. Eva paid the pioneers a visit in the forest. Though his aunt was not his mother, Billy was glad to see her. She played with him and told him stories. Will asked Eva what she had heard from Nora. Nary a word from Nora, said the loyal sister of his disloyal wife. He suspected she was lying but he didn't say so. Soon Eva married Bob Bruce and offered to provide a home for her motherless nephew. Will told her angrily that Billy already had a home and he had a father and it would be better for him if she didn't keep coming round reminding him of his mother. Before long Billy stopped asking about women who gave him a kiss and went away and didn't come back.

Entwistle to Winnipeg is nine hundred miles. Will never did find out just where Nora and Walter had gone. After a while the widow Ransom, who didn't insist on marriage, helped him put Nora out of his mind.

Lorna's mind was on her career. During four years in Winnipeg, she made friends with journalists, acted in plays, hobnobbed with writers, and bore a healthy but time-consuming baby. Given the many pressures of the professional life, it seemed the best thing to do was to send the child to England to grow up with its aunt and uncle, who had no children of their own. Lorna worked for the *Winnipeg Telegram*, the *Tribune*, and the *Saturday Post*. In 1917 Walter took an accounting job in Minneapolis, where Lorna continued her newspaper work. The exact details of her employment have been obscured by various retellings. Interviewed ten years later by her friend Alma Whitaker of the *Los Angeles Times*, Lorna remembered coming to America at twenty (she was thirty-one when she and Walter crossed the border) and "writing about the theater" for the *Minneapolis Journal.* But on another of Whitaker's pages Lorna was "writing up the theaters for advertising purposes." To *Century Magazine* Lorna declared: "For years I wrote syndicated editorials for the daily papers." She clearly recalled her signed review of Cecil B. DeMille's *Male and Female*, in which she "razzed him wickedly" for inserting a Babylonian orgy into a Scottish play about an English butler. DeMille read the review, she said, and wired: "If you think you can do better and you're not just a smart aleck, come to Hollywood and try." But in another version, Lorna didn't write a review, she wrote "a saucy letter." In yet another, she met DeMille before going to Hollywood, and they corresponded "for months." That supposed correspondence is missing from the files, as are Lorna's signed reviews and her editorials, syndicated for years.

I would guess what actually happened is that Lorna wrote about movies coming soon to the New Lyric Theater, went to see *Male and Female*, and sent a letter to the director saying she could do better. Father did like spunky women, especially if they were panting to take orders from him. He must have answered: "Come and try," because a few weeks later Lorna was at Paramount working on the script of Cecil B. DeMille's *Affairs of Anatol*, starring Gloria Swanson. This remarkable leap from quasi-marital obscurity beside the waters of the Minnetonka to the artist's life among the flaming reels and burning ambitions of Babylon was not one of Lorna's "high-powered fabrications." It was as real as hauling water in the forest of Alberta, but it also marked the arrival of the mythical Lorna Moon, daughter of Highland chiefs, child bride, war widow, auburn-haired divorcée. As Lorna wrote to Eva: "For the sake of appearances, I shall now have to 'divorce' dear Walt, a man I have never been married to." Eva showed the letter to Annie, who sniffed: "I suppose in Hollywood everything is possible."

Walter had known, of course, that Lorna was driven by ambition, but she had seemed so happy at the *Journal*. Who would have expected her after eight idyllic years to run off and leave a responsible provider, a respected member of Rotary, with no more hesitation than when she had deserted a futile, failing farmer! Pride would not permit him to admit he cared. He took his betrayer to the train, kissed her, and wished her well. Nine years later, when she died, he married affectionate young Helene La Foille, who had waited five years for him to get over Lorna. They lived together in childless bliss until his death at eighty-one. In fifty years he didn't complain about having been cast off by "the first Mrs. Moon." But he left a sign. At eighty "the second" Mrs. Moon was still her predecessor's greatest fan. On the phone from Manistique she read me a poem Lorna had written. She said:

You know, I practically tore my house apart looking for pictures of her to send you, and I couldn't find a *thing*! My husband must have destroyed them all. I don't know when he did it. He had taken my photograph album and *cut* every *one* of them *out*! Here he had been gone ten years, and I was spitting *mad* at him! If I'd known he did *that*, I'd've pinned his ears *good*!

When the heartbreaker of Minneapolis stepped off the train in Glendale, California, her past had disappeared. In Hollywood, Nora Low Hebditch would be a name unknown. Only one or two close friends would learn that there was such a place as Strichen, Aberdeenshire. Lorna was Lorna of the Movies, connected somehow with Scottish nobility, recently divorced from Moon, whoever he might be.

Cecil B. DeMille's *Affairs of Anatol* was said to have been "suggested by" Arthur Schnitzler's play, much admired in Vienna in 1893 for its witty contrast of virtuous love and base philandering. Snobbish highbrow movie critics thought DeMille should have stuck closer to the play, but *Motion Picture News* said: "As a box-office magnet the picture cannot fail. . . . [It is] sure-fire for big cities and little towns alike." Robert Sherwood, of *Life*, agreed: "[Mr. DeMille's movie] should be enormously popular with those who think Schnitzler is a cheese."

Lorna received screen credit for *The Affairs of Anatol*, but it was her one and only picture with DeMille. She had talent and worked hard, but she didn't understand that a motion picture is a story told by the director. She kept bringing up Schnitzler. Father tried to charm her with Shakespearean hokum: "Surrounded as I am by stars, do you wonder I sigh for the moon?" He tried to bend her to his will with Belasconian bluster. He uncoiled his vixen whip, stinging, cutting sarcasm. Moon endured everything but seemed to learn nothing. Father sighed to be rid of her. A year later she confessed:

> Convinced that I was an idiot, I crept out of the firing line for a few weeks and counted my scars. Then I began to realize that the scars were not a total loss and that I had learned something from each of them. I went back to write for Mr. Lasky. The public likes what I have written, and so does Mr. Lasky.

Producer Jesse Lasky set Lorna to writing Gloria Swanson's next picture, to be directed by Sam Wood. "Lorna Moon, the scenarist, provided a good idea for the story," said *The New York Times*. Titled *Don't Tell Everything*, it featured two young husband-hunters tracking the same man, one "the eternal feminine," the other "the new sportswoman." Drawing on her once unwelcome knowledge of the outdoor life, Lorna wrote a comedy in which silk stockings, satin slippers, and fluffy negligee proved more deadly to the male than bird shooting, horse jumping, flannel shirt, and high wool socks. "Highly enjoyable," said *The New York Times*. Lorna's next assignment was to write *Too Much Wife*, a comedy about a woman who meddles in her husband's business and tries to run his life. Her fourth picture in six months was *Her Husband's Trademark*, a "society melodrama" about a wife (Gloria Swanson) kept as a trophy by a wheeler-dealer on the skids, until she falls in love with a rich, successful engineer. Conveniently, the wheeler-dealer is killed by Mexican bandits. One might think Lorna was saying success is an aphrodisiac, but in fact her task here was merely to adapt a story written in New York by Paramount writer Clara Beranger.

It was easy to write movies. They were fairy tales for grown-ups. The upper-class characters were drawn from British comedy, the lower-class from Dickens. And Hollywood had better weather. Lorna found a place to live near the studio. She decorated it herself, everything the way she liked it, warm California colors, palm green, date brown, desert yellow, sun red, rich fabrics from the downtown stores. Her beginner's salary was unheard-of wealth. She had come out of the wilderness into the promised land. For a while, just at first, Lorna missed dear Walt. It was nice to have a man. But Walt's head was full of bricks and numbers. One couldn't talk to him about stories or ideas.

For Paramount Pictures, 1921 was a busy year. Twenty-two films would be released between May and August. Director William Desmond Taylor, soon to be terminated by Mary Miles Minter's jealous mother, was putting the final touches on *Sacred and Profane Love*. Comedian Roscoe "Fatty" Arbuckle, soon to be condemned for crushing the hopes and bladder of Virginia Rappe, would appear in *The Travelling Salesman*, "a screamingly funny presentation." And writer-director William de Mille, soon to be a pallbearer at William Desmond Taylor's funeral, was finishing *The Lost Romance*, written by him and Olga Printzlau. It was their ninth story collaboration in four years. William liked working with lady writers. Since 1915 he had worked with Margaret Turnbull, Marion Fairfax, Jeanie Macpherson, and Olga Printzlau. The first two ladies were attached, and Jeanie was in love with Cecil, but Olga was free as a bird except for having a little daughter. Her apartment on Hollywood Boulevard was on William's way home. As William recommended for writer-director teams, he and his collaborator had developed a close bond. But *The Lost Romance* would be their last picture together.

"She left him for Christian Science," Agnes said, briefly amused at her father's much deserved discomfort. Christian Science or not, Olga had written a one-act play, which was in rehearsal at the Mummers' Workshop. To William's considerable annoyance she told him she was taking her play to New York. Early in 1921 William was left without a close bond and without the help he needed to adapt the Broadway hit *Miss Lulu Bett* for the screen. Coming to his aid, Paramount sent Clara Beranger out to be his lady writer. Clara's friend Rita warned her: "When you get to Hollywood, watch out for the DeMille boys!" Whatever the reputation of the DeMille boys, Clara was thirty-five, separated from her husband, a mother, and a professional woman. She had come to work, not play.

Lorna was also thirty-five (passing for early twenties), twice separated, twice accouched, and a professional woman. She was well aware of William, noted playwright on the Great White Way, second in Hollywood only to his flamboyant brother. The studio was a small community, where friends and colleagues went to each other's parties. Veda Buckland, wife of Wilfred, Cecil DeMille's art director, invited a group that included Frank and Ella Reicher, George and Beulah Marie Dix Flebbe, the Tully Marshalls, Helen Belknap, William and Anna de Mille, Clara Beranger out from New York, and Cecil's new writer Lorna Moon, out from who knows where.

A young boy opened the door and said: "Please come in. I'm Billy." He was the Bucklands' only child, a soft, cherubic boy, not at all like Billy Hebditch, who was firm and wiry; Billy would be twelve now; a braw laddie, Eva said. Lorna went round the room with Veda meeting various guests. They wouldn't interrupt Anna de Mille, lost in a discussion of the Single Tax, but in the opposite corner, William de Mille was explaining the world to a spellbound throng. He spied the newcomer approaching and was glad to meet her at last. By all reports this Lorna Moon had stood up to Cecil in defense of literature. A woman who could do that would pique

William's interest. And he liked the look of her and the sound of her Scottish burr. He smiled with great benevolence and resumed his lecture.

Liberty, said William de Mille, is the right to be wrong. The people's mistakes have injured the people, and the injury forces them to correct their mistakes. The few cannot think for the many, but the dynamic few can guide the static many ("dynamic" and "static" attesting here to the speaker's former studies in the Columbia School of Mines). However, drama is not easily made the servant of reason. A book may appeal to the few who will read it for its ideas, but a play must please the many, who will see it only for its story. The dramatist who wishes to lift the people's minds must first get his hands on their hearts. The drama is the democrat of the arts.

This man is brilliant! Lorna thought. And he speaks so well. What a pleasure it would be to know him. What a joy to work with him.

A tall, handsome woman came in with a young girl. They greeted William with delight. Lorna withdrew to observe. The young girl drifted in her direction, and Lorna engaged her in conversation. She was pretty but rather shy. She said her name was Frances. Her mother was Clara Beranger. They had just come to Hollywood. Her mother was going to write for William de Mille.

Seven years after that party, William and Anna were divorced, Clara Beranger married William, and Frances acquired two stepsisters, Agnes and Margaret de Mille, who lived with their mother and didn't care to know the daughter of the woman who had stolen their father. A lovable and amusing girl, Frances soon won Margaret's heart, but Agnes could never quite forgive her for being close to the father who had not loved Agnes enough.

In the years that followed, Frances had her own career as an actress on the stage. She had admirers by the dozen and one great and tragic love. She married and had children. At seventy-five she lived alone in a lofty apartment overlooking an elegant park, surrounded by pictures of family, friends, and roles she had played on Broadway and out of town. One day she received a letter from a man she had met once long ago, who was now claiming to be more or less her brother.

Fran-Sis: My earliest and most recent memory of you is of a raven-haired beauty coming down the staircase in our house in Laughlin Park. I was nineteen. I stood at the bottom of the stairs marvelling at your glory. I don't suppose you have changed.

Frances was undeniably vain, but she deserved all compliments to face, form, and character. She said she was glad to get a brother, she had always wanted one. To exorcise the sins of youth, she had written a memoir of her life and loves. She quoted the dedication: "To William de Mille, whose love and understanding helped me erase the 'step' from 'stepdaughter.' " All the same, when we talked, she called William "your father." Though she was thirteen years older, she treated me like a big brother. We talked for hours about the past. She remembered the Bucklands' party:

Lorna Moon was there. My first impression of her was vivid. I thought she was stunning, lovely-looking, what we used to call willowy. Dark, well dressed, and very chic. I was twelve and very self-conscious about being too tall for my age. She talked to me for quite a while and made me feel less awkward. She was kind and very warm. I think it was her eyes. It must have been the first time she had met William. She drew me aside and questioned me about him. We went into a corner and talked. I remember her Scottish accent. She said how witty he was, how brilliant. She said: "He's the most fascinating man I've ever met."

CHAPTER 17

Our Lady of Definite Opinions

"*Oh! That's* all so long ago! Why bring it up *now*?"

Agnes didn't want me to write about her father. When we talked, Lorna was "your mother" but William was not "our father." William was Agnes's father—adored, lost, resented, pitied, in the end almost forgiven. He belonged to *her*, and of course to some extent to her—not our—sister Margaret. Everybody got one father. Mine was "Uncle Cecil," and I should remember that. I shouldn't go poaching other people's fathers, especially when I barely knew them. I hadn't even been *born* when these things happened. I didn't know the other woman—well, in a way I knew her, but not to put down on paper what they said in the *bedroom*! "I mean, it's unconscionable! It's effrontery!"

"It's my life, Agnes."

"Oh, *Richard*!"

Agnes was her father's eldest child, the inheritor of the childhood home—which hurt sister Margaret's feelings, but they made up later. Then when Agnes was fifty-four, she woke at two-thirty in the morning in a Boston hotel to hear from Cousin Cecilia that Cousin Richard, whom she hadn't seen for years, was her little brother. It was a terrible shock. In old age she could discuss it calmly.

"Father always wanted a son. It must have been a great sorrow to him that he could seldom see you. I'm sure he must have suffered." She sent me a chapter she was writing about the brothers de Mille, to get my opinion "as to whether anything should be changed" and (though she didn't say so) to see if I would object to the following line: "Father sired an illegitimate son. . . . Richard de Mille. . . . He is, of course, my half-brother. . . ."

"How can you let her *say* that!" Ann del Valle had spent four years directing Father's public relations, putting our best foot forward. In Ann's professional opinion, "illegitimate" wasn't our best foot.

"It's true," I said, "and she needs to say it."

"*Why* does she need to say it?"

"First, her father abandoned her when she was barely out of her teens and still hungry for his love. Then years later it turned out that in a moment of utter self-indulgence he had also tossed away her honorary position as his eldest son. Agnes wants her reader to know that in spite of all injuries and insults, she alone is her father's legitimate firstborn. Nothing can ever take that away. A few things in her manuscript do need to be corrected, but that isn't one of them."

"I think it's terrible."

"It's the author's authentic voice, especially the 'of course.' 'He is, of course, my half-brother.' There was no 'of course' about it, until I told her the jig was up."

Like Frances, I had long admired Agnes. As a freshman at Columbia, I saw her dance in the Ballet Theater. She had composed a comic ballet about a very scruffy devil tricking three virgins into hell to the tune of Respighi's *Ancient Airs and Dances*. Agnes was one of the virgins, the dominant, priggish, fanatical one. It was a funny ballet, and she was funny in it. She had a comic gift. After I saw *Three Virgins and a Devil* I was no longer only her cousin, I was also her fan. I visited her and Aunt Anna in their apartment at 25 East Ninth. I went to see her performances. Once the two of us had a soda sitting at a little table in Walgreen's Drug Store with Martha Graham. Fifty years later Agnes invited me and (my) Margaret to lunch in that same apartment. She was in a wheelchair, paralyzed on one side. It didn't stop her. She went on composing

William de Mille wryly observing the follies of mankind.
CBDeM kept this picture on his desk

Lorna's children together for the first time: Richard, Mary, and Bill in 1970

Mary Moon, youngest reporter for the Leeds Guardian

Cousin Evelyn Scott, determined to clear up the mystery of the Low blue blood

Mary Moon, blond bombshell, 1935

*The White Horse on the Hill of Mormond, sheltering the village from the North Sea blast.
On the skyline, the Hunters' Lodge*

High Street, Strichen, Aberdeenshire, looking west, 1984

13 High Street. At the bottom of the garden stood Da Low's cottage, "Number Ten, Downing Street"

Ruined Hunters' Lodge atop the Hill of Mormond, Lorna's final resting place

Charles Low in 1861 with his Grannie Elenora, who taught him to be an upright man

Margaret Benzies Low, RdeM's Scottish grandmother, dressed to visit her English grandson, Bill

The Lows of Strichen in 1897: Nora, "the queer one," sitting next to her father, Charles Low; Annie, "the big one"; Sadie, "the little one"; young Charlie Low, the "saft" one; Margaret Benzies Low, their grim, responsible mother; and Eva, "the bonnie one," ready for mischief

The Charleses Low, son and father, in South Africa after the Boer War. Young Charlie had to sail for New Zealand in a hurry

Annie Low, village belle

Annie Low and Jim Lyall, newlyweds, in 1906

Ingrid Lyall, when she was still Annie's darling granddaughter

Jim Lyall and son Charlie, father of Ingrid, Charles, and Penny. Ingrid thought Charlie looked familiar across a hotel lobby

Eva Low, black ewe pretending to be a lamb

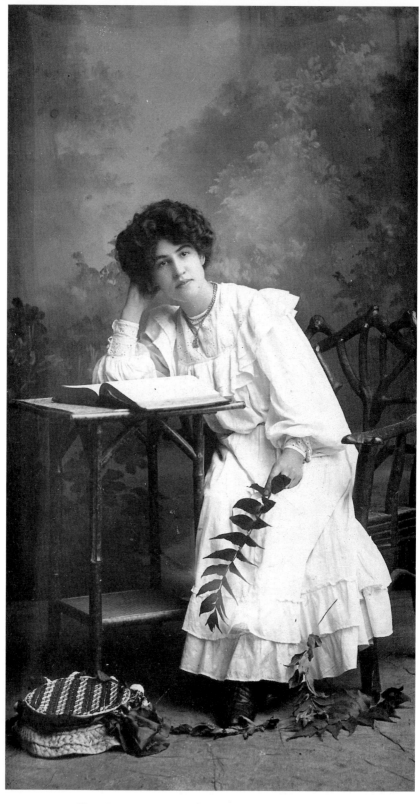

Nora Low, October 1907. One can see she is a reader

*Watchmaker Will Hebditch and his wife, 1908.
He had never in his life known anyone like Nora*

*Nora with her firstborn, clutching his
mother for safety*

Train day at Entwistle, Alberta, 1910. A postcard Nora sent to Sadie

Walter Moon (rhymes with Doone). He thought Nora didn't belong on a farm

Nora in her husband's forest, 1911

On the back she wrote, "Mostly hat and teeth"

<small>ABOVE AND FOLLOWING:</small> *Lorna coquette, 1913. Pictures kept by Charles Low in a special frame*
he had carved to hold them

*Constance de Mille in front of her house at
4 Laughlin Park, in the 1920s*

*Lorna, 1925, with new nose and
bob fit to make a fetching woman or
a bonny corp. Inscribed "To Walt
from 'Bunchie'"*

I Have a Better Time than Most of You Folks — **and get More from Life who have Good Health**

them. I will not go away and leave them sitting there.

But also, I know that I shall rise from this bed and run fast again. I will rise and go to Scotland. For I must know again the beauty of sweetbrier roses growing in a lane. I must smell once more the bitter scent of broken bracken stems; I must listen to the fey calling of moor birds upon a misty night, and watch the wind's long fingers flattening the heather on a hill.

But I am writing this principally to show that tuberculosis, far from being a handicap to creative writing, is in fact an asset. I cannot think of a single other thing that is so helpful to creative writing, unless it be a life sentence in prison. But in prison there are chores to be done, whereas in tuberculosis all chores, social and domestic, are wiped out. Life is simplified down to two or three things: to getting well; to being in love (for who ever heard of a "lunger" who was not in love?); and to writing a book.

No bores to meet and take to luncheon; no tedious dinners which *must* be attended

for business reasons; no moving-picture openings; no terrible dinner dances in stuffy rooms; no books to change for a sick friend; no silk to match for Aunt Jemima; no sitting on backles benches to watch polo because that is the smart thing to do; no dashing down to pick up Cousin Nellie, who has an appointment with the dentist—nothing! All responsibilities are lifted from my shoulders and deposited neatly on the shoulders of my friends.

They, poor things, must hasten out in their brief luncheon hour to "change a book for poor little Lorna," while I lie on a broad cool bed in an airy room thinking my thoughts, untroubled, uninterrupted.

Milly sends me gardenias to wear on my white satin pajamas, but Milly does not expect a note of thanks, for "poor Lorna" has no strength to expend on such notes. Edith tells all tedious people that I am too weak to receive visitors. Frances sends her car to bring all the visitors I am not "too weak" to see.

It is true that my strength is limited, but there is a limit to *(Continued on page 135)*

*Lorna, 1929,
like a houri in
a convent*

Lorna in art deco, 1930. Her son turned right past the page

The de Mille house
atop a mount of olives

Cecil de Mille's office
in the "West Wing" at
home, where he told
RdeM, thirty-three,
who his natural
parents were

MARY NICHOLS

CBDeM in 1915, his
second year in
Hollywood, directing
opera star Geraldine
Farrar in Maria Rosa
her first movie

and directing ballets till the final curtain. After a long lunch, with a nice red wine, I said:

"Agnes, I'm fed up with being your cousin. From now on, I'm going to be your brother. If you don't say it, I will." She started to cry.

"Oh, *Richard*! Family relations are so difficult! You have no idea how *awful* I can be!" I said:

"I know *exactly* how awful you can be, Agnes. I've known it for years. And I'm going to be your brother from now on."

Agnes could be pretty awful. A few years earlier she had lectured at the university in Santa Barbara. My Margaret and I attended. After the lecture I introduced them. "Well, you *are* pretty!" Agnes said. She had heard it from other members of the family—Richard has a pretty wife—and now she made it official. She introduced us to some other visitors. "This is my cousin, Richard de Mille, and, and . . . and his wife, Margaret." She turned to Margaret and said, "I *can't* call you 'Margaret de Mille.' You understand why." The unstated reason, which seemed obvious to Agnes, was that Margaret de Mille was *her sister*, who had died six years before, and the name was still too sacred to be given to another. Agnes cultivated her feelings like an exotic garden for others to appreciate, but others didn't always appreciate them. On the way home, my Margaret said:

"I've been Margaret de Mille for thirty years. I think I have a right to use the name."

Toward the end of Agnes's life, we spoke often on the phone. Our typical conversation started like this:

A: Hello?
R: Agnes!
A: Yes?
R: Richard.
A: Richard who?
R: Richard de Mille, who else?
A: Well, there are several Richards.

In 1989 Margaret and I were invited to New York to accept membership in the Emerson Radio Hall of Fame for Father and

his Lux Radio Theater, a favorite on the airwaves from 1936 to
1945. There were other inductees, Lowell Thomas, Fibber McGee
& Molly, Jack Armstrong, the All-American Boy. Joan Benny accepted for her father. Orson Welles's granddaughter accepted the
trophy for *The Shadow.* When we arrived at our hotel, I dialed
Agnes's number.

A: Hello?
R: Agnes! Richard.
A: Richard who?
R: Richard de Mille. Margaret and I are in New York.
A: *Why?*

This close, affectionate bonding had begun ten years before,
when Cecilia, always the family manager, sent me a copy of *Where
the Wings Grow,* a memoir of childhood. It was Agnes's ninth book
but the first one I had read. I found it touching, sweet, nostalgic,
and poetic. I thought it was very good indeed. After thirty years
of estrangement my fanship was rekindled. I wrote the author a
letter. She was very pleased, and we started talking. She was eager
to be loved but couldn't make the first move. If you smiled at
Agnes, she would open like a flower, then quickly close again sus-
pecting your love was not sincere or would be forgotten next time
you met. If you didn't write or call, you would hear nothing from
her. "I dropped out of the family quite completely for a long
time," she said. She paid little attention to other family members
and complained that they neglected her. Some years before we
resumed our friendship, she had come to Santa Barbara to narrate
for her dance troupe. Did she ring me up and say, "I'll be there
soon and hope to see you"? That would have been too risky. A
printed notice came from the ladies' auxiliary. I was still too proud
to pay court to my regal sister, that pontificating grande dame who
would call me only cousin, so we didn't go.

When someone else took the risk, Agnes could be lovable. In
April 1984, I spent a week in New York and visited her three
times. I took her out in her wheelchair and wheeled her around
Washington Square. It was a warm sunny day. A lot of people were
out. Some boys were doing "break dancing" on the pavement.
Agnes didn't approve of break dancing. We sat in the sun and

talked. I told her I had been her fan in 1942 and had wanted to be closer to her, but she was too busy. She thanked me for being so persistent now. She shed a tear, and we kissed. She would have liked it that way all the time, provided anyone who loved her would ask nothing in return and would recognize her as the center of the world. Being the center of the world was a family foible, but Agnes had it worse than any of the rest of us. If you drove a hundred miles to have lunch with her, she would arrive two hours late talking about her hectic day and expecting sympathy.

When her book *Reprieve* came out, describing her refusal to be defeated by a stroke, she commanded me to buy it. "Of course I'll buy it," I said. "I'm studying your works." Which made her a little uneasy. What does he mean, studying? Is he going to write about me? If any writing was to be done, Agnes wanted to do it. Still, she couldn't resist talking to me about her life. In childhood she had realized that the world wasn't treating her right and probably didn't intend to. She was a special flower, and they forgot to water her. In books, lectures, and interviews she had often complained about her father and her uncle. They didn't care enough for her. They took little interest in her work. In Hollywood in the twenties both of them had been powerful and wealthy, yet they hadn't bothered to endow a film archive of early choreographies, now lost forever. Raking in their vulgar profits, they didn't do their duty to support genuine artists. President Reagan was equally guilty when it came to tax money. This shameful failure stemmed from woeful lack of taste. For all their commercial cleverness, influence, and prominence, these men lacked artistic refinement. William's aesthetic appreciation was deplorably narrow. Cecil's taste was atrocious. The less said about Reagan, the better. Frankly, father figures were a terrible disappointment.

In the manuscript she sent me, Agnes contrasted William and Cecil, measuring them by various standards. Agnes's standard of art, implicit in many things she said, is easily brought out. At the top are great artists like Chopin, Keats, or Martha Graham. Then there are the lesser artists like Agnes de Mille, genuine artists but not great. Next come the failed artists like William de Mille, a should-have-been, a would-have-been, a talented man who lost his nerve. And at the bottom of the pole, there is Uncle Cecil, the world-famous philistine.

Agnes contrasted the brothers in character. Cecil dynamic, practical, and ruthless. William intellectual, reflective, and considerate
(except to special flowers who wanted to be dancers). Cecil wary,
William too trusting. Cecil disciplined and hard, William self-
indulgent. Cecil surrounded by reporters, William slipping into obscurity. Cecil the "old guard" Republican, William the Jeffersonian
Democrat. Cecil the traditionalist (which Agnes called "reaction-
ary"), William the progressive. William dedicated to the public
good, Cecil the rugged individualist, the free-market robber baron,
"believing in independent enterprise by no matter what confiscation of public rights." Confiscation of public *rights*? What is Agnes
talking about? I asked her.

"Well," she said, "I'm a Georgist." There it was—her grandfather, the unseen guest at every party. Henry George (1839–
1897), author of *Progress and Poverty* (1879), was a newspaperman,
social reformer, and economic visionary, who ran as Labor candi-
date for mayor of New York in 1886 and would have been elected
if votes hadn't been stolen from him by the Democratic political
machine. Henry George proposed to tax bare land and nothing
else—not the buildings on the land, not crops or herds or irrigation
systems, not any other property, not any other income, certainly
not wages, just the rental value of a piece of land as it would be
in its natural state. Agnes quoted her grandfather: "When we tax
ground values, we take from individuals what does not belong to
them, but belongs to the community and cannot be left to individuals without the robbery of other individuals." Uncle Cecil had
bought land and seen its value rise simply because population and
production grew around it. Then he sold it at a profit or collected
high rent from it. Whether Cecil knew it or not, he was robbing
other individuals. Henry George had said that a wise and moral
society would reward production, not speculation in land. One
thing men did not produce was land. Land was given to them by
God and rightly belonged "to all the people." To exercise the
people's right, the whole rental value of each piece of useful land
would be collected from the private landholder by the people's
agent, which was the government. In effect, all land would be
nationalized. Some might call this socialism, but invidious labels
are beside the point. The point is to be fair.

Among Henry George's fair-minded followers were his daughter

Anna and her husband William and their daughter Agnes. Inspired by his prophetic tone, clear prose, and moral fervor, these partic-ular de Milles overlooked some thorny questions. How, for ex-ample, did "the people" of San Francisco come to own Nob Hill? Henry George had said that the *pueblo* (that is, the town) of San Francisco received a grant from the King of Spain. Very well, but how did the King get land in California? Did he get it directly from God, or did he get it from Stone Age people living by the bay, who, one supposes, got it from the Great Spirit? And if he got it from Stone Age people, *how* did he get it? One hopes he didn't take it by force. That wouldn't be fair.

Another question was: If Single Tax takes all the rent from land, land itself will have little market value. How then will the gov-ernment assess its tax value? Well, that's not so hard. Farseeing public servants will imagine all possible uses of the land and cal-culate the land's potential rent. Government will tax potential rent. Some may call this arbitrary. What they call it doesn't matter. What matters is to be fair.

Henry George believed that taxing nothing but the land would completely free production by removing all its tax burden, but a hundred years later the free-market economist Friedrich Hayek said that was an illusion. Though he called the Single Tax "the theoretically most defensible of all socialist proposals," he found it to be impractical because "the original and permanent powers of the soil" could not in practice be distinguished from "the dif-ferent kinds of improvements." The best Milton Friedman, an-other Nobel economist, could say for the Single Tax was that it was "the least bad tax." With all due respect to Agnes's extraor-dinary, influential grandpa, Single Tax is not the perfect cost-free solution the Georgist de Milles believed it was.

Such academic nit-picking didn't bother Anna, William, or Ag-nes. They were uplifted by noble purpose. When they looked into the mirror they saw the fairest citizens of all. And they felt sorry for the unenlightened. Father, for example, didn't understand that owning a piece of land was confiscating public rights. He foolishly believed he was giving his tenants opportunities to produce and getting a fair reward for risking his money. His refusal to obey the higher economic law proclaimed by Henry George was always counted against him by the moral wing of the family. "He made a public show of being a good man," Agnes said, "but what he was mainly interested in was money. He didn't live the life of a generous Christian."

This opinion, I'm glad to say, doesn't square with the facts. Behind the scenes, Father committed unauthorized, unregulated, unnoticed acts of kindness. One of his former assistant directors, having bouts with the bottle, said scurrilous things about him, which got back to the Boss. How did the moneygrubbing hypocrite get his revenge? When the griper's health went bad, Father paid his rent and hospital bills. He was loyal to his crew and made allowances for their faults, as they usually did for his. He helped people in distress with no thought of compensation, making many so-called loans he knew would never be paid back. Jeanie Macpherson's assistant, Cora, came down with tuberculosis. She went home to Iowa in the dead of winter and rapidly got worse. Her mother wrote: "My heart aches for my poor sick girl. Last night she said to her father, 'Papa dear, I am so tired. Will I never get rested?' " A letter came from Miss Macpherson. Cora was to come back and be treated by Dr. Francis Pottenger, whose patients came from around the world—Mabel Normand, the movie star, Manuel Quezon, president of the Philippines, a U.S. ambassador to Spain, a grandson of Emperor Mutsuhito—TB was no respecter of rank. At first Cora believed that Miss Macpherson was her benefactor, but then letters came from Gladys Rosson, and Miss Macpherson brought Cora a present from Mr. de Mille, a bottle of champagne from his private cellar (illegal under Prohibition). Dr. Pottenger said she wasn't well enough to drink it yet, and Cora wrote to Father:

"I have it under lock and key and am guarding it with my life." Seeing the bitter truth of that, the plucky girl added: "Ha!"

Dr. Pottenger wrote to Father: "Cases of this kind often disappoint us." Cora lived for a year.

Not realizing that at the final trump he would be called to judgment by his high-minded niece, Father neglected to send Agnes a list of his good deeds. She did recall his gifts to her when she was a child, always more fun than those her father gave her. She mentioned Uncle Cecil's delightful interest in her girlhood dancing. So where did he go wrong? It was when she was twenty-five and just beginning to be noticed as a dancer, and Father wouldn't appoint her as his dance director! A big player in the West Coast capital of nepotism, he didn't want to be accused of promoting family members. Suddenly the kindly uncle turned into a callous movie mogul. Sixty years later Agnes wrote: "I never heard of Cecil's helping a young talent." This was far from the truth. Father recognized Agnes's young talent and offered to send her at his expense on the road with her own dance company, but she wasn't ready. He hired her to compose and perform a dance in *Cleopatra*. She wouldn't take direction from the famous director and was shocked by his reluctance to defer to her superior taste.

Religion was another place where Father had gone astray, even more than William. William was polite about religion in public, but on the wall at home he had pictures of monks laughing fit to die while censoring pornography. William laughed along with them. Agnes despised the pictures, not for being antireligious but for being bad art—like Father's Bible movies. She agreed with some other nonreligious writers who criticized Father for trading on religion when he was not a sincere believer. How did she know he wasn't sincere? Well, in addition to voting, twice, against Adlai Stevenson and making a profit trading land, he had had three mistresses. She compared him to Jimmy Swaggart, who didn't practice at the motel what he preached on TV. She called his movies "superficial propaganda for religion." I said perhaps she couldn't see that Father was sincere, because she wasn't religious.

"You don't know *that*!" she said.

"I know it very well," I said. "Religious people don't talk about 'propaganda for religion.' They talk about sacred stories. I don't want people who *are* religious accusing my dear secular Sis of writing about a subject she doesn't know the first thing about." Agnes was startled by the idea that there was a subject she didn't know the first thing about. She said:

"Well, I *am* an agnostic, but I have a pro*found* feeling for human emotion and the human response to beauty. I believe in what John Keats said: 'Beauty is truth, truth beauty.' Uncle Cecil and the people he reached with his movies may have felt strong emotion, but their aesthetic was clouded and confused. It wasn't truly or deeply religious."

I said that would come as a surprise to Catholics with garish holy cards stuck to their refrigerators and Christian believers who weep every Easter at *The King of Kings*. I said: "I think you just don't like the way he told the story."

"I certainly don't," she said. "His aesthetic was *very* faulty."

Agnes's religion was art. They have things in common, of course—dedication, inspiration, daily striving for elevation, and for flagellant monks and ballet dancers mortification of the flesh—but the beauty of art is made by artists; religious truth comes from a higher source. The closest thing to a higher source in Agnes's pantheon was Henry George.

In the end Agnes wrote: "Richard de Mille disagrees with much of this interpretation." And she quoted me at some length. I was astonished that she would do that. I told her she was generous to let me have my say in her book. I said she wasn't nearly as awful as she professed to be and I didn't regret making her my sister. "Well," she said, "somebody had to do something."

Agnes found it hard to take another person's point of view. She did it rather well in her portraits of dancers, especially Martha Graham, but she couldn't do it with Father. She said he had neglected William in his years of illness and Clara had resented it. "I don't know where she gets this idea," Frances said, "but it's not true. Cecil often called William, and William loved his calls. I was there. She was not. At William's funeral Frank Reicher said it was amazing how devoted these two men were to each other when they were so different."

Agnes said Father had "somehow managed to publicize" his refusal to pay a dollar to the radio union "as a national crusade for liberty." It's the *somehow* that gives it away. She didn't understand what *he* thought he was doing, which was opposing unconstitutional acts of union bosses. Congress agreed with Father and rewrote the law, but one doesn't have to agree with him to understand his campaign or why it succeeded. On top of that, incongruously, she called him "a conformer." She said: "He did not state a belief and hew to it and fight for it and if need be go down fighting for it." But that is exactly what he did do. When he was gravely ill, Father traveled to Washington to testify before the House Labor Committee. He didn't have to do it. He knew his time was short. He wanted to do his duty. First, last, and always, he was a fighter for the right, a bold champion of principle—like his opinionated niece. On opposite sides of most questions, they were both honest, brave, and true and worth listening to about things they understood. Agnes understood the dance. Father understood liberty under the law.

Agnes was proud of her long memory and relied upon it, sometimes a little too much. President Ronald Reagan had infuriated her by being stingy (with my money) to the National Endowment for the Arts. "Reagan!" she said. "I could *kill* 'im!" A few years later he awarded her the National Medal of Arts for lifetime achievements in the theater. She didn't tell him she wanted to kill 'im, but it was still on her mind. Describing turmoil and hard times in her book *Martha*, she wrote: "The President was shot but not killed, which made him a national martyr." Yes, I remember the movie. Preston Foster played the lead. It was 9:35 p.m., Wednesday, the 15th of February. The President had just finished speaking to the crowd. Suddenly shots rang out. Mayor Anton Cermak of Chicago was fatally wounded. The President told reporters: "I held him all the way to the hospital. I said, 'Tony, keep quiet, don't move. It won't hurt you if you keep quiet.'" The President's coolness under fire and gentle care of Cermak made a very good impression on the public. That was 1933. Agnes was writing about the Depression. The President was Roosevelt. None of the bullets hit him. He became a hero not a martyr. Agnes had him mixed up with that stingy Ronald Reagan, who was shot but not killed in 1981. Since *Martha* was already published, I didn't say anything to Agnes about Mayor Cermak.

Agnes was steadfast in her beliefs. Her faith in the people's fair, wise, and helpful central government survived every test. At seventy-seven she complained about being "hounded" by the IRS. She had donated her film archives to the New York Public Library Dance Collection and had taken a deduction. The IRS didn't buy it. They contrasted Agnes with serious artists like Danny Kaye and deemed her archives worthless. She went before the tax tribunal to defend her case. They treated her like a tax evader, as big a cheat as William, whose "every penny" Agnes said they had confiscated. They spoke to her rudely and imposed a heavy fine. The curator of the Dance Collection tried to comfort her. Agnes said it was her own fault; she should have hired a better lawyer. The curator protested that the hearing had been rigged to make an example of her. Agnes said it was un-American to be so cynical about the system. In Agnes's world of noble purpose, fathers couldn't be counted on, but you could trust Big Brother.

She was fearless in her expression of ill-founded opinions. Father got a lot of publicity out of pretty feet. Paulette Goddard supposedly landed the role of a sexy half-breed in *North West Mounted Police* by striding into his office and planting a naked foot on his desk. In the 1890s, when Father was growing up, it was very exciting to see the flash of a shapely ankle stepping down from a buggy. Helen Twelvetrees, movie star in the 1930s, wore an anklet that promised "Heavens above!" Father made that promise one of his movie trademarks, along with battles, bathtubs, and very tame orgies, little guessing what teasing toes would mean to psychoanalysts. Agnes had been to a psychoanalyst, and in a TV interview she called Father a "podophile." Now she was saying it in her chapter. I wrote to her:

> If a man likes breasts, is he a mammiphile? Psychiatric jargon doesn't belong in a literary essay. Anyway, you're using it wrong. A podophile *prefers* feet to genitals. He substitutes the part for the hole. Are we to believe that if Cecil B. DeMille got his hands on a woman, he would stop at her *feet*?

Agnes relinquished "podophile."

She had mixed feelings about feminine beauty. Distracted by the charms of Venus, foolish men would overlook finer qualities in a woman. A publicity photo shows her at twenty-nine on the set of *Cleopatra* with Father and Katherine DeMille. Katie has come in costume from the set of Mae West's *Belle of the Nineties*. The two women are standing on either side of Father, one the ascetic dance artist in a plain black dress, the other a glorious sex object. Agnes's arm is linked with Father's, but he is looking adoringly at Katherine. Agnes would have liked to be Anna Pavlova, Martha Graham, George Eliot, *and* a glorious sex object.

She wanted to write better than her father, but they were too different for easy comparison. He was adept at satire, she had a gift for lyricism. His best writing was in his wry little comedies, hers was in her heartfelt memoir of childhood. His secondary gift was drama, hers was biography, of which the crowning achievement was *Martha*. Inheriting writing talent from both sides of her family, she added music, movement, design, indomitable spirit, readiness to endure loneliness and privation, and relentless hard work. It was her pride that she outdid him, and it was her sorrow. William had had three careers—stage, screen, and university. As the first two passed him by, he proudly stood his ground, unwilling to change his track shoes and catch up. His teaching career was secure, but it lacked the influence and glory he had dreamed of —guiding the people, lifting their minds, bringing the nations together. His life was a story of bright beginnings followed by somber disappointments. Agnes had had two careers and had triumphed in both of them. She became the hero she had wanted him to be. Unlike him, she never gave up. After her stroke, she learned to write shaky but legible words with her left hand and wrote three books that way. She conducted rehearsals from a wheelchair. Her husband of forty-five years, Walter Prude, suffered a lingering illness, and Agnes was left a widow. Asked by an interviewer what kept her working under such trying conditions, she replied: What else should I do? Either I work or I lie in bed alone. It gives me something to hang on to.

About Lorna, she said only: "It's a pity she got sick. I mean, that's tragic." But there was one question she wanted me to clear up. Had Lorna broken off with William before he met Clara? I said I hadn't worked the timetable out. That wasn't good enough for Agnes. She had to nail it down and get it on the record. In *Portrait Gallery* she wrote: "It is an incontrovertible fact that four months after the birth of [Lorna's] baby William de Mille and Clara Beranger started their love affair." When I worked the sequence out, it wasn't four months after; it was eight months before. Agnes had mistaken 1921 for 1922. For her it was a very comforting mistake. She had already convicted her father of destroying her childhood family. She didn't want me or anyone else accusing him now at this late date of two-timing his second wife with the mother of his son. She would be his biographer, accuser, and defender. Other people could write about fathers of their own. Though I must respectfully decline to obey her, I salute our lady of definite opinions, my reluctant, difficult, admirable Sis.

CHAPTER 18

The Love Affair

I remember that during this time I saw him with another woman
and asked him chidingly if he was two-timing Lorna. He answered:
'No, Neil—at least I am faithful in my infidelity.' " Neil Mc-
Carthy's daughter said he could really dream stuff up, and maybe
he dreamt up that conversation, but "faithful in my infidelity"
does sound like William, and if he said it, I would believe it. William didn't tell everything, but he was too proud to lie. Frances
said Clara went through a crisis over William and Lorna.

It was much later, after they had been married for maybe
twenty years. I know it was after my daughter was born. William used to keep a diary. He was a very private person, and
nobody could touch his desk, not even the cleaning woman.
Mother didn't know what was in his diary, but one day he
asked her to look up an old date for him, and she noticed a
little notation—like a mystery story—where he had written
the letters "LM." She asked him what it meant, and he said
it was an appointment with Lorna Moon. I don't think they
said any more about it. I was amazed at Mother's reaction, it
was so dramatic. At first she was very mysterious. She wanted
me to go out with her in the car. She didn't want William to

hear. We parked at the end of a street looking out over the ocean, and she told me what she had found. She was shaking. She could hardly talk.

R: She thought he had been romancing her and Lorna at the same time.

F: She was sure of it. She asked me not to tell anyone, and I never did until after she and William had died and Margaret came out from New York and told me you were William's son. Margaret was as amazed as I was at Mother's reaction. To us it seemed like ancient history, something that had happened long before they were married, but Mother didn't look at it that way.

R: Did she ever know about me?

F: No. That would have made it worse. She always thought you were Cecil's son.

After her father died, Agnes had wanted to collect his papers. She asked Clara about his diaries. "And she told me she had *burned* them! I said, '*Why!*' and she said, 'There was nothing in them but facts.' Nothing in them but *facts*! Everything that had happened to him in Hollywood for *forty years*!" Like Agnes, I deplored the loss of an irreplaceable record, but I didn't realize that something more was at stake—William's honor in affairs of the heart, his reputation as a gentleman.

When Margaret got back to New York, she told Agnes what Clara had discovered in the diary, and Agnes understood why Clara had burned it. William's divorce had been bad enough. No one wanted any more scandal. When I proposed to write about him, Agnes was far from pleased, but at least no one was going to tell me about the diary. Then one day I said to her how much I enjoyed talking to Frances and what a darling person she was and how many things she remembered. After a pause Agnes said, in a very subdued tone: "I didn't know you knew Frances so well." A few minutes later, as if introducing a brand-new subject, she asked me whether Lorna had broken off with William before he met Clara. She wanted to find out whether Frances had told me about

the diary. Frances hadn't told me yet, so I said I hadn't worked it
out. Agnes couldn't rely on that. She published her "incontrovertible fact" to counter any rumors that might be spread by less responsible, upstart biographers.

One thing is not a rumor. On or about the twelfth of May 1921,
most likely in Lorna's apartment, which would have been the saf-
est place, she and the most fascinating man she had ever met were
locked together body and soul in reckless eager carnal delight. In
those days a gentleman didn't like to break the mood by bringing
up unpleasant subjects, such as birth control, which men considered women's business. In spite of being, as William believed, in
her early twenties, Lorna had been married and must be an ex-
perienced woman. He confidently expected her to manage her re-
productive rights in a sensible way, asking for whatever male
precautions might be necessary (but he hoped none would be) as
his other ladies had done. It is clear she didn't. At first, he was
very glad of that, counting himself a lucky man to have found such
a competent lover, who would not deprive him of the sharpest
pleasures. For William, the price of this indulgence was lifelong
regret mixed with bitter satisfaction at having gotten a son at last,
though a son he had to give up to another man, a very good man,
it is true, but not a man who would teach the boy tennis, fencing,
and Single Tax, or show him how to play a swordfish in the Catalina Channel, or sit with him at the Tuna Club smoking a fine
cigar and discussing the failure of Goethe's theater. For Lorna, the
price was disaster.

I feel for the unlucky lovers, but I wouldn't save them. If I did,
I wouldn't be here to do it. Mum and Dad took a chance in the
lottery of lust, and I cashed their ticket. Their bad luck, after much
delay, became a story about them which they couldn't tell, and
writers know the story is the thing. Many details of the story are
hidden but can be imagined. How they got into such a fix is the
easiest thing to say. Each had heard good reasons to admire the
other. Each believed the other to be footloose and fancy-free. Each
was aching for a new and wonderful lover's touch. One enchanted
evening across a crowded room they saw their fate and rushed to
meet it, mistaking it for a harmless, delicious opportunity.

When were they first alone together? Both were working at Par-

amount. I would guess he invited her to come and sit in his office
and talk about the art of the film and other professional topics.
Why wasn't Clara there? Presumably she hadn't yet begun her
work with William. How did they progress to courtship? With
literary allusions, clever repartee, and caressing voices, not to mention one or two seductively adoring glances. William was monu-
mentally vain. It didn't take a cliver quine from Strichen to see
that.

When did they make their first assignation? After about an hour.
Art is long but life is short. Gather ye rosebuds while ye may. The
same flower that smiles today, tomorrow will be dying. What—
dear Agnes, up there in heaven keeping the saints on their toes,
rehearsing Three Angels and a Republican, looking down in disapproval—did they say in the bedroom?

Lorna, ransom of the lovelorn, where have you been these forty-three
years!

Well, my dear, most of the time unborn or in the cradle.

Which was pure deception. She was born when he was eight.

Did they love each other? It depends on what is meant. Looking
at Lorna through William's eyes, she has much in common with
his erstwhile colleague Olga Printzlau. Both are tiny, well dressed,
charming, and amusing. Neither will be jealous or possessive. Both
will be discreet. Then the differences begin. Though she is sur-
prisingly well informed for her years, Lorna in her youth will look
up to William, certainly more than Olga did, as a teacher of drama,
literature, and life. Lorna has not written a play and won't run off
to New York to compete with senior playwrights. She has no children to get in the way. She despises Christian Science. Olga was
a New Yorker and a familiar type, but Lorna is exotic, colorful in
her speech, a woman with an unknown past, exciting in her mystery. It is a pleasure to talk with her. She understands everything.
Her eyes have something in them that he cannot name. One moment she treats him like a father, the next like a playmate. She is
warm, she is passionate, she is ready for every thrill erotic love can
bring. God in heaven! What man wouldn't want her!

Did Lorna love William? Four years later she gave him a copy
of her little book of stories, inscribed not quite discreetly: "To my
friend William de Mille, very tenderly, Lorna Moon." A fragment

of an ancient urn, it is her only testimony to that fatal tenderness. William kept it in his study. Seldom did he look at it. On the flyleaf was his sorrow, and sweet recollection. When he saw his death in the mirror, he gave the book to his brother, to keep for his—their—son. Thus, though he didn't know it, he spared his jealous widow-to-be the painful need to find the book, open it, and burn it.

And who could blame Clara for getting rid of the evidence? She had dedicated herself to cherishing William, protecting him, helping him in everything he might wish to do, urging him to do more, keeping him alive, smiling at his wry jokes about weak martinis, nursing his silent pain, hiding her tears as he clipped the third cigar of the day, which the doctor said would kill him, but she couldn't take them away. William would die before he would change. At the beginning of their love, when he couldn't leave Anna, when he was still bound to his wife by loyalty and compassion, Clara had waited and endured. The worst was hearing from Anna's lips that they were still sleeping together—God, it was an insult!—and she hadn't reproached him with it. He would have to work it out. He was worth waiting for. Then to find those hideous little marks in his diary after twenty years of marriage! She knew in an instant what they were. Suddenly she was hurled back into that awful meeting with Anna, into the betrayal and humiliation of sharing him with another woman. She had been through hell with him. And she would do it all again.

On an old shopping list in a bleak and empty house Frances read her mother's last reflection: "I'm living on iron will since William's death." Clara would live less than a year. Surely it had been her duty to destroy that diary. Who knew what else it might contain! The world respected William. His students venerated him. Let him be remembered not for peccadillos but as the daring playwright, the subtle film director, the Academy President, the dignified professor, the hilarious after-dinner speaker, the seventy-year-old tennis player, the husband happily married at last and for many tranquil years. His memory must not be sullied by a passing adventuress trading on his weakness to further her career.

Lorna had nothing up her sleeve. She was swept away by William. She had no thought of using him. She wanted to please her brilliant lover. She was happy in the affair. She thought she had everything under control. In June she missed her period. She didn't tell him right away. She wanted to be sure. She had been through it all before. She could arrange it somehow. She was making very good money. In the flush of her new prosperity, she had even written to Will offering to put their son through good schools in California if he would send him down to her. Will didn't answer the letter. Eva said he tore it up.

William couldn't raise the child. His wife would never agree to that. But Lorna could hire a nurse. If she had to find herself in a family way, like a lovesick milkmaid, how glorious that it was his! No doubt he had always wanted a son. Well, now he would have one. She'd have to go away for a while. But she could write anywhere. She could take assignments and send her pages through the mail. Maybe she would rent a house at Carmel-by-the-Sea, a quiet place for writers.

Both of them were working hard. Lorna was laboring to adapt Clara's story for *Her Husband's Trademark*. It was her second picture with director Sam Wood and her third with Gloria Swanson. Sam liked the script so far, but Gloria wanted one thing and Sam wanted another and Lorna had her own ideas. There were many conferences. It wasn't easy to get away to meet William during the day. William longed to see Lorna, but he too was very busy, transforming the stage dialogue of *Miss Lulu Bett* into equivalent silent scenes. Clara had written fifty pictures and was turning out to be his best collaborator. She was quick to see exactly what he wanted. She had a lovely sense of humor. He was at ease in her company. And she was an attractive woman, tall, graceful, and well formed. At times he felt drawn to her, but he would be true to Lorna, as long as it lasted. Lorna would expect that. He expected it of himself.

CHAPTER 19

The Conspiracy

Lorna recognized the signs. Food cravings, odd dreams, tender nipples, swelling breasts. She had never had morning sickness. William praised her new glow, calling her a passionflower, Rhine maiden, water sprite gleaming forth a lovely light. She couldn't keep the secret forever. Smiling at him mysteriously, she clung to the joyful moment. Afterwards she turned serious. Dearest one, I have something to tell you. It came as a surprise to me. I hope it will make you happy. He stared at her in alarm.

There's going to be a little William.

An iron hand gripped William's gut. He had wanted a son, but not outside of marriage, not—in the cold light of reason—from a woman he hardly knew. Was there ever a bigger fool than William C. de Mille! How could she let this happen! Cecil didn't have such troubles. He chose steadier women. Until now, William had chosen steadier women.

The mother of his third child was looking at him steadily. She was speaking to him. I don't want to distress you. It's my responsibility. I can support a child. You can see him whenever you like.

William was shocked. Of course I'll support the child. And you must have the best care. Will you go away? Before the baby shows, she said. I'm thinking of taking a house at Carmel-by-the-Sea. You could visit me there. She smiled. After bittersweet farewells, William left the apartment in a daze.

Every day Lorna felt tired by midafternoon. She called William and told him she must be coming down with something. Whatever it was, she didn't want him to catch it. He said, of course, he understood, and she must take good care of herself, especially now. She told him he was sweet. He said: Be sure to ask me for anything you need. She said: I have everything I need if I have your love. He said she would always have that.

He couldn't concentrate on his work. Clara kept him going. Clara was the port in the storm. She could see he was upset. She guessed he was having trouble at home.

Lorna would finish *Her Husband's Trademark*, then she would take some time off to look after her health. She felt a little feverish. She got a nagging cough. She went to Dr. Barnard. Dr. Barnard painted painful throats with silver nitrate and soothed nagging coughs with cherry syrup. The nurse said: Hold this under your tongue. Over a hundred, the nurse said. Dr. Barnard peered through the hole in his mirror into Lorna's ear. He pressed a dry stick on her tongue and scrutinized her tonsils. He put an icy stethoscope up underneath her blouse and thumped her back and listened. He said she had bronchitis. She should go right home to bed and drink lots of fluids. She said: I have a script to finish. You won't get well that way, he said. We don't want this to turn into pneumonia.

Every day she went to work, until the script was finished. Sam called it a very good job. Gloria said it was grand. Sam said: Lorna, go home now and don't come back until you're in the pink.

In the night she woke up coughing. It was hard to stop. When she turned the light on, she saw a dark spot in her handkerchief. She stared at it. She didn't move. She had waked in Callie's bed because Callie was coughing. Callie had chronic bronchitis. That could give you a terrible cough. How they used to laugh together! Until they had to stop because it made Callie cough. That was twenty years ago. There couldn't be any connection now.

Dr. Barnard said it wasn't something to take chances with. She must go to a specialist. Luckily the best man was right there in Los Angeles, downtown at Fifth and Spring.

Lorna didn't tell anyone. People would be afraid. It wasn't something you talked about. You couldn't ring your lover up and say: I can't see you today, I've got a touch of TB. She'd have to tell him, when she knew. If it was true. These days, many recovered. She was afraid, not of dying but of losing everything. All her dreams could blow away like dust. Lorna Moon, screenwriter, daughter of Highland chiefs, mystery woman invented by an unknown village girl, could vanish without a trace, unpublished, unremembered. It couldn't be true after all this time. Dr. Barnard must be wrong.

He was right to send you, Dr. Pottenger said. We'll make tests at the sanatorium, but I have little doubt.

Will I be there long? she asked. I have to make a living.

You can make a living when you're well again. First, we must get you well.

Can't you treat me at home?

We haven't had success with that. Patients left on their own get worse. Patients with active tuberculosis need a very strict routine, especially pregnant women. If the tests show that you have TB, I will recommend immediate termination. The strain of carrying a child is very dangerous for the mother. Fortunately, it's early in the pregnancy.

I don't want to lose the baby.

That's the mother speaking, and it's very commendable, but this is your third child. The danger increases with each one. It would be risking your life.

It's mine to risk, and I want to have the baby.

If that's what you decide it will be all the more important to have the best possible care, for your sake and the child's.

Can I have him in the sanatorium?

Him?

It's going to be a boy.

I see. Well, in any case, it wouldn't be good for you to leave. You'll be under the most stress at the time of delivery. My first training was in obstetrics. I have delivered babies in the sanatorium and I will be glad to deliver yours, if that's what you decide.

———

𝓗ello, my dear.

Lorna! I called, but there was no answer.

I said I'd be going away, and I've gone a little early. I'm in the Pottenger Sanatorium.

Good God!

I hope so. I'll be here for quite a while. I can have the baby here. But I can't take care of him. I don't like asking you to help, but I can't work while I'm in here. You're the only one I can ask.

Of course! I'll talk to Dr. Pottenger.

He wants me to have an abortion.

Because the baby . . .

No, the baby will be fine. But he says it's risking my life. I told him my life is mine to risk and I want to have the baby.

You must do what's best for *you*, Lorna.

You want me to have the abortion?

No, no. I mean, I can't tell you what to do. It's your life and your health.

You're leaving it up to me?

I must.

I'm glad. If I don't come out alive, you will have a son.

You're *going* to come out *alive*, Lorna.

Oh, I mean to, dear one. I have a lot of writing to do. And I'd like to see *you* again.

𝒲illiam went to his younger brother. C, you are a man of the world. You manage much better than I do. I don't know what to do about this. Lorna can't take care of the baby. I can't take the baby.

His younger brother passed no judgment. He said: I'll talk to Constance about it. She's very good with these things. She's fond of you and she's very fond of babies. He allowed himself the ghost of a smile. It could be a boy, he said.

𝒞ome in, Bill. Neil McCarthy shook William's hand.

And thank you for coming down. I think we have this matter resolved along the lines you discussed with Cecil and Constance.

They will take the child and raise it as their own. You and Lorna will agree to make no claim of parenthood. Lorna will agree not to see the child. You will see your nephew or niece from time to time on family occasions, as an uncle would.

Dr. Pottenger expects the child to be born healthy, but for its own protection it must be immediately removed from the mother. Lorna cannot hold the baby or be in the same room with the baby, which means that she will feel less attachment to the baby. Under the circumstances, that is good.

Lorna is asking for nothing except help with the hospital bills, which may be extensive, but I think it's fair. She says the money is just a loan and she will pay it back as soon as she can work again. She is very independent. If you wish to help her further, after she is well, you are free to do so, but I advise against it. Unexplained gifts can arouse suspicion and invite unwarranted questions.

I have advised Cecil and Constance to defer formal filing of the petition for adoption for several years. This will avoid early scrutiny by the court and, in the event that Cecil and Constance both predecease you while the child is still a minor, you can more easily claim the child, if that is what you then wish to do.

Cecil proposes that, when either you or he dies, the other should inform the child of its natural parents. I advised against that, but Cecil says he'll talk to you about it. Certainly it should not be done unless the child is old enough and prudent enough to be trusted with the information, which could be a long time.

We plan to leave the child at the sanatorium for several months. The more time we let pass between Lorna's leaving Hollywood and the baby's arriving there, the harder it will be for outsiders to make a connection between Lorna and the baby. Constance suggested that at the proper time the baby could go to the Castelar Creche, where she is on the board. She would then notice the baby and decide to adopt it, as she did with John and Katherine. It's a very good idea. The press will like it and accept it.

To avoid connecting you with the matter in any way, all payments to Dr. Pottenger will be made from Cecil's office. You can resolve financial matters directly with Cecil. He has helped other patients at the sanatorium, and Lorna can be just one more former employee he is helping. A few of her friends will know she is there, but if she keeps her promises no one will know about the baby. No birth certificate will be filed. When the baby is old enough, I will arrange the transfer to the Castelar Creche. About a year from now you will read in the papers that Mr. and Mrs. Cecil DeMille have given a good home to an infant whose parents have disappeared. We did it with John and with luck we can do it again.

After you have read and approved this agreement, your signature will be required to make it valid, binding, and enforceable. Among other things, we want to ensure the privacy of all the parties—you, Lorna, the child, Cecil and Constance, and your family. I think we've caught this early enough to keep anything from leaking out. If all goes well, this document will never be made public. The press would love a Paramount scandal starring the DeMilles. It would be bigger than Fatty Arbuckle. The wild card is Lorna. We have to trust her to keep the secret.

A fine premise for a drama, much like *The Woman*. William wished he were the playwright controlling the events rather than the reckless lover betting his future on the whims of a water sprite. How powerful an author is! How helpless a character in a play!

Monrovia was a small town sheltered by the San Gabriel Mountains, ten miles east of Pasadena, twenty miles from Hollywood. In 1903 Francis Marion Pottenger, M.D., had risked eight hundred and fifty dollars to buy eight and a half acres dotted with large boulders among which ran a meandering stream. Planting flowers and young oaks, he created a private park populated by quail and rabbits, visited by deer and fox. The townspeople were up in arms when they heard that he would take patients with consumption, "the white plague" feared by everyone, but he managed to reassure them. The Pottenger Sanatorium fulfilled a dream he had conceived as a young doctor in Ohio. On the last day of June 1895, when he had been married one year, he heard his young wife coughing. Examining her, he was filled with horror. She died three years later, and he devoted the rest of his life to saving victims of the disease that killed her. Peaceful surroundings, good food, milk from a private dairy herd certified free of tubercle bacilli sustained patients who were suffering through their final days and helped others rise up again and return to their occupations. But it was solitary. Until they were well on their way to recovery, patients stayed in their rooms alone. All their meals were served on a tray.

Dr. Pottenger knew how to keep his patients cheerful. Starting the morning rounds at seven, he visited every patient. He came into the room solemn but with a twinkle in his eye. He said the secret of recovery from tuberculosis was the patient's immunity, her powers of recuperation. She must heal her own disease. She must remain hopeful. With proper care and strict routine her chances were very good. She should also have something to do, something to keep her interested in life. Writing would be a very good thing. All it took was pencil and paper.

And a writer, Lorna said.

Lying in her little gray room, she remembered an old song.

> *Speed, bonnie boat, like a bird on the wing.*
> *Onward! the sailors cry.*
> *Carry the lad that's born to be King*
> *Over the sea to Skye.*

The year was 1746. Charles Edward Stuart—born to be King of Scotland and, in his own opinion, King of Ireland, England, Wales, France, and their dominions, an inspiration to his nation, but a very poor general—had just been utterly defeated at the battle of Culloden, where at the order of the evil English Duke of Cumberland, ever after known as the Butcher, wounded clansmen were slaughtered like sheep as they lay helpless on the Moor. Planning to fight another day, Bonnie Prince Charlie hasted away to the western shore, where he embarked for the Isle of Skye, aided by young Flora Macdonald, heroine of Scots.

> *Though the waves leap, soft shall ye sleep;*
> *Ocean's a royal bed.*
> *Rocked in the deep, Flora will keep*
> *Watch by your weary head.*

Sighing in her narrow bed, weary and full of fever, Lorna thought of Flora Macdonald saving the lad born to be king. The lad growing in Lorna's womb had brought this illness upon her, but she bore him no ill will. It was all her own doing—or her undoing—sneaking out to stay with Callie, throwing caution overboard while sailing on a tide of joy, getting pregnant once again like a witless warlock. Now came the reckoning. She must bring the lad to shore, as Flora had done for the Bonnie Prince, and he must do his part as well by keeping up her spirits. He was her work in progress, her anonymous creation, to be revealed someday at a time she couldn't guess but hoped she'd live to see.

Dr. Pottenger did not hide the truth from his latest lunger. Every bit of strength collecting in the growing child would be taken from the mother and from her recovery. Strengthening him would weaken her. Well, she was a young woman and she would have strength for both! Or at least for him. She would *not* be defeated by her passionate mistake. One or both of them would live. She would be mother to three children she might never see again.

Dr. Pottenger was descended from a Scottish family. That was reassuring. A *pottenger*, he told Lorna, was a maker of pottage. Perhaps his people had been cooks. His parents had named him Francis Marion after the Swamp Fox, hero of the American Revolution. Lorna smiled at superstition, but she thought it was a good omen that the man who must keep her alive had the same name as her friend Frances Marion, the screenwriter. It meant that Lorna would be going back to Hollywood. It meant she would recover and still make her mark in the world. William's son would know her name.

My mother was a writer. Her name was Lorna Moon. This is a book she wrote.

Through the bay window she could see the bungalow beyond, then the towering mountains. Two nurses were walking along the path. Birds were hopping and chirping on the shingles overhead. This simple little house, quiet, all her own, would be a good place to rest, to think about the past, to have a secret baby without giving up her life, to dream her way into stories about people she had known.

CHAPTER 20

The Short-Story Writer

Writing was easier in the morning, when the fever was down. If you could get them to leave you alone, with their thermometers and their sputum cups. The bay window in Lorna's cottage reminded her of the ones in Selby, but she didn't want to recount the ordeal of Mrs. Hebditch. She was remembering Strichen. She had started village stories in Minneapolis, but none of them were finished. She wouldn't call it Strichen, of course. "Drumorty" was a good name for a Buchan village. It had the rhythm of Rosehearty. "Drum" meant ridge, to match the Hill of Mormond, and made one think of "drumly," meaning a cloudy, troubled sky. There had been plenty of those in Strichen.

Only a few weeks earlier, in Jesse Lasky's office, when life was good and the future was bright, Lorna had met Sir Gilbert Parker, a Canadian writer knighted for his glorification of the British Empire, and showed him one of her Scottish tales. Sir Gilbert sent the manuscript to his friend Glenn Frank, editor of *Century*, who wrote asking Lorna to finish it and write more. Now she had nothing else to do, except stay alive and have a baby. No one could reach her on the phone. No one would interrupt her, outside of nurses, doctors, janitors, and on good days Neil McCarthy. There was a dashing Irishman! A few more visitors like him would do a girl a lot more good than certified milk and strict routine. Little hope of that.

She set to work on the first story, writing with dark humor, funny if you were reading it, not so funny if you had to live it. Jessie MacLean, seamstress of Drumorty, is still unmarried at thirty-six. The undertaker knows her age, because he remembers having the pleasure of burying the tax collector the morning she was born. Jessie has waited fifteen years for farmer Jock to propose marriage, but he can't make up his mind whether to level the rowan tree and build a bedroom on the east or move his peats and build it on the west. A more practical woman would gently but firmly herd him into the marital trap, but after waiting so many years Jessie is too hurt and proud not to make him come the whole way on his own, which he can never do. Each of them settles for the dismal comfort of complacent loneliness. The story is a warning against failing to seize the day, a lament for those who shrink from life. Lorna had seized the day all right, and look where it had landed her. She wasn't going to apologize. She had no time for despair.

Glenn Frank accepted the story for the December issue and asked the author to tell her readers why she had written it, and to write a bit about herself. Lorna answered that she felt compassion for old maids, indeed had often longed to be a man so that she could bring some romance into their lives. Then she made the mistake of saying that all her life she had wanted to write as well as J. M. Barrie. This came out in the magazine as "wanted to write like Barrie." The revision plagued her from then on, perennially repeated by eager publicists. Lorna didn't want to write *like* her famous countryman, only as *well* as he did—a grand ambition, certainly, but not beyond all reason. Apart from being fellow Scots, they were not much alike. Barrie was known for *Peter Pan*, for comic fantasy, and for being sentimental. Lorna cut closer to the bone. A Scottish novelist would say of her Drumorty tales:

> Lorna Moon quarries the same hard granite as Barrie, but her work has more rugged realism. When it comes to a touch of charm and a wistful tear, Barrie stands alone, but realism is

not his forte. Lorna Moon is the realist. Her book is a little storehouse of truth.

They did have things in common. Lorna was a plasterer's daughter, Barrie a weaver's son. Both had practiced journalism. Both were social critics who wrote with irony based on penetrating observation. Lorna looked up to Barrie and down on him in the same breath, calling him (in private) "that dear old whimsical bastard," protesting statements that she wrote "like Barrie," saying she "might as well be buried as Barried," but sending him her book hoping for a quotable comment. The dear old w.b. didn't answer.

Two months after her first story was published, Lorna's movie *Her Husband's Trademark* was released, and her third child was born. The third event was celebrated in private. Dr. Pottenger called Neil McCarthy. Neil called his client Cecil DeMille. It's a healthy boy, he said. Lorna is out of danger and doing as well as can be expected. Cecil called his brother. His brother said it was good news. He said their father would have been glad to know the line would be carried on. They agreed to name the boy after their great-uncle Richard and to preserve the enigma of his double paternity by giving him no middle name.

Flowers came to the sanatorium addressed to Dr. Pottenger. A nurse brought them to Lorna's bungalow. There were two cards in the box. One said: Congratulations on your latest triumph and a speedy return to Hollywood! It was signed: *Cecil.* Father was a master of cryptic ambiguity. His kind remarks would serve as well for *Her Husband's Trademark* as for a newborn child. The second card quoted lines from a heroic poem:

> *The boldest knight did bow his head*
> *To see a warrior's courage*
> *Spring from a woman's heart.*

It was signed: *W.* How like the brothers, one inviting her to return, the other commending her from afar. Would she ever see William again? Impulsively, she scribbled an answer.

Freeze the rivers, dim the sun,
Let the day and night be one.
Take the babe and dig my plot,
If my heart yearns and yours does not.

Having got it down on paper, she didn't want to send it. The child would be her message to a receding lover, and her gift of love. Anything more would be up to him.

After the delivery, she managed to work two or three hours nearly every day. Her second story was published four months after the first. It is a tale of marriage ruined by a woman's foolish insistence on getting the perfect proof of love. Lorna would not make a man prove his love for her. She would take love as it came and give it as she felt it and let it go when it would. She would neither be nor keep a prisoner. Fifty readers wrote to *Century* about the story.

A third story, published in July, brought back the lonely spinster Jessie MacLean, whose empty arms, Lorna said, had been reproaching her ever since the loss of farmer Jock. A village girl falls in love with a summer visitor, who leaves her with a baby and no goodbye. Cast out by the elders, the teenage mother is taken in by tenderhearted Jessie, who soon begins to treat the baby as her own. Penning a note of apology, the girl runs away, leaving the child in Jessie's no longer empty arms.

Like Constance de Mille, Jessie MacLean is an older woman who adores children but cannot have (any more of) her own. By taking the younger woman's baby she rescues it from the almshouse (the foundling home) and protects the single mother from village condemnation (bad press in Hollywood). The author gives the babe no name, but of course it is a boy. She defines mother love as "compassion for the helpless," which is part of mother love but not quite all one expects. The girl believes her pregnancy was "cruelly thrust upon her," but in fact she lay down willingly and often with the summer visitor, and everybody knows what happens when a girl does that. Nora Low had done the same, but her summer visitor paid the marriage penalty and saved her from disgrace.

Jessie fiercely defends the girl against the village elders, accusing them of hypocrisy. She speaks "brave words" in private to reassure the outcast, but the author thinks it wise not to tell the reader exactly what those brave words are. A writer has to know her market. It is 1922. D. H. Lawrence and James Joyce are having trouble with the censors. The editor of *Century* would not like to receive fifty angry letters condemning impudent excuses for immoral conduct. "These things," Lorna writes (that is, these impudent excuses for immoral conduct), "are written by the angels and only mothers may read them." Such literary sleight of hand excuses not only the reckless girl but the reckless author as well.

The baby lies screaming in Jessie's lap, because "he cannot yet see how near is Jessie's lap to the tender heaven of her heart." This is a vagabond mother's hope for the happiness of her child cradled in the love of his foster mother. Lorna wished all of her children well in their new situations, and two out of three times it worked out. As the luckiest of the three, I must let the reader judge the lawless baby maker. Unruly red-haired girl gleaming forth her naked light, conceiving me, protecting me, she's all the baby maker I've got.

In September Dr. Pottenger brought word from Neil McCarthy: it was time to go ahead with the transfer of the baby. Lorna penned a note to Neil:

Dear Mr. McCarthy.
The enclosed letter covers the ground, I think. I am so glad that you have decided to have Mrs. Mc. accompany you—we women you know! The nurse's name, if you should run into her, is Miss Copsen. Say as little as you can. Just thank her. She is very *keen* (*Irish* extraction!). Good luck.
Sincerely, L.M.

She enclosed a pitiful note suitable for pinning to an abandoned baby. Two photos sent a month earlier show the baby plump and in good spirits in the arms of a smiling nurse, presumably Miss Copsen, who has been taking care of him at the sanatorium under Doctor's strictest orders to avoid all gossip about whose baby he might be. The baby's cheery look tells us that he doesn't know he is missing anything when Nurse Copsen gives him a bottle.

Many years later Neil wrote to Cecilia that he and Mrs. Mc-Carthy had gone to pick up Lorna's baby at the hospital where she was—true so far—but then he said the hospital was in San Francisco, which was one of his false trails. On 12 October 1922, when the baby was eight months old to the day (Neil had a very orderly mind), the McCarthys came to the sanatorium in their green Locomobile, greeted Dr. Pottenger, spoke politely to Nurse Copsen, and took the baby away. For reasons of secrecy and health they didn't visit Lorna and Lorna didn't say goodbye to the baby. They drove to their house on South Ardmore Avenue, where Mrs. McCarthy called the Creche and announced breathlessly that someone had left a *baby* in their *car*! She didn't add: "Just like Charlie Chaplin's smash hit *The Kid*, which we all saw last year." She said she would bring the baby in tomorrow. By the time the baby arrived at the Castelar Creche, he had acquired a French name and lost his date of birth. They guessed his age by size and weight and put him down as "6–7 months," noting at the same time: "Child cries incessantly. Probably spoiled or frightened." Or missing his first love, smiling Irish Nurse Copsen.

Perusing the *Los Angeles Times*, one sees that for the next thirty days life went on in the city in the ordinary way. Cecil B. DeMille was conducting a public contest to find a good idea for his next movie. Sir Arthur Conan Doyle, an expert on the spirit world, described the current conditions prevailing in heaven. A man afraid to die alone shot and killed his teenage brother so as to have his company in the heaven Sir Arthur had described. A dead baby was found in a paint can. An infant girl was abandoned in Ocean Park. A man of thirty-one found the mother he had been told had died when he was an infant. The silent movie *Lorna Doone* opened at the Kinema Theatre. On 12 November, in the Sunday *Times*, Cecil B. DeMille announced the contest winner. His next movie would be—*The Ten Commandments*!

The following day, Dr. Fish sent word from the Castelar Creche that I had whooping cough, and Mother came right down to get me. She or someone else who knew it must have told a reporter my true age (miscalculated at the Creche), because shortly after that, Lorna Moon and William de Mille read in the *Hollywood Citizen*:

Nine months is a tiny enough span of life, but in that time whatever chance the Castelar Creche had of learning something about the waif's parentage has grown less and less, and finally disappeared. He was found in a motor car belonging to Neil McCarthy. That is the only fact known about his babyhood.

Neil had done it again! Lorna wondered whether she would ever meet her son. William was glad to be out of trouble but sad to be only an uncle. Now and then it crossed his mind that he had taken a serious risk by kissing a person with tuberculosis, but he had faith in the prophylactic power of a good cigar.

As Dr. Pottenger had warned her, if she wouldn't give up the baby, Lorna was not improving. Each story was taking longer to write. The fourth, published in November, relates the pathetic downfall of old Kirsty Fraser, the prime village mourner. Departed souls would be deprived of the honor due them if Kirsty were not there to wail as the lid is screwed down and fall in a fit as the coffin is carried out. Her eyes roll up and her legs grow stiff. A lad runs for the doctor to bring the poor woman round. Without Mistress Fraser it would be a sorry funeral. Then she has the bad luck to scoff at Mrs. MacNab's butter the day before Mr. MacNab chokes to death on a potato. The vengeful widow bids the neighbors, all except Kirsty, to the house of sorrow, where she astonishes everyone by throwing the mother of all fits and becoming the new champion wailer of Drumorty. An author who is not improving explains to her friends why there won't be any funeral.

Lorna wrote in longhand and sent her pages to Hollywood for typing. Letters came to her at "Box A" in Monrovia, but few of her correspondents knew what she was doing there. In January 1923, she sent a letter to editor Glenn Frank describing the story she was working on. In July she wrote again, admitting she had accomplished nothing because of having "engine trouble and a flat tire" and, "in spite of these, falling in love and out of love with the rapidity of a professional tumbler." She hoped, she said, in a couple of months to go into the desert, where she could work in peace, "if there aren't too many sheikhs." In January 1924 her fifth story was published. She had lost a year to illness, none of it to sheikhs, but now for the first time Dr. Pottenger was encouraged, and Lorna's story reflects new hope. It is a comedy of young love, sparkling with good humor.

With no delay she plunged ahead into "The Courtin' of Sally Ann," a lighthearted duet between a conceited farmer accustomed to success with "quick-eyed saucy lasses that were loud in their laughing and free at tossing gibe for gibe" and a shy glove maker "steeped to the lips in mortification at her mother's constant angling after a man for her" but dreaming "rash and glowing dreams of flashing lovers who would not be denied." Dark touches lurk in the background. A consumptive brother has a cough "like to split him in two." A father deaf as a doornail takes his Sunday walk along the railway tracks.

> They gathered him up piecemeal and brought him back in a gunny-sack, and there had been nothing to dress up and show the neighbors. All the expense and work of a funeral and none of the pleasure.

Religion, the author tells us, is a pious sham. God is "a big deaf face," who doesn't care about people as much as ministers say he does. Departed souls get buckets of tears after they are gone from hypocrites who never said a single kind word to them when they could still hear it.

Lorna began to think about living in the world again. She asked what was going on in the Lasky office. Was William de Mille directing a picture? Who was writing for him? William's latest was *Locked Doors*, a daring society melodrama in which a dutiful daughter marries a rich old man because he will provide a home for her invalid father. Promptly she falls in love with his junior partner (who one hopes will supply an equally good spare room for Dad). As any gentleman would do, the understanding husband graciously steps aside. The story was by Clara Beranger, who was now writing William's pictures. Rumor had it they were lovers, though nobody thought Mrs. William would graciously step aside.

This melancholy news brought forth a declaration of emotional independence:

> *Broken I am because I love,*
> *But do not pity me;*
> *A branch I was that grew above,*
> *Now stricken from the tree.*

A branch I was, with running sap
That warmed to every spring,
And ardent buds that would unwrap—
A glad, but songless thing.

Echoes I have of songbirds now;
Song where I once was mute;
For Sorrow's hand that broke the bough
Has fashioned it a flute.

Work would fill the lonely hours. Art would free her from desire. While the poem was on the stands, Lorna wrote her darkest story. Jean expects to marry Sandy, but when she turns to wave at him across the harvest field she is pulled into the thresher. "Sandy came to the hospital, silent and down-looking, and every time he came his stay was shorter." After many evasions, he admits he has no use for a one-armed wife. Jean learns to do her work better than most two-armed workers, but her lonely hours are bitter. The story is strong, swift in telling, not a bit like Barrie.

Dr. Pottenger sent her out to walk among the oak trees and along the country roads. Lorna began to feel almost like a normal person and hoped it wouldn't spoil her writing. Overnight the world was back, asking to be conquered. Late in 1924 she said goodbye to her mountain view but not before Dr. Pottenger gave her a lecture on staying well. A TB patient is never cured. She would live the rest of her life on the edge of an abyss, and she must walk carefully. Lorna nodded solemnly, hiding her impatience. She would not walk carefully. She would gallop at full speed.

She went to San Francisco to resurrect herself out of Hollywood's view, staying first at the Plaza Hotel, then at the Cloister, an apartment house on Green Street. She met Charles Dobie, the playwright, and together they wrote a play based on two of her stories. Maxwell Aley, former managing editor of *Century*, said he would try to place the play. His new employer, Bobbs-Merrill, asked Lorna for a book. They didn't expect to make any money on a volume of short stories, but they wanted to capture Lorna and the novels she would write before some other publisher could do it. Editor David Laurance Chambers said: "We certainly want to bind her to us with hoops of steel." He wrapped Lorna in flattering letters and prepared to cinch her tight with a binding contract.

Lorna wasn't ready to sign. Though she had promised three more stories in the next three months, in April she admitted she had written none of them. Her head was buzzing with novels. One, called "Flutes and Lovers," would be "the sex life of a woman from sixteen to thirty-five . . . the inside of a woman written from the inside," showing what the men in her life "bring to her and take from her." Another would follow three generations, grandmother, mother, and daughter, all talented musicians but only the last possessing both the public appeal and the strength of character to succeed. Chambers wanted a book of short stories for the fall, not a novel next year. Lorna parried his complaint. "An up-and-coming publishing house"—she didn't mention the name—was clamoring for a Hollywood novel, "as if I were a candy machine" —the publisher puts his penny in and gets the flavor of his choice. How can a publisher know what Lorna Moon should write? Chambers agreed to receive fewer stories. Lorna listed her contract terms. Bobbs-Merrill accepted them.

In the days when he had been rebuilding San Francisco, Charles Low had sent every penny he could spare home to his family. To honor his uprightness, Lorna wrote her last Drumorty tale, about the money that comes from America too late to buy food and medicine for a dying child. Out of foolish pride, the grieving mother wastes the money on an expensive funeral to prove her husband's worth to their spiteful neighbors.

Hoping the title would sell the book, Bobbs-Merrill proposed *Doorways in Drumorty*, which echoed Barrie's well-known *A Window in Thrums*. Dazzled by this marketing magic, Lorna said she liked the title, an endorsement she would soon regret. The book was published in October. One reviewer reminded readers how much they had enjoyed Miss Moon's delightful earlier volume, *A Window in Thrums*. In a radio interview Lorna said J. M. Barrie was a whimsical old dear, but to members of the California Writers Club she called him a son of a weaver and a bastion of Scottish literature. She badgered sold-out bookstores about ordering more books, went to parties on Nob Hill, and cheered at polo matches. She told her editor not to believe reports of her engagement to a cavalry lieutenant. "I've just swept the whole male sex from my life forever (again) and am settling down to the book." God, she said, should have made all men repulsive, so that even the drudgery of writing would be more desirable. But she risked everything to make herself desirable.

A photograph of Lorna appeared on the book page of the Sunday *San Francisco Chronicle* (with the recommendation: If you liked Barrie, you'll love Moon) and Lorna sent a print to Eva. On the back she proudly wrote: "My new nose and new bob." The photograph is in profile. Lorna's nose is shorter and the bump is gone. A year earlier she had mentioned her wish for a better nose to Dr. Pottenger. You must *never* do that! he said. Anesthetic gas could destroy those damaged lungs. Lorna nodded solemnly. To Eva she said: "In any case, I'll make a bonny corp."

CHAPTER 21

The Novelist

A slim volume of Scottish tales and a novel in progress wouldn't pay the rent. On New Year's Eve Lorna was back in Hollywood. From 1926 to 1930, six M-G-M movies would list her name in screen credits. Frances Marion, favorite writer of Boy Wonder Irving Thalberg, was the star of his scenario department. She was versatile and prolific. Beulah Marie Dix declared that Frances could write a tearful tale for Mary Pickford with one hand while writing a roaring Western with the other. And she was hardheaded. Knowing that producers, not writers, had the first and last word on stories, she described her craft as "writing on the sand with the wind blowing." Two years younger than Lorna, Frances had come from San Francisco expecting to work in advertising, but she was so beautiful that she was promptly listed as "actress, refined type." They met while Lorna was at Paramount. Since neither would tell her true age, each saw in the other an admirable, capable, likable younger woman. At eighty-five, Frances would remember Lorna as "a very great friend," notable for "blithesome flights of fancy" and a rare sense of humor, "a fascinating intellectual type, to me very beautiful, with her red hair and deep topaz eyes." Frances introduced Lorna to Irving Thalberg.

Thalberg's favorite actress was his wife, Norma Shearer, also a "refined type," best known today for her roles as Elizabeth Barrett (of Wimpole Street), Juliet (to Leslie Howard's Romeo), and Marie Antoinette. In *Upstage*, Lorna Moon's first M-G-M picture, Miss Shearer played a small-town girl with theatrical ambitions—and some endearing bad habits, conquered by the end of the seventh reel. In *Women Love Diamonds*, a naive girl manages to free herself from a scheming older man played by Lionel Barrymore. In *Mr. Wu*, Lon Chaney played both grandfather and grandson in a tale of racism, hate crime, family murder, and revenge, with a happy ending. *After Midnight* featured Norma Shearer as a nightclub hostess who knocks a holdup man cold, falls in love with him as he lies handsome and unconscious on the floor, and steers him into a better life as an honest taxi driver. Except for *Upstage*, Lorna had little to say about the plots of her M-G-M scenarios. She wrote to editor D. L. Chambers: "I hired myself to the movie brothel for fifty thousand a year. I'm going to work here two years and then retire to write only books I want to write." It was not an idle boast. Forty weeks of steady work at Lorna's contract rate (actually twenty-five thousand a year) would purchase a mansion in Beverly Hills or five years of freedom to write novels in a garret. The key phrase was "steady work."

Despite the pace of movie writing, Lorna had been working at home on "Flutes and Lovers," the sex life of a girl named Nancy told "from the inside," and sending chapters to Chambers. As diplomatically as he could, Chambers said he missed the wistful charm of the Drumorty tales. He wondered what if anything would happen to Nancy besides sex. Lorna didn't answer for five months. Then she said she had done her duty by the charm of Scotland; now she was going to show the other side. After so long without a letter Chambers knew better than to disagree.

Since leaving the Pottenger Sanatorium Lorna had been living as though she had never been sick a day. She bought a small new house on Graciosa Drive in the hills above Hollywood. From the big window on a clear day you could see Catalina Island. She decorated in her colors and hired a cook and a gardener. She was happy and on her way. In the spring of 1927 she began to cough. Dr. Shulman sent her to bed and told her not to work for six months. What did he think she would do there? Entertain her lovers? She had to stay on salary or use up her savings. She and

Frances Marion transmuted *Anna Karenina* into *Love*, a script for Greta Garbo and John Gilbert, but the producers saw a problem. Most exhibitors wouldn't stand for an ending where the heroine is run over by a train. However loud he may roar, *"Ars gratia artis!"* the M-G-M lion keeps his eye on the bottom line. The exhibitors would have a choice—a sad last reel by Tolstoy, a happy one by top screenwriters. A studio secretary came to take dictation at Lorna's bedside.

Summer brought red handkerchiefs and fever. In August the *Los Angeles Times* reported that Lorna Moon was just finishing "Flutes and Lovers." Lorna wished it were true. With her vain straight nose she couldn't go back to Dr. Pottenger. In October she entered the Hillcrest Sanatorium, at 2300 feet in the mountains above Tujunga, where she had a tiny suite with bed-living room and bath, a sleeping porch, a radio with headphones, and meals served on a tray. Visitors were rare. One was Sara Haardt, literary protégée and later wife of H. L. Mencken. Sara too had hired herself to the movie brothel, most of whose inhabitants she thought "dull and ordinary," but in Lorna she recognized a literary peer, with whom she shared both purpose and affliction. She too had written stories in a sanatorium and published them in *Century*. She too wrote about unfamiliar folkways, hers in Alabama. Though an acute observer, Sara was led astray by Lorna's elegant Hollywood living and her imaginary childhood in a Highland castle. As she wrote to Mencken: "This afternoon I am riding up the mountain to see Lorna Moon. You perhaps know about her. . . . She has wealth, beauty, and I think a very real talent for writing. I remember some very lovely things she did for *The Century*."

By December Lorna weighed eighty-seven pounds. At first she paid the bills herself, but soon her bank account was flat. She rented her house, but it wasn't enough. William was going through a divorce, suffering snubs by former friends, and guiltily giving up his fortune to a wronged and shattered wife. Even if Lorna had wanted to ask him, she couldn't add to his troubles or intrude on his new life with Clara. Reluctantly she turned to Father. Father put money in her account and said he would do so every three months. "Don't let repayment worry you," he said. "You may repay when and if you can."

She lay dreaming about the life of a girl named Nancy. Editor

Chambers's complaints about too much sex had made her angry. Later she would speak her mind: "It is revolting to me that a woman's virtue rests entirely upon her hymen. In a civilized world there wouldn't be a 'fallen woman' any more than there is a 'fallen man.' " Still, an author will not be read unless her book is published. Only the year before, Arnold Bennett, the leading British book reviewer, had contrasted French- and English-speaking standards of propriety:

> Here and there in . . . Marcel Proust's complicated and endless epic of fashionable society occurs a page for publishing which a British publisher would come into painful contact with the police; but Proust does at least enfold his audacities in a film of misty phrases. The newer French novelists waste no time in paltering. What they desire to say they say plainly.

Though Lorna had apparently dismissed her editor's prudery, she had then quietly begun to steer "Flutes and Lovers" away from plain-spoken audacities into unrequited love, retaining only a few passages like the following from *Dark Star*, which she hoped would not embarrass her respectable English-speaking publisher:

> She was growing a woman now, and men's eyes lingered upon her as she passed. In the eyes of most of them she saw a thing that made her angry and afraid. . . . if she met one alone and his eyes made free with the tender rise of her breasts beneath the blue print of her too narrow frock, she would blaze at him with angry defensive eyes till often he would redden and turn away.

But anger and pride could be weakened by desire:

> She fought him more feebly as his arms locked about her more tightly. She had a fancy that there were two of her, a white prim one that fought and pretended, and a black savage one rolling up like a warm sea on a hot still night. The white one struggling because it *ought* to struggle, pushing with feeble silly hands, the black one heedless of it, sweeping up in long languorous waves.

Having heard nothing for ten months from his headstrong author, Chambers wrote to her on Graciosa Drive, where he thought she was still residing in good health. She answered from the Hillcrest Sanatorium:

Your letter found me, pencil in hand, glaring like a truculent old man at the nurse who came to interrupt me. I've been in bed for months casting my gore upon the wind. There is something in my chest like a chil's rattle. I play games with it when I breathe, calling it "my orchestra." I have to do that because it is the one symptom of this disease that unmans me—not the ache, not the fever, not the terrible sinking-through-the-bed tiredness, just this one little noise. I am at present in the building of the "Moribundi." From here one goes either in a wheel chair singing praises to the Lord round the corner to the convalescent building or most unobtrusively down the hill to the morgue. With my usual perverse determination to live, I shall once more blast the hopes of the undertaker.

Now about the novel. For a long time I've been wanting to have a talk with you. Do you think you are the people to handle my kind of stuff? Is there profit in it for either of us? I don't think so. "Doorways" almost broke my heart, such a shabby little book, the printing was so small. No amount of asking for it at the book stores seemed to do any good. I think my sort of thing needs a personal interest behind it. I don't suppose Bobbs-Merrill could sell a hundred copies of either of my next two books. This one is about a bastard who kills herself at eighteen. The next will be about patients in a TB sanatorium. What do you think? Would you like to wash your hands of me, for your good and my own? By the way, the title isn't 'Flutes & Lovers' now. You didn't like it much anyway, remember?

Lorna's correspondence with Bobbs-Merrill was a constant jockeying for advantage, relieved by humorous anecdotes, medical reports, and flights of fancy masquerading as memoirs. The publisher's in-house memos buzzed with maneuvers to keep this maverick in the corral. Chambers's letters to Lorna are flattering, beguiling, often sycophantic. He urged her not to abandon Bobbs-Merrill and promised first-rate publication. Lorna answered: Very well, but he should keep in mind that almost "every publisher" in America and England had written asking for the novel, each one swearing to "concentrate all his forces upon it." If she could earn a living writing fiction, she said, she'd never go back to the movies, but so far no publisher had made her independent, and she had no "talent for being a kept woman."

By March 1928 things were going better. Lorna had gained back twenty pounds. She wrote to Father:

> Dear Cecil,
> I would have written long ago to thank you for the deposit, but for weeks I had my right arm and shoulder strapped. The least movement would dislodge the only thing between me and extremity, which is a clot of blood that keeps my lung from bleeding. Now I am making progress, and I write to thank you. Almost my only visitor is a dear old Irish priest who comes up from Tujunga. He goes easy on my sins since he learned that I was raised on the Songs of Ossian. He and I swap poetry in the Gaelic by the hour.

The visiting priest may have been Father Denis Falvey, pastor of Our Lady of Lourdes. Whether Lorna allowed the poor man to think she was a believer, let alone a Catholic, there is no reason to suppose she had read Gaelic as a child or ever, but a scene in which a hoary man of God saves a sinful redhead by chanting heroic rhymes with her would surely appeal to Cecil B. DeMille.

In the meantime she was writing to magazine editors offering her unfinished novel for serial publication. Arthur Vance of *Pictorial Review* said he would pay a thousand dollars down and nine thousand on completion "to our satisfaction." Lorna was elated, until that last phrase caught her eye. She wrote to Chambers:

> What does he mean "to our satisfaction"? Is he planning to have off and tell me how to finish the story? I thought only motion-picture supervisors, with their long experience of pressing pants and making button holes, would tell an author

how to auth. Maybe it is just a way to get his thousand dollars back if I muck up the job in my haste to get the rest of the money. Little does he know me.

Four days later she wrote:

I'm shooting an awful temp again. The excitement of selling the serial rights made me leap at the novel. I broke a few rules about rest hour. Lay awake nights mulling the story. Now they've taken most of my papers away. They keep putting their heads in to see if I am writing. To them it's like taking dope. NURSE: I'm sorry but I can't let you write any more today. ME (sternly): This is important. NURSE: Doctor will be cross. ME: Doctor is a fussy little rabbit. NURSE (very sweetly): I'd like to take your pulse now, dear. Really, it's very hard to write a novel in a hospital.

Chambers implored her to "be a good girl" and take care of herself. She answered: "Every night I pray, God bless my tuberculosis and make me a good girl for Christ's sake! He always seems to bless my tuberculosis, but so far he has not made me a good girl."

On a scrap of paper overlooked by Nurse, Lorna wrote these lines:

If ever I rise up again and walk the busy street,
If ever I rise up at dawn with eager, lightsome feet,
If ever I can breast the wind or bide the lashing rain,
Or feel the sea upon my face and meet my friends again,
Oh, if that day will ever come, when I can walk on grass
And smell the mouldy smell of earth and watch a bird fly past,
I'll be a better girl—maybe. But maybe I'll be worse.
It isn't in me to be good except inside a hearse.

During April she sat in bed holding a pencil and a yellow pad, dozing forward on the paper, unable to think because of fever. In May the crucial clot dislodged, the fever rose, the gore spewed out, the arm and shoulder were strapped again. In June she wrote to Gladys Rosson:

> I've started new injections. Sometimes they strain my heart and I faint. Must wait a month for X-ray to see if there is healing. You were so kind to call on my birthday. I'm not "courageous," Gladys, just philosophical. TB is not the worst thing in the world, and if it were, why not me as well as another?

In July she wrote to Father:

> I can't get any work done here, but I'm broke and can't move till your July deposit. When I finish the book I'll get enough from *Pictorial Review* to keep me safe for a year and a half. I won't need any more loans. I know I have to trim my sails to suit this handicap. Other writers with TB have done the same and done good work. But I am only thirty-two. I've had so little time to play. I have such a zest for life. It's hard to give everything up.

Back in Hollywood Lorna wrote to Chambers, saying she would finish *Dark Star* and then look after her health. He protested that a book wasn't worth her health. She didn't agree.

> I'm fed to the teeth with being nursed. I'm worn out by my friends' worrying about me. A weakling would by now have become a professional lunger. I still work and think like a healthy human being. I'm not going to die for many a year, despite hemorrhages and fevers. As mehitabel the cat would say: There's a dance in the old dame yet. Toujours gai, kid, toujours gai! Besides, I've fought this fight before. As a kid from nine to eleven I lay on my face in a plaster cast with TB of the spine [this is an invention], but at thirteen I climbed trees. I'm down again, but what of that? I'll get up and run hard a short while once more. Don't say that if I'm careful for a long time I'll be well. I'm not going to spend my youth getting back my health. What use to get up well

after the leaf is sere and yellow? Give me high noon, and let it then be night!

In her private journal for 22 August, Lorna wrote:

On this day of our Lord the novel is sixty-seven thousand words long and my lungs are improving. I believe I win once more!

A week later:

Gore! But not much. I just wouldn't let it. I reached my arm up into the cosmos again and held on to the skirts of my female god. This is not a setback. My temperature is no higher. I'm on the last lap of the book.

In September:

I get stronger every day. Dr. Shulman is cross as a bear that I don't die and prove him right. I knew I could write my way out of this. I've done it before.

1 October 1928:

For a fortnight I have not gone higher than 99. This is my lowest temperature in two years. The book is finished and I am not! Far from it.

CHAPTER 22

A Zest for Life

Frances Marion's secretary typed the last few pages. Lorna wrote to Father:

> You are a great darling to let me lean on you this year. I have completed my novel and sent it off. I don't expect any slip-up about acceptance, so in a couple of years I shall be able to pay you back, most likely, but I cannot pay back your being the only person in the world that I could turn to. I am much better since leaving the pest-house. My own house is a better place to live in, and to die in if need be. I've been reading about you in the papers. I'm trying to imagine you on the M-G-M lot, where they have never seen an office with stained-glass windows, bear-skin rugs, and gold-inlaid revolvers. I *do* hope I out-live you, Cecil, because if I do I shall surely put you into a book—with admiration and a smile.

Chambers wired acceptance of the manuscript. Lorna answered:

> Your wire and letter have made me so happy. I really did try to save Nancy from suicide because Vance moaned so much about killing off a lovable character. I hope he will feel dif-

ferently when he reads the end. At any rate, I can't change it. From the day she was born Nancy was on her way to prove her noble birth by joining the noble Fasseferns in death.

Last week I was very adventurous and had some pictures taken which I will send on to you. In two of them I stood up! I confess that after each pose I collapsed into the arms of a hovering young man, mostly because he was so handsome.

A hovering young man. Frances Marion recalled that when the telegram came, Lorna said to Everett Marcy, "Laddie, hold me in your arms, or I'll soar wingless into the blue!" The rumor was she had met him in a sanatorium, but twenty years later he would die of whiskey drinking and pneumonia, not of tuberculosis. Everett was just twenty-four, tall, blond, elegant, according to Sadie very handsome, an aspiring author somewhat in awe of his glamorous paramour, who was a proven professional, a mysterious older woman, how much older she never told him. He found out when he took her ashes to Scotland but, like the gentleman he was, he didn't tell anyone back home. Everett Marcy came from Olean on the Allegheny in western New York. Fresh from college he volunteered to work at *The New Yorker*, met the Round Table literati, made no recorded impression on Ross, went West in search of D. H. Lawrence, and ended up in Hollywood, where Lorna Moon, La Bohémienne of Graciosa Drive, Camille aux Manuscrits, received him with delight as lover and cavalier-in-waiting.

John Jay Curtis was president of Bobbs-Merrill. Lorna wrote to Chambers:

The Curtises have just been here, and all afternoon I've been hearing Mrs. Curtis calling you "Dear Laurance." I always wondered what the D. L. was for in D. L. Chambers. Now I know—Dear Laurance! I told Mr. Curtis the story of my next book, "Macabre." It made him "shed a bitter tear." Mrs. Curtis shed buckets. It is the story of a TB sanatorium told by an inmate. Thomas Mann's *Magic Mountain* is a good book, but he is a well man writing about lungers. Nobody knows a lunger but another lunger. Their gaiety, their courage, their

queer grim humor, their passionate often beautiful love affairs. I spent four years in one san. There were 160 of us
between the ages of seventeen and twenty-four. Why has no
one written about it? Katherine Mansfield should have done
it, but she died. They have all died but me. So now it's my
job. I really don't want to, but I must. Consumptives want to
ignore their illness. I ran from it also, laughing loudly like the
rest, till one day I looked into the mirror and said: "You are
a consumptive." I think I have the strength now to be at once
detached and sympathetic. But I am probably boring you
talking about my next child when I have just given you a
child to bring up for me.

Arthur Vance was not prepared to horrify the gentle readers of
Pictorial Review with the plainspeaking he found in the manuscript
of *Dark Star*. Lorna reported to Chambers:

Vance is in a tailspin over "maidenhead" and "holy bitch."
He has wired Frances Marion. I must make the language
purer than leaf-lard and may even have to bring the boy back
from Paris to make an honest woman out of Nancy. This is
worse than the movies. At least they pay you very well for
doing violence to a story. If I didn't need the money, I'd tell
them all to go to hell. *You* are not going to make my villagers
talk like club women, are you?

Chambers said: Your villagers are perfect. A week later, Lorna
admitted:

I have tried the book out on three intelligent women, "pillars
of society," and all three are stampeded by the word "maidenhead." This gives me pause. It's the right word, of course,
but changing it to "virginity" won't change the story. I don't
want my book to be called obscene or kept out of libraries.
Do you think "holy bitch" will be too much for Miss Amelia
Proudbosom, president of the book club?

Chambers said: Forget Vance and club women—let's publish right away. Lorna answered:

If we publish right away, I'll have to go back to movie work instead of starting another book. I'm counting on Vance's money to keep me for a year and give me peace of mind, which is the biggest part of getting well. But there's a reckless streak in my heart that makes me hope his demands are too ridiculous to grant. Then we'll have to publish!

Like the M-G-M lion, Vance wanted a happy ending—girl gets boy and wedding cake. Lorna gave up his ten thousand dollars and trusted fate to pull her through. Chambers scheduled publication of *Dark Star* for spring. He asked Lorna for chapter titles. Chapter titles are tripe, she said. If you want them, write them yourself. You're right, of course, said Chambers—no chapter titles. And please rewrite our jacket copy giving it your distinctive touch. Lorna requested promotion copies for literary friends she had met in Hollywood: Robert Benchley, Dorothy Parker, novelist Joseph Hergesheimer. She approved publicity photos—or didn't.

Laurance, you are breaking my heart! What perversity made you pick this terrible old picture? I don't look like *that*! Cameramen and electricians write mash notes calling me "cutie"! Use one of the new ones.

She drew a mustache and a goatee on the picture and sent it back.

Joe Hergesheimer will give us a blurb, I saw him last week. He has done it only once before, for a novel by James Cabell. Joe now feels he is the Daddy of my book and wants to get it to Mencken and such people. Laurence Stallings will write something for us. Dorothy Parker is leaving next week for New York. She is such a flighty sparrow. If I get the pages in time, she can take them on the train. If not, you'll have to send them to her at the Algonquin Hotel. There is a slight strain between us because of a certain blue-eyed gent [Everett Marcy, whom Parker had known in New York]—my fault, I'm the nasty bitch, as Rebecca West would say—but Dorothy is swell, and she might review the book in *The New Yorker* or *The Bookman*.

Frances wants a comment from Lillian Gish. I don't think it's worth the trouble. She certainly won't like the book. At heart she's a perfect prude. She won't even understand it. One day I met her on the staircase at the studio, and she exclaimed, "Oh, Lorna darling, I've just read the *cutest* story of yours!" It was "Wantin' a Hand," pure pain and sorrow from the first word to the last. Frankly, I think she's an awful pinhead. Don't let the designer burst into stars on the jacket! Given our title, it's just what he would do.

I've been very bad lately. Frances threatens to tell on me, so I'll spike her guns by telling you that my new blond swain carries me out to his car and we go careering off into the jasmine-scented night and come back with the milk in the morning. I like to sleep on sands and on the mountains and wake with the chipmunks and the birds. Some healing thing comes out of the ground that never comes out of a bed. These adventures make me cough, but one must save one's soul alive, one's romantic soul I mean, even at the expense of the body. It's hard to convince loving friends of this.

Daily bulletins flashed between them. "Stallings has been drunk ever since he read the first half of the book (not the effect of the book). I'll send his comment when he stops wrestling with pink spiders." Knopf announced a spring novel titled *Dim Star*. Lorna telegraphed Chambers in alarm. He reassured her: *Dim Star* is delayed till fall. He sent the *Dark Star* jacket. Lorna called it a "knockout." But there was a painful shock. After printing the author's text exactly as she had written it for 341 pages, the publisher cut three words from the climax of the story. And with very good reason. Without the cut, the last page would start with a short line, which is bad typography.

"I never heard such hooey!" Lorna protested. "Suppose the printer wanted to fill up the last page and added the Lord's prayer!" Chambers promised to put the words back in the second printing, but the first was off the press and on its way to reviewers. Publishing is a subtle art not well understood by authors.

Chambers said he agreed with Frances Marion that a beloved
movie idol could help sell a novel—even if the author thought the
beloved movie idol was a pinhead. Lorna wanted the book to sell:

I'm going to Francie's house tonight to dine with your dear
Lillian. Instead of kicking her under the table after every
vapid comment, I shall smile and purr at her, so she will tell
George Jean Nathan that I have written the *cutest* book.

Frances lived atop the highest hill in Beverly Hills. Lorna rode
ten miles each way through the winter night with Everett at the
wheel. The following day she had "much temp," but she had done
her duty to promote the book.

Publicists at Bobbs-Merrill talked to magazine editors about the
most exciting young author on their list. *Cosmopolitan* editor Ray
Long, who was publishing Rupert Hughes, Edna Ferber, and Som-
erset Maugham, invited Lorna to contribute a story. She wrote
"The Wedding of the Wheat." Long said her price was steep, but
he paid it and asked to see all her future work, especially her next
novel. Now that she was established at *Cosmopolitan*, he said, she
didn't need to bother with an agent; they all want their commission whether they do any work or not.

Dark Star was published in March. Holding the volume in her
hands, Lorna rejoiced at the scarlet jacket, the bold black title
edged in gold above the menacing North Sea wave, the vines of
intrigue and desire curling up and down the spine. She admired
the sturdy binding easily opened to lie flat, the red-bordered title
page, the rough-edged leaves, the elegant type, the ornamental
running heads, the pages carefully composed not to start with a
short line. She told Chambers the book had "it." She inscribed a
copy to Father: "To C. B. de Mille, who made possible the writing
of this book. In friendship, Lorna Moon."

She made lists of journalists who might review *Dark Star* and
spent hours on the phone arranging local promotions. A lecture on
her book would be given at the Ebell Club. M-G-M would permit
a table of books in the commissary. The Hollywood Bookstore
would send a postcard to every member of the Motion Picture
Academy. A San Francisco store would do the same for members

of PEN. "These sales schemes," Lorna wrote, "make me feel like a fishmonger."

Dr. Shulman begged her to slow down. She sent a note of thanks to Gertrude Atherton for calling *Dark Star* "the most notable first novel of our time." A cousin of Benjamin Franklin, Gertrude Atherton had published her first novel in 1888 under the pseudonym "Frank Lin." It provoked instant outrage, as did the thirty-six books that followed, many of them banned, most of them about women who claimed the right to think for themselves and did not apologize for having sexual desires. Widowed at thirty, Atherton had not married a second time, because she prized freedom "too much to sacrifice it to any man." She was known for audacious themes, ill-constructed sentences, and absurd figures of speech. One of her heroes "had nostrils so thin and flexible that when they were not quivering like the wings of a captured bird they lay limply against the septum." Lorna refrained from comment on Atherton's distinctive style. An endorsement from the Queen of Literary Amazons, who had been a best-selling scandal for forty years, could hardly hurt a book about a passionate young woman seduced and abandoned by a selfish man.

Every Sunday, rain or shine, I ran down our front steps to get the Sunday comics. Eagerly searching for Happy Hooligan and the Katzenjammer Kids, I didn't pause for an Art Deco drawing titled in big letters "Lorna Moon." I was learning French at the Hollywood School for Girls, where boys like me (and Joel McCrea and Douglas Fairbanks, Jr.) were tolerated in the first two grades. Virginia Parsons, fourteen, was in the upper school. Virginia called Father "Uncle Cecil" and came to movies at our house. She grew up to be an author-illustrator of forty children's books. In 1982 our fellow alumna from HSG, Evelyn Flebbe Scott, told me that Virginia Parsons had a story for my book. Virginia wrote from London:

> The way I was involved very briefly with your mother was through a mutual friend, Mrs. Palma Wayne. She was a writer and I think knew your mother very well. We were all neighbors on the hill. Lorna must have told her, I'm sure in

deepest confidence, that ever since you were adopted she had not been allowed to see you and didn't even have a picture of you. Since I was at school with you, the two of them cooked up a plan for me to take a snapshot, but Mother thought it would look odd for me to go down to the lower school and start taking pictures of Mr. DeMille's little boy, so she asked Miss Harpe to do it. Miss Harpe was the art teacher. To avoid suspicion, she took pictures of several children and gave me the picture of you. You were in short pants. I went with Mrs. Wayne to Lorna's house, so I could meet Lorna and give her the picture. I remember the house was dark, with curtains drawn against the sunlight. The whole impression was dark and tragic. It's sad to think that only a few years later medical advances would have saved your mother's life, and someday you would have known her.

Fondly, VIRGINIA

Lorna had been planning for that better future. She wrote to Laurance Chambers:

I have five novels in my head and most desperately wish I were well enough to come to Indianapolis and talk them out with you. I don't want to write any more short pieces. I need a big canvas and many people. Which brings me to "Macabre." I'm sure of it but also I'm afraid of it. It's too big a job for me, but I don't know anyone it wouldn't be too big for. No magazine will take it as a serial. I don't know how you are ever going to sell it to booksellers. And yet it is the child that moves in me and wants to be born. Are you afraid of it? It is laughter and passion and death—laughter that is too gay, passion keyed too high, death that comes too often, but life too, and hope, that never-ending hope.

I haven't any money. The movie rights aren't sold yet. The government descended on me and took five thousand dollars in taxes and penalties. When you have a book out, everyone thinks you are rolling in money. My doctor sent me a bill for two hundred dollars. It was always fifty before. Can you send me advances to keep the roof over my head for the next few

months so I can fiddle at "Macabre" instead of thinking up
tricky dialogue for the movies or equally tricky stories for Ray
Long? I'm really not fond of money, but somehow I can't live
under eight hundred a month. It's the gardener and the nurse
and the secretary and my Chinese servant, Wong. Lord knows
I never have anything but a few pajamas. I had a letter from
Miss Johnston saying you are in New York. I must say I don't
like it a bit when you don't stay home and answer my letters
yourself. Is Lillian Gish in New York by any chance?

Suspiciously, LORNA

CHAPTER 23

Go China
by Lorna Moon

An awful thing has happened. Yesterday Wong said to me:

"Miss Moon, I go China." I said:

"Don't be silly, Wong. You can't go to China."

"Pletty soon I die, Miss Moon."

"*Die*! *You* can't die! I'm the one that dies in this house. You are here to get me well."

"Pletty soon you well, Miss Moon. I go China die."

"You'll do *nothing* of the *kind*! What am *I* supposed to do while you are dying all over China? Who will make the soup? Who will bring the tray?"

"Nephew in kitsen. He more better. More stlong cally tlay. Pletty soon you well."

"You're leaving me because I'm getting *well*?"

"Two year I want go. You too much sick. I stay see you die. Die more better."

"Die more better?"

"When die, no more cough. Pletty soon you well now. Tlain go six o'clock."

Publisher's Note: This story was told by Lorna Moon in letters to her editor. The description of her Chinese servant is conventional by the standards of 1929.

"*Tonight!* After eight years you're leaving me *tonight*!"

"Nephew in kitsen, Miss Moon."

"What the devil does *he* know about what I want?"

"He in kitsen two week. I show everything. Put yellow soup in gleen bowl. Put white soup in blue bowl. Put vegebel soup in yellow bowl."

"You've been training him in *my* house for *two* weeks, and you never said a *word* to me?"

"He know everything. Goobye, Miss Moon."

I struggle with my new Chinaman. Soon I shall be dead. He is a student, and very proud, carrying out the tradition of his venerable uncle. But he is not Wong. When I was in the sanatorium, Wong would come to cook me special dishes. At home, when I would hemorrhage and everyone else would lose his head, Wong would call the doctor. Wong would get the ice bag. Wong would say: "Pletty soon well." It was a fiction to call him a servant. He was the boss of the house.

"Wong, please buy me some caviar."

"Too much money."

"All the same I want it."

"Too much money."

When the book jacket came, I showed it to him wrapped around a book.

"How much?" he said.

"Two dollars and a half."

"Too much money."

If I said: "I'm not well today," Wong said:

"Too much parties."

He believed I was sick because I washed my hair so often. Every time the hairdresser came, Wong would paddle about the room murmuring: "White lady all time sick, all time wash head. China lady no time sick, no time wash head. White lady all time cough, all time wash head, all time cough some more, pletty soon die."

"China lady no time die, I suppose."

Once the hairdresser phoned that her car had broken down and she wanted someone to pick her up. I asked Wong to go.

"Wash dish," he said.

"Go now. She is waiting."

"All dish dirty."

"Go *now*!"

He went. The hairdresser phoned to say no one had come. I told her to take a taxi. She arrived and began her work. The phone rang. It was Wong.

"Lady no here. I come home."

"Where are you, Wong?"

"Corner Hollywood Gardner."

"You silly ass! I told you Hollywood and Garfield."

"More better no wash head. I come home."

"You stubborn old mule! You don't need to come home. Stay there till somebody runs over you."

An artist came to paint my portrait. Wong did not approve. He thought I would get too tired. He stood for a long time watching. The painter put color on with a brush, then took some off with a rag. Wong turned away in despair. "All time put on, take off, never finish." When the thing was finally done, Wong surveyed it solemnly. "Too much neck!" he said.

Wong knows nothing of Scottish speech. He said to Frances Marion: "Miss Moon no speak good English. She no go to school?" He is beside himself with glee that anyone would publish anything I write when I can't even speak correctly.

There was a knock at my door. I said: "Come in," and what did I see? A figure dressed in spotless white under a silly round white hat, a solemn moon face saying:

"Bling tea now?"

"*Wong!* You're *back*?"

"Bling tea?"

"I thought you were in China. Why have you come back?"

"Six month."

"Six month what?"

"Stay six month."

"You're going to stay six months?"

Silence which means "yes."

"You've postponed your dying then?"

"Bling tea?"

It could be a fever vision. I will make a test.

"Wong, please buy me some caviar."

"Too much money."

He is *back*! Don't ask me why. Calamity is put off six months. He went as far as San Francisco. Did he know I missed him? Does he know I care for him? Maybe he lost his money in a fan-tan game. Whatever it was, my roly-poly Buddha is going all about the house swiftly and silently taking care of everything. Pletty soon I well.

CHAPTER 24

Last Rites

Chambers was not in New York with Lillian Gish. An associate said he had collapsed from overwork and had been ordered to take a long rest. Lorna wrote to his assistant: "Life is a trackless waste without him. No one who is needed so much has a right to get sick. Besides, he is stealing my stuff." To the invalid she wrote:

What could prove my devotion to you more than the fact that, on hearing of your illness, I proceeded to have hemorrhage upon hemorrhage. Not big but frequent. I hadn't done this for a year and really thought I was getting out of the woods. If I didn't have "Macabre" to write I'd take the good old cyanide. This doesn't mean that I'm going to check out on you. I have known hundreds of lungers and lost twenty-five close friends, but I have seen many get well and walk out into the world again.

I am writing about T.B. as a lunger sees it, in its ugliness and its beauty, for there is beauty in young people making the same fight together with laughter and hope and queer grim humor like the humor in the trenches. I'm writing with as little emotion as I can, but when I told one of the more grotesque incidents to a hard-boiled New York playwright, the man sat and wept! When he was restored, I asked him if he didn't think it was also funny. He said: "I can see that *they* would think it was funny. That's why it's so sad."

Near the end of September, Lorna had a worse hemorrhage, and Norah, her Irish nurse, quickly assembled aids to stop it. Watching Norah rushing about, Lorna resolved to remember her actions. They would be useful in "Macabre." In October she was relieved to find Chambers back at his desk.

Dear Laurance: This will be short and not sweet. I am the bunk. Two weeks ago I had a twelve-ounce hemorrhage in the morning and two more in the afternoon. They shot me with enough fibrinogen to coagulate a regiment and gave me a blood transfusion, for I was damned near out. Otherwise, I am gaining weight and my temp is better. It would be just like me to get well and then bleed to death. The point is that my important cavity is over the main artery of my lung. I laugh heartily and whoops! How can a person learn not to laugh! But a hemorrhage is a local accident. The rest of the lung may be healing all the time. Of course, healing won't profit us much if a hearty laugh carries me off.

Lorna's article "Flat on My Back" was published in *Cosmopolitan*. The illustration shows the author clad in silk pajamas lying seductively on her bed under a large crucifix, like a houri in a convent. She asks the reader to believe that she feels sorry for her healthy friends, harassed as they are by daily chores and social burdens. Tuberculosis has given her the gift of long quiet hours in which to practice a lonely art. She lists great writers who were forced into productive solitude by this unrelenting illness. They died young, but Lorna has five novels in her head and will not die till she is ready. Indeed, she will outlive the friends who feel sorry for her and be carried past their tombstones chortling in her coffin. She admits it is an arrogant thought. The article brought an avalanche of letters, many from lungers it had buoyed into defiant optimism. Lorna explained her kind to Chambers:

I have never met a lunger who wasn't flip about T.B. The occasional terrified one dies off after a few months. Sister Mary of the Angels would be pained to learn that T.B. doesn't bring people to God. It makes them more what they were before. If religious, they lean more on the Lord; if pagan, they become more pagan. There is nothing softening about it. You can't be soft and fight T.B. Never will I forget "Sick Boy." He was twenty-six years old and had been in bed for fourteen years. As he fought for every breath, our chests ached with the sound of his panting and gasping. At the end they brought him a priest and we heard the murmur of prayer and then Sick Boy's dying cry: "When I see . . . your God . . . I'll spit . . . in his face!" I will spare you further details, because I must not use my strength for anything but the book. My love to you all.

Thursday, 24 October 1929, the market crashed on Wall Street. Ruined speculators plunged from office windows. Monday M-G-M announced the popular run of *Dynamite*, Cecil B. DeMille's first talking picture. William de Mille had been elected president of the Motion Picture Academy. And the *Los Angeles Evening Herald* reported a crisis on Graciosa Drive.

> Lorna Moon, red-haired girl, who wrote "Dark Star," was dying today. Her condition has been growing worse for a month. At her home in the Hollywood hills they said she probably wouldn't live until night. Two physicians and two nurses were at her bedside most of the day. Dr. Leon Shulman and Dr. E. B. Woolfan said there was virtually no hope that she would rally from this latest sinking spell.
>
> This year she published her first—and last— novel, "Dark Star," which became a best-seller and made her famous all over the United States. Long before that, she was known as one of the three best scenario writers in Hollywood.

Six weeks later the lately lamented author wrote to Chambers:

My Sweet Lamb, *of course* I'm interested in your "basal me-
tabolism," also in your erythrocytes, polychromatophilia, and
eosinophiles. Further than this, I cannot go, you being married an' everything.

Let us say nothing about my recent "death." It was all too
grisly. Someday when I'm strong again, I will regale you with
its funnier moments. The pneumonia that followed did me
no good. I'm thin as a scarecrow and weak, but I am not dying
or likely to die. In fact I'm in a fair way to get on my feet in
a few months. The thing that worries me is that my mind is
flat and arid. I have been in adversity too long. I am starved
for gaiety and happiness and good fortune. Do you never
come out to California? I'd love to see you at last. What would
it take to bring you here? An introduction to Lillian? I could
arrange it.

On the last day of the year:

Your lovely yellow roses came. How sweet of you to remember that I like yellow roses. Let me tell you about my
"wake." I had been in a coma for twelve hours. At midnight
the doctors said death was an hour off at most. Norah, my
Irish Catholic nurse, called a priest to give me the last rites.
My friends filed in to say goodbye before the priest should
seal my lips. Poor Frances had the job of rousing me. I don't
know how long she had been speaking but finally I heard her
say, 'It's Francie, darling. We have a priest here—just for
your father's sake." Hazily I thought: "Now what's the matter
with my dad that he should need a *priest*?" But I couldn't
answer her. She said: "It's so I can tell him that you had a
priest at the last." "The last of what?" thinks I. Then she
sobbed and tears fell on my face. "Can you hear me, Lorna?"
she said, and I realized that it was for *me* they had called the
priest! Rage surged through me like new life. I opened my
eyes and glared at them, weeping and groaning and having a
jolly time at my expense. I roared at them in a great voice:

"Hysterical buggers! I'm not going to die! Throw that priest out of the house, and bring me ham and eggs!" Then I passed out for a day, but that rage had released enough adrenaline to carry me through the crisis. So you see, the man of God did save me after all. As soon as he had left the house, my friends got drunk in the living room. Most of them had been up two nights. The clipping bureau sent me a hundred notices of my death. After reading them all, I felt I should apologize for still being around. I'm thinking now that I will be able to finish "Macabre" in May, if my health is all plain sailing from here on. At this moment I'm sitting up in a chair.

The day after the crisis, reporters had called to confirm the death of Lorna Moon. She answered the phone and told them she had decided not to die. Nurse Norah said: "Miss Moon is the gamest person I ever saw." It was a season to be game. In February, Mabel Normand, film comedienne, thirty-two, who had been at the Pottenger Sanatorium for a year, was conscious to the last. A week later D. H. Lawrence died in the south of France. "It's so wearying and painful being ill," he had said, but "while we live, we must be game. And when we come to die, we'll die game too." Lawrence never gave up hope that he would recover. Lorna likewise persevered, but the work was getting harder.

Oh my God, how I hate to write! I loathe writing and I loathe "Macabre." I grit my teeth each morning and say: "Come on, you grisly bitch." I wish some fat old gentleman with kidney trouble and a million dollars would take a fancy to me, so that I might never have to do this drudgery any more.

The last letter in Lorna's hand was sent in March to Anne Johnston, Chambers's assistant:

"Macabre" and my cough between them have got me down to 85 pounds. In place of my darling Wong I have an elephantine nurse. Let no one tell you an elephant never forgets. This one forgets everything. My best beau has gone to New York for a month. Can you send a substitute? Must be over six feet, blond hair, blue eyes. Back of the head must be well shaped. You know, not one of these Teutonic flat-backs.

Lorna couldn't afford to go into a sanatorium until *Dark Star* was sold to the movies. Frances didn't tell Lorna, but she thought it wouldn't sell. Motion-picture exhibitors who didn't want an unfaithful wife to throw herself under a train wouldn't want an abandoned girl to leap from a cliff. She was about to ask Lorna to let her pay the hospital bills, when she had an impudent thought. Hundreds of stories were submitted to M-G-M each year. Supervisors were busy men and didn't have time to read them all. They hired "readers" to do that and pick out the hot prospects. At the weekly conference, no supervisor could recall reading Lorna Moon's *Dark Star*, but one said: "Anything dark sounds gloomy."

"It's anything but gloomy"—Frances sprang into the gap. She proceeded to expound a rip-roaring comedy of her own design, about the hard-boiled proprietress of a waterfront hotel and her uncouth boyfriend, skipper of a fishing boat. The supervisors' eyes lit up, picturing Marie Dressler in the role of flophouse Min and Wallace Beery playing rowdy Bill. Soon Lorna received a check for seventy-five hundred dollars and a letter promising to make a smash hit out of her riotous farce.

"What is going *on*!" she said. Frances described the story conference. Laughing as heartily as she dared, Lorna said: "Bless you, lassie!" She put the money in the bank and prepared to save her life, but she knew the odds were getting longer.

Before Everett left for New York, Lorna had instructed him on how to take her ashes to Strichen if her luck ran out this time. Everett's youth and beauty, not to mention his adulation, had been a joy to her. Though he might never be a writer, he was an intelligent reader and he had made useful comments about her work. He understood passion with restraint, important for good writing, and for keeping one's lover alive if she was a lunger. Lorna was glad he wouldn't see her limping into exile. She wanted him to remember her in the room she had decorated, surrounded by desert colors, wearing a chiffon velvet robe or green satin pajamas, extending a graceful arm to accept a cup of tea from Wong.

Had it really been nine years since she and William saw each other across the Bucklands' living room and Anatol fell for Satan Synne and Lorna last saw Cecil? Living only a mile away, with the son she had given him, Cecil might as well be on Mars. But he had never failed to help her when the going got too rough. Lorna asked Gladys Rosson to come and see her. They talked about her plans and about the odds of staying alive. She wouldn't bother to make a will. If she didn't die penniless in the sanatorium, she would come out with her next book, the true story of the lungers told by a lunger. Either way, the time had come to square accounts with Cecil. The house would cover what she owed him. She would sign the deed over to him. If she returned to Hollywood, he could rent it back to her. If not, he could sell it and recover his money.

Father accepted the house with a sigh. Four years later, he sold it at a profit. In the meantime he had learned that Lorna had a young daughter in England. Father instructed Neil McCarthy to send the profit to Lorna's daughter as though it were part of Lorna's estate. The girl didn't have to know the details. Mary received the money with joy. It made her a woman of property and got her a terrible husband. It wasn't a story at bedtime or a kiss while snuggling down, but it was a sign of her mother's love, distant but abiding, like the jade necklace. In the last reel of *Great Expectations* the true benefactor is revealed. It isn't the person the orphan Pip had thought. Mary left the theater of life before the story played out and never knew that her small fortune had been a gift from Mr. DeMille, whose daughter she had yearned to be all the years she worked for him. It's better to stay for the last reel.

A friend, Alexina Brune, helped Lorna pack and went with her on the train nine hundred miles to Albuquerque, where on 23 April Lorna entered St. Joseph Sanatorium. According to the record, the patient was a novelist, thirty-four years old, born in Scotland to Charles and Margaret Cameron, divorced from Walter Moon. No need to destroy the legend just for a few months' convalescence.

At St. Joseph Sanatorium the Sisters of Charity prayed for all, no less for a patient to whom God was a big deaf face. When Lorna told them she must write, they brought her extra pillows and gave her pad and pencil, and took them all away again when she nodded off. Work would have to wait a while. Rest was what she needed now. When she wasn't racked with coughs she lay dreaming about the world she had left behind. Dad had sent an article published in Aberdeen. Instead of going to church on Sunday, Scots were spending the morning in bed, and they were not resting! Lorna could hear him laugh at that. She longed to see sister Sadie, now a woman and unhappy in the life she had settled for. Mother wouldn't like cremation. How could you have a proper funeral without a bonny corp? Dad would see it her way. He had always understood her. He had always been proud of her. And he would be proud again. She would live to write her book and take it to him in the cottage she had seen in Sadie's photos. She would rise and run fast over the sea to Buchan fields to catch the color and the scent of sweetbrier roses growing in a lane, to hear the moor birds calling on a misty night, to watch the wind's long fingers flattening the furze and ling on the slope of Mormond Hill where Dad would scatter the pale dry grit out into the four winds and down with his burning tears into the sleeping heather.

The patient had no visitors. Some letters came from California. Tuesday she didn't open her mail. Thursday morning her pulse was weak. In the afternoon it failed. Dr. Mulky put the time of death at 2 p.m., 1 May 1930. The sky was blue in Albuquerque and the day was warm. On Saturday John Barrymore would "literally come to life" at the Sunshine Theatre, where through the magic of Vitaphone audiences would thrill to hear him speak from the screen in his first talking picture.

CHAPTER 25

Lorna Moon at the Belasco

The same winding Santa Fe rails that had brought Father West seventeen years before brought the corp of Lorna Moon, once bonny, now wasted, caught between a last breath and a dream yet to come, no more cough, no more fever, no more beautiful love affairs, rocking gently through the canyons back to the Hollywood Crematory to be put into the fire, purified of all corruption, vanity, ambition, weariness, and pain and crushed to coarse dry bony sand, ready for a pagan rite on a hilltop far away. The *Los Angeles Times* reported:

> By a strange coincidence the last short story writ-
> ten by Lorna Moon dealt with death and brought
> out her dislike of funerals. Her friends will re-
> spect her wishes and let her passing go un-
> marked by ceremony of any kind. Miss Moon,
> who was 31 years of age, died . . .

". . . at the age of 30," *Publishers Weekly* perfected her youth. "Her husband was killed in the War," *Variety* chimed in. "Her second novel," the *Times* reported, "was nearing completion" and—according to the Los Angeles *Record*—would be finished by "Everett Marcy, a young author with whom she was collaborating."

Lorna's British publisher, Victor Gollancz, wrote to Laurance Chambers expressing a sense of personal loss at the death of Lorna Moon, recalling the wonderfully brave letter she had sent recently, and inquiring whether her work in progress might be in such a state that it could be published "with some little touching up." Chambers said he was doing his best to find out "if anything can possibly be made of it." Fortunately for the true story of the lungers told by a lunger, all efforts to save the project failed.

Mother spent a lot of time at her little telephone table talking to people I didn't know about the Children's Hospital or the Hollywood Studio Club, a residence for young actresses founded by her and Mary Pickford. Poe went there to deliver things. Poe was our chauffeur. Sometimes I went with him. The floor of the club had big square tiles. We weren't allowed to go upstairs and see the actresses. One day Mother was talking about "Grahsiosa Drive." The name caught my attention. It had a ring of mystery. Poe had to go there. I wanted to go with him, but Mother said: Not today. I never forgot the way she said "Grahsiosa Drive," or the ring of mystery.

In November 1930 Frances Marion's rip-roaring comedy, *Min and Bill*, opened at the Capitol Theater in New York. Newspaper ads and screen credits declared that the film was "based" on Lorna Moon's *Dark Star*. "An unsavory version," said Mordaunt Hall of *The New York Times*, rowdy and sometimes coarse, which now and then "rises to slapstick comedy," as in the runaway speedboat sequence. Undaunted by faint praise, Marie Dressler won an Oscar. Bobbs-Merrill and M-G-M arranged book-movie tie-ins. *Dark Star*, the book, was issued in Britain in a mass-market edition subtitled "The Famous Novel on which the Film *Min and Bill* is Based." Contracts required that the movie and book titles appear together in all advertising and promotion, but there were complaints. *Woman's World*, a British weekly, published the story of *Min and Bill*, the movie, but the editor didn't want to mention *Dark Star*, the book, because readers would be perplexed by the "total dissimilarity" between the book and the movie. In Spain *Dark Star* became *La Fruta Amarga*, Bitter Fruit, which tie-in victims from

Barcelona to Jerez de la Frontera searched in vain for the flophouse brawl and the runaway speedboat.

As a child, I examined miles and miles of Father's bookshelves upstairs, downstairs, in the East Wing and the West, but I never came across a copy of *Dark Star*. Father had a dozen copies in a box in the attic—perhaps a gesture of support for a first-time novelist—but it was prudent not to keep a copy on the shelf where an inquisitive boy might find it and see his secret mother's name.

On 1 May 1939, Walter Moon acknowledged Bobbs-Merrill's payment of the last thirteen cents of Mary Moon's royalties from Lorna Moon's *Dark Star*. I was seventeen. Lorna's book was out of print, out of stock, and out of mind. Nine years after being "famous all over the United States," she was gone and forgotten. In September of that year Barbara Stanwyck and William Holden played in *Golden Boy*, a movie about a boxer and "a dame from Newark." Father had it on the screen, and the family saw it. From start to finish we heard the name of the dame from Newark, which didn't ring a bell with me. It rang a bell with Father, who just sat and smoked his pipe and looked wise for another sixteen years. When I was thirty-three, he told me about my other parents, by which time I had forgotten *Golden Boy*.

Thirty years further down the line, when I was working on this book, I saw a film called *Frances*, starring Jessica Lange, about Frances Farmer, an actress in the 1930s. Before coming to Hollywood, where she got into terrible trouble, Frances Farmer got into trouble in New York by falling in love with Clifford Odets, the celebrated playwright. In 1937, Odets had written his play *Golden Boy*, which opened in November at the Belasco Theatre with Frances Farmer playing the dame from Newark. In 1982, Jessica Lange played Frances Farmer playing the dame from Newark, and this time the bell rang. The name of the dame from Newark was Lorna Moon.

It's not a name you expect to find in the telephone book. Why would Odets use the name of another writer? I began to investigate. Margaret Brenman-Gibson, a professor of psychiatry at Harvard Medical School, had been Odets's psychoanalyst, friend, and biographer. In her book, she explains the psychodynamic origin of the name Lorna Moon and how it must have occurred to Odets when he was writing his play. "Lorna," she says, is derived from "lovelorn" and "forlorn" and from a pet name Odets gave to his first typewriter, which he talked of as a mistress. In 1928 he wrote to a friend: "I had a machine once that I really loved. I called it 'Lovelorn Corona.'" "Moon," the psychoanalyst explains, signifies "the eternal symbol of cool, inhospitable, unattainable Woman."

These metaphorical speculations may explain why Clifford Odets *liked* the name Lorna Moon, but they don't tell us whether he invented it (that is, reinvented it thirteen years after Nora Low invented it the first time while running away with Walter Moon to Winnipeg). I wrote to Dr. Brenman-Gibson saying I was working on the life of Lorna Moon, not Odets's dame from Newark but the author of *Dark Star*, a novel published in 1929. She was startled to learn that Lorna Moon had been a real person. She stated her opinion that Odets would not by any means have knowingly used the name of another professional writer in a play. I sought confirmation. Luise Rainer, the actress, was briefly married to Odets and living with him while he was writing *Golden Boy*, which he dedicated to her. She said he never spoke to her of a living Lorna Moon. Herman Kobland, Odets's lifelong friend and his secretary while he was writing *Golden Boy*, was sure Odets had invented the name.

Dr Brenman-Gibson does not tell us how or why the two psychodynamic symbols, "moon" and "lorn," came together in Odets's unconscious to form the single name Lorna Moon. She explains the symbols only separately. Meteorologists point out that the moon can have a corona, and perhaps the lunar corona supplies the missing link to Odets's lovelorn typewriter, but I think there is a more direct explanation.

From the age of seventeen Odets was constantly trying to write a novel. By the spring of 1929, he had written 65,000 words about the life of a musician. Living most of his youth in New York, Odets was a critic of other critics of literature and drama. In March 1929 *The New York Times Book Review* ran a full-page ad trumpeting *Dark Star* in letters three inches high, "a novel by Lorna Moon," with a picture of the author. Similar ads appeared in the *Times Book Review* on six successive Sundays. The *Times* reviewer outlined the story of the novel, about a girl whose heart is broken by a self-absorbed musician, which echoes both Odets's musician and his own self-centered treatment of women. Other ads and reviews of Lorna Moon may have struck Odets's critical eye in *New York Herald Tribune Books*, New York *World*, *The Nation*, and the *Saturday Review of Literature*.

Unlike the typical New York theater person, Odets was interested in movies. In November 1930, when he was an aspiring actor rehearsing in a play for the Theatre Guild, the movie *Min and Bill* was playing at the Capitol. Posters on the street and ads in the papers proclaimed the film's origin from Lorna Moon's novel, and Mordaunt Hall of *The New York Times* began his panning of the "unsavory" movie version by exonerating the novelist, Lorna Moon.

Though I quite agree with Dr. Brenman-Gibson that Odets would not deliberately have assigned the name of another writer to a character in a play, I think he read the name Lorna Moon in 1929 or 1930, felt its emotional pull on him, fell under its lunar spell, saw its lovelorn corona, breathed its fragrance of the mistress, and promptly forgot it for seven years until it came to him out of nowhere when he was writing *Golden Boy*. No doubt he was pleased with his invention, as Lorna had been with hers. Odets was only thirty-two, good-looking, intellectual, newly acclaimed, and already not getting along with his wife. Lorna would have written to him: "How dare you give my name to a *blonde*! Lorna Moon is a *redhead*! Either come here and apologize or read in my next novel about a scurvy bald scoundrel named Clifford Odets." But if she could have written the letter, she would not have been forgotten, and Odets would not have used her name in a play. The blonde from Newark would have been some other lonesome typewriter—Elsie Smith, Mona Underwood, or Solitaire Royale.

Her Son's Impressions

Lorna told her publisher that she had a son. The publisher wrote a note to his publicity department: "Would her son give us his impressions of his mother?" Assuming they were referring to me (brother Bill's impressions of our mother would not have pleased the publicity department), I was not ready to reply. I was only seven years old and had not been near my mother since the hour of my birth, when to protect my health and other people's reputations we were separated forever. I had bonded not with her but with smiling Nurse Copsen and have always been glad to see a pleasant woman with buckteeth and a receding chin.

After Father died, I pursued my secret mother for thirty-seven years, seeing her in various lights. At first she was a shadowy figure, someone I would never know, but she had done three things for me. She had brought me into the world. She had given me half of her genetic code, whatever that might lead to. And by a very odd set of hidden circumstances, she had given me full but far from ordinary membership in the family of William and Cecil de Mille. Though I would never be with her again, she would always be at the core of my life.

When I learned from my sister Mary and my brother Bill how they had been cast off by her, my opinion of Lorna fell. Obviously, she was not the mother I had been looking for, the woman eager to have a son, the woman whose blood boomed around me like the engine of a ship on a stormy ocean, lulling me, comforting me, teaching me the rhythm of life, on whose glistening belly the midwife laid me down red and dripping to hear again the familiar beat of her joyful heart and feel the inspiration of her triumphant breathing, who suckled me at swollen breasts till the age of two, kissed me and held me close, knew my wish before I spoke and granted it without delay, told me stories, laughed with me, understood my purposes, bound my wounds and praised my efforts, and remained young, strong, vibrant, and beautiful till I left her for another woman. Maybe I was expecting too much.

While sister Mary lived, Lorna was her mother more than mine. That was fair. I had grown up with two parents, she had grown up with none. Not until Mary died did I read our mother's books, whereupon I realized that my urge to play with words had not come exclusively from William. Much of it came from Lorna. Today my words appear on the page more like hers than like his. On the other hand, he had started out to be an engineer, and I was for some years occupied with science. He was drawn to Henry George, I to Kant and Wittgenstein. Lorna, a stranger to abstractions, was as concrete as a cough, a laugh, a kiss, a sigh, a peach. She had mothered not my thinking but my wild impulses, my rebellious streak, my hunger for the lyrical, urges William may have felt but could not put on paper. Lorna's words throb with passion. William's are the wry comment of a wise man in a tree looking down on the follies of mankind. He does not care to tell us much about his joys and sorrows.

Did Lorna love William enough to raise his child if she had been able to? Would she have tended the child herself instead of turning it over to nannies? I doubt that she could love any man that way or ever think of dedicating herself to a child. Lorna did love men, as the bee loves flowers, as the cavalier loves the courser. Men were stallions, great beasts that could carry her away and take her where she wanted to go, to England, to America, to the bowr of earthly blisse. Rarely would she drop the rein as she did with William. Men were lovely but not essential. She could live in pain without them. She could not live without her work. She liked to play the femme fatale, but she was mainly solitary, a constant reader like her father, a prisoner of unfolding stories that she was condemned to write. Work came before pleasure, before life if one had to choose, certainly before children, who were not really persons until they were thirteen. Having a baby, if it happened, was a personal achievement, something her mother had proudly done and she could do as well. She told editor Chambers she had given him a child to bring up for her. She meant her book, *Dark Star.* A book or a child was something she created and gave to someone else to care for, whether a husband she deserted, or the child's paternal uncle, or a publisher.

Why did she want a picture of me? I think it started as Palma Wayne's idea. They were talking in Lorna's bedroom, and Palma said Virginia Parsons was at the Hollywood School for Girls, where she had seen Richard de Mille in the lower school. Everyone in Hollywood knew that William and Cecil de Mille sent their children to that school. Very few, like Hedda Hopper, knew that William was my father. Lorna confided to intimate friends that she was the mother of Cecil de Mille's younger son, which in a way was true, but was not allowed to see him. The ladies naturally assumed that Cecil had adopted his own natural son. Lorna enjoyed misleading them. That way, she could still go on protecting William and his family while taking center stage in a heart-wringing, glamorous, private melodrama. Lorna wanted a picture of me to see what she had created. For once she had borne a child to a man she greatly admired, a prominent man, a brilliant man, a man who could teach her much about her profession, a man she had been wild about. Necessity had parted them, but she had left a mark on him no other woman could rub out.

Though an individualist intent on living as she chose, Lorna chose to follow much of the traditional moral code. She kept her word and was honest in her daily dealings. She meant to pay her own way. She refused to be a victim or an object of pity. She didn't complain about misfortunes or blame others for her mistakes. She was strictly disciplined and faithful to her purposes. She attracted and kept many women friends, who wanted to do things for her, introduced her to their employers, helped promote her book, took her into their houses when she needed a place to stay. Sister Sadie always wrote. Sister Eva defended her and took her as a model.

Walter's wife, young Helene, worshipped her from afar. Frances Marion's falling tears roused her from a coma.

How can I call her honest when she told so many false stories about herself? Those stories did no harm. No one counted on their being true. What about that crucifix on the wall behind her bed? Frances Marion believed it was there because Lorna's father was a Catholic. Frances wasn't religious and wouldn't have been shocked to learn that Lorna's father was an atheist. But that would have damaged the legend of Lorna Moon, which Frances and the rest of world enjoyed more than they would have liked the facts. Besides, the crucifix was an antique from a church in Guadalajara. It was stylish decoration, 1920s sophistication, Christmas Communion with cocktails and plum pudding. It was defiant flaming youth. Let him watch me with my lover and strike me dead at the height of pleasure, if he is really up there. It was fellow feeling. He and I suffer and die but drink the cup we are given.

Did she ever regret anything? If she did, she didn't say so. Whatever she wanted to do she did and took the consequences, unless they happened to be children, in which case she gave them away. Around the time of World War I, not caring to raise one's children was thought to be reprehensible, but in a world where the womb is more dangerous than the subway I must count my rogue mother among the maternal angels though not, like Constance de Mille, among the saints.

Lorna was Woman nearly Unlimited—relentless artist, fastidious lover, bearer of three healthy babes, she could have it almost all. Her first son had a father who loved him. Her second was fed on milk and honey with a silver spoon. Only her daughter had bad luck, in a foster family that had seemed like a rather good solution at the time. In any case, having a mother was a mixed blessing in our mother's opinion. She herself had little desire to see her own mother again. After reading for weeks about Dorothy Ellington, on trial in San Francisco for killing her mother, Lorna wrote to her editor:

> Since receiving your letter, I've been having the flu, and next to killing one's mother having the flu is California's most fashionable pastime. My mother is in Scotland, so I had to content myself with the lesser excitement.

Lorna was little, refined, and sparkling. Men took one look at her and wanted to protect her. They didn't know she had steel in her. They didn't know she was holding the rein. Lorna cast a spell on them with nimble conversation and deep topaz eyes, which promised what no man could fathom. Much of it was simply play, like choosing Lillian Gish to be her imaginary rival for Chambers's imaginary affection. When Lorna lived with a man, she didn't say: I will stay with you till death do us part, my strength will support you in whatever you may wish to do, my tenderness will care for you. She said: My life belongs to me, my body and my thoughts are mine. I will stay with you as long as it is good for my career. She did have romantic dreams of sacrifice for love, which she portrayed in *Dark Star*, but when she woke she sacrificed lovers to ambition. Love came and went in waves. It burned her, healed her, bore her aloft, dashed her to the ground, left her bleeding but not dying. Art was hard to master, yet it was obedient. It was satisfying. It was being in control.

In writing as in life, Lorna's weakness was in love. She believed in courtship, bitter failure, and marital hate, but enduring love did not seem quite real to her. Marriage was a trap. If it didn't go tragically wrong, it became an amusing picture postcard. She was adept at comedy. She was earthy and direct. She didn't care for tricky tales like *Orlando* or *The Bridge of San Luis Rey*. "I too have read French novels," she said. She didn't like adopted styles. "A writer should write in his native voice." She wasn't afraid to recognize faults in her writing.

Already *Dark Star* seems far from well done to me. I should have held back in the last two sections. Several critics said I shouldn't have rushed at such a pace. I think that is a very just criticism.

She was versatile.

Mr. Curtis seems to think that it is wise to follow up a success with a similar book, but you know, Laurance, I don't think I'm ever going to write "similar books." "Mother Superior" will be a very airy satire. "This Mortal Sappho" is the inti-

mate journal of an amoureuse. "The Three MacPhersons" is
a struggle of genius through three generations of women to
express itself.

If Nora Low, at sixteen, had not disobeyed her mother by slipping out into the night to lay her head on Callie Birn's fatally
infected pillow, what would we say today about the writer Lorna
Moon? Arnold Bennett, author of *The Old Wives' Tale*, was the most
prominent British journalist of his day. His weekly column in the
London *Evening Standard* "confirmed his position as quite the
most powerful and important reviewer of books in England." He
was the first British critic to appreciate Chekhov. After reading *The
Brothers Karamazov* in a French translation, he caused the novels
of Dostoyevsky to be published in England. He was an early com-
mender of James Joyce, though he wrote of Joyce's *Anna Livia
Plurabelle*: "it is utterly incomprehensible to me, and will be to
you." Dickens bored him, Henry James gave him "little pleasure,"
Dostoyevsky he "adored." He was a great discoverer of young
writers, the first in Britain to recognize Hemingway and Faulkner,
an early champion of Waugh and T. S. Eliot. Among new writers
hailed by Arnold Bennett was Lorna Moon, of whose novel he
said:

> It is captivating to read for the author has both a gift for
> narrative and a style which is distinguished and original. . . .
> Some of the scenes are admirable and have power, especially
> the suicide of the heroine, which is a little masterpiece of
> poetic felicity in ten lines. [The book] is vitalised by one of
> the rarest of all qualities—passion. I could write two columns
> in depreciation of it; but I salute it and recommend it.

An evenhanded judgment. Bennett did not ignore the defects
of the books he praised. "It is clumsily constructed. . . ." This was
not written about *Dark Star* but about *Soldier's Pay*, William Faulkner's first novel. However clumsy he may be, "Faulkner is the
coming man," Bennett wrote in 1930. I am not suggesting that my
captivating mum was in a league with Faulkner, but other noted
critics praised her, and I think she would have proved to be a

serious writer and would have written notable novels, as she learned her trade and learned more about love.

Cecilia advised me not to write this book. "You shouldn't do that to your mother," she said. Agnes didn't want anyone else to write about her father. Ingrid Lyall was keeping memories of her Grandmother Annie locked in a black box. My man in Buchan hesitated to tell me that my Scottish granddad got his start on the wrong side of the wrong blanket. If you go digging up the past, you're bound to find some skeletons. In his *Autobiography* Father revealed that in 1553 the Holy Roman Emperor Charles V imposed a fine on Adam de Mil, a glove maker in Flanders, for splitting his stepfather's head with an axe. Father himself left his estate in uneven portions, and his spelling was atrocious. William de Mille gave up too easily. Katherine and Richard de Mille couldn't feel the love of their adoptive mother. Agnes was often a pain in the neck. Margaret George de Mille was "bristly." Some were even socialists.

But people want to know who they are and where they have come from, and search for parents they have lost. Eighty years ago, it was said that man is only what he is trained to be, but that is foolish. A horse raised in a birdcage will not sing. Today biologists will tell you, after closing the office door, that heredity counts. People want to learn about their genetic relatives, and it's not all good news. Aunt Annie was a hard worker, witty, and lots of fun, but she heartlessly rejected a little girl who adored her. Aunt Eva played with her children and wrote an entertaining book, but she was a hell-raiser and a family outcast. Sadie was a dutiful daughter, but traded four persons' happiness for a fancy house. Lorna gave her life for mine but abandoned Bill and Mary. People do good things and bad. My purpose has been to tell a true story about some people who are gone, some of them famous, some obscure, whose lines crossed one afternoon to produce their chronicler. Heredity may account for the fact that these two families abound with writers. Richard Mead De Mill was a theologian. Henry, William, and Cecil were dramatists. Agnes and I were biographers. Among the Lows, Lorna and Eva were novelists. Mary, Don, and Sadie's daughter Jean were journalists. And younger writers come after them. I have labored to correct errors published earlier. One fanciful account said that Lorna had four children (she had three), lost a husband in a war, then married a Canadian (her only husband, an Englishman, lived to be eighty-two), wrote her stories in New York (where she never set foot), and died in Albuquerque on the way from Los Angeles to Phoenix (which requires a trip round the world).

Would I have liked to grow up calling Lorna "Mother"? Would her sparkle have brightened my days, her wit and humor gladdened my heart? There is no way to think as you would if you had lived a different life, but after living thirty years longer than Lorna did, I see her more as a long-lost daughter than as the mother I should have had. I judge that I was better off with cool, reliable, saintly, unsatisfying Constance than with an artist who didn't want kids and never wrote about a child as if he were a person.

Would I have preferred William to Cecil as a father? That's a harder question. Cecil and I had little in common, but he was heroic and warm. In youth I was much like William, intellectual and distant. William was a kindly uncle. He played his Bert Williams records and we laughed together. He gave me a set of the *Jungle Books*, in pink leather with gold trim. Inside he wrote: "with love." He said he hoped Kipling's stories would give me as much pleasure as they had given him. They did give me pleasure, but the volume I actually read had belonged to Father when he was a boy. I treasured that book and wrote my name in it right under his.

Lorna loved the pleasures of life and had more than her share of pain. She was a connoisseur of men but dedicated herself only to telling stories, beginning with stories about her village:

> I know all these people through having grown up amongst them. In some cases I haven't changed so much as a freckle. Some I met when I was nine and never saw again. The rest I haven't seen since adolescence. Yet Divot Meg is more vivid to me than people I see every day. The only one I've been afraid of libelling is the librarian. In real life he sat as I

picture him, towering behind the great table in the lower hall, his noble head set upon the torso of a giant, his face beautiful, or at least so it seemed to me when I was a child. Seated, he inspired awe, but when he stood, he didn't rise. His legs ended at the knee in round feet like an elephant's. He did go to Aberdeen, to the university, and soon returned, because the people in the streets would laugh at him. His tragic love is fiction, but I believe just such a love must have happened to him. It is always hard for me to know where truth leaves off and I begin. I was whipped so often for that when I was little!

She was a wounded minstrel.

In the summer of 1927 a succession of pulmonary hemorrhages laid me low. For six months I wrote nothing. Then one day I found myself day-dreaming "Dark Star." I thought to myself "this is good, but I don't want it all to be in Scotland. It will sell better if I move Nancy to the Continent, say Paris or Vienna." Immediately she turned into a wooden doll. Finally it came home to me that I was betraying the story, caring too much about money and success. I saw that I had been sterile for years because I was trying to be a popular writer instead of singing my own simple song. My body had sickened because I had betrayed my art. At the time I was very ill, and the thought preyed on me that I should just die, having killed my song. Yet I wanted to live. I wanted to redeem myself.

The struggle was fierce, bloody, and grim, but she wouldn't give in to despair.

19 Jan. 1928. Hillcrest Sanatorium. I'm working now every day. I've come to believe that this is the only way I can pay off the demon that afflicts my lungs. I bought my way out last time with the Drumorty stories. This time I must do it with the novel.

27 Jan. 1928. I am still working faithfully, so of course my

lungs are better. All this work should have made my temperature go up, instead of which it has dropped. All will be well with me if I keep on working.

Feb. 1928. More gore! They say I'm getting better but I *know* I'm getting worse. I'm always worse when I lie flat like this. Why can't they see that they break my hold on life when they keep me from writing?

May 1928. I had hoped to finish by June, but everything went wrong. I've been in bed almost a year, and the result is nothing, worse than nothing. The trouble has spread, the fever is higher, the little rattle in my chest is a big rattle now. I can't stand or sit in a chair. And most terrible of all is that way at the back of my bravado I think I'm licked this time. I shouldn't have listened to the doctor. I'm going to start working again before I get too toxic to write. Barring a hemorrhage I can still finish the book.

She did finish the book and would live two more years on Graciosa Drive, about a mile from our house. Every day on the way to school I would pass beneath her hill and again on the way back. Her death would be on the front page, imminent when I was seven, ultimate when I was eight, and I wouldn't notice it. She would appear in Art Deco, and I would turn right past the page. Knowing nothing of her struggle or of the risk she had taken for me, or of the picture she would examine to see if the product was worth the price, I was already learning my craft, mastering phonics in the first grade, getting ready to tell the story of my secret mother's life. My conceiver and protector, the storyteller who didn't want kids, would have been glad to know that.

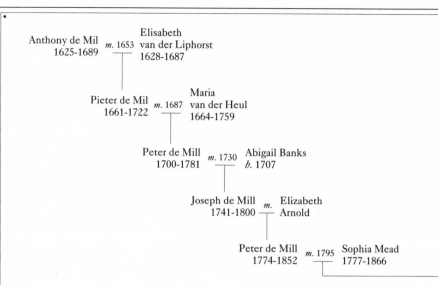

Anthony de Mil   *m.* 1653   Elisabeth van der Liphorst
1625-1689   1628-1687

Pieter de Mil   *m.* 1687   Maria van der Heul
1661-1722   1664-1759

Peter de Mill   *m.* 1730   Abigail Banks
1700-1781   *b.* 1707

Joseph de Mill   *m.*   Elizabeth Arnold
1741-1800

Peter de Mill   *m.* 1795   Sophia Mead
1774-1852   1777-1866

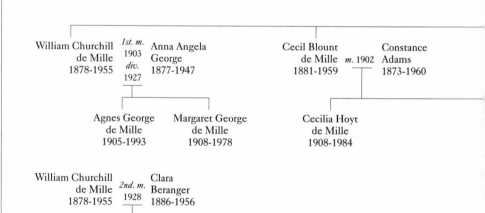

William Churchill de Mille   *1st. m.* 1903 *div.* 1927   Anna Angela George
1878-1955   1877-1947

Cecil Blount de Mille   *m.* 1902   Constance Adams
1881-1959   1873-1960

Agnes George de Mille
1905-1993

Margaret George de Mille
1908-1978

Cecilia Hoyt de Mille
1908-1984

William Churchill de Mille   *2nd. m.* 1928   Clara Beranger
1878-1955   1886-1956

Frances Beranger
1909-

William Churchill de Mille   —#—   Lorna Moon
1878-1955   1886-1930

Richard de Mille
1922-

THE de Mille FAMILY

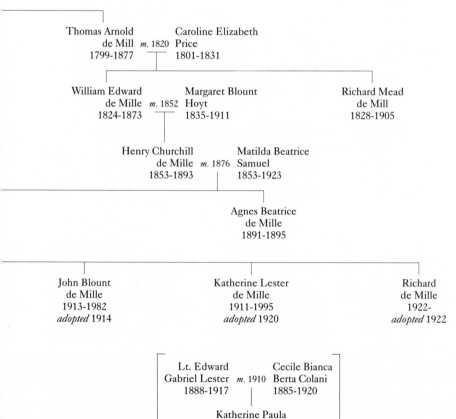

Thomas Arnold
de Mill *m.* 1820
1799-1877

Caroline Elizabeth
Price
1801-1831

William Edward
de Mille *m.* 1852
1824-1873

Margaret Blount
Hoyt
1835-1911

Richard Mead
de Mill
1828-1905

Henry Churchill
de Mille *m.* 1876
1853-1893

Matilda Beatrice
Samuel
1853-1923

Agnes Beatrice
de Mille
1891-1895

John Blount
de Mille
1913-1982
adopted 1914

Katherine Lester
de Mille
1911-1995
adopted 1920

Richard
de Mille
1922-
adopted 1922

Lt. Edward
Gabriel Lester *m.* 1910
1888-1917

Cecile Bianca
Berta Colani
1885-1920

Katherine Paula
Lester
1911-1995

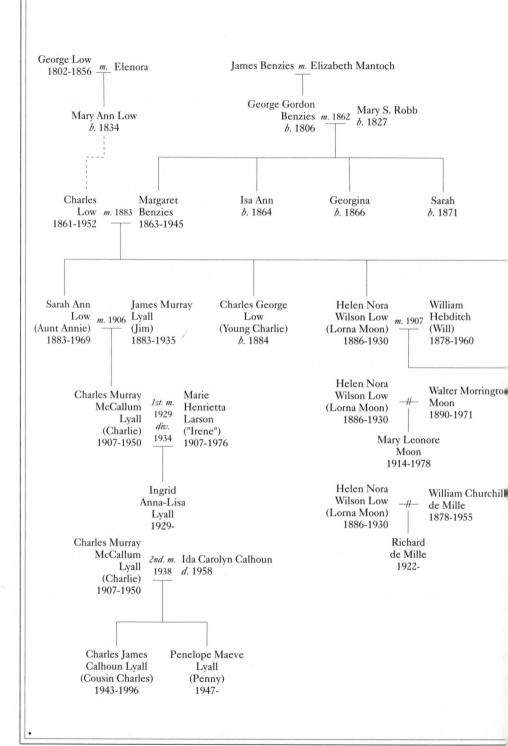

THE *Low* FAMILY

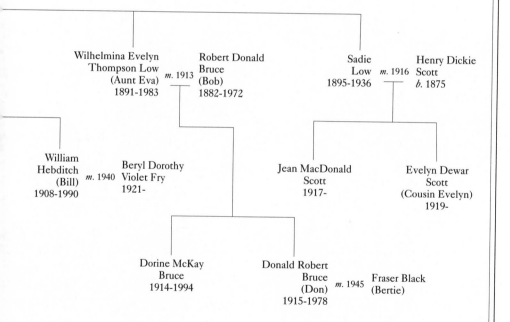

Wilhelmina Evelyn
Thompson Low
(Aunt Eva)   *m.* 1913
1891-1983

Robert Donald
Bruce
(Bob)
1882-1972

Sadie
Low   *m.* 1916
1895-1936

Henry Dickie
Scott
b. 1875

William
Hebditch
(Bill)   *m.* 1940
1908-1990

Beryl Dorothy
Violet Fry
1921-

Jean MacDonald
Scott
1917-

Evelyn Dewar
Scott
(Cousin Evelyn)
1919-

Dorine McKay
Bruce
1914-1994

Donald Robert
Bruce
(Don)   *m.* 1945
1915-1978

Fraser Black
(Bertie)

Notes

CITATIONS

Lorna Moon's *Dark Star* (Bobbs-Merrill 1929, first edition) is cited in the form DS22, meaning page 22 of *Dark Star*; the 1980 Gourdas House edition, reproduced from the Victor Gollancz edition, has different page numbers and is not cited.

Lorna Moon's *Doorways in Drumorty* (Jonathan Cape 1926) is cited in the form DD22; the 1981 Gourdas House reproduction has the same page numbers; the Bobbs-Merrill first edition, of 1925, is not cited because it contains only six of the eight stories.

PAGE

vii   Woman of Mystery—Bobbs-Merrill memorandum; Lorna moonshine from LM ltrs (esp. 22, 24 Dec 1928) and publicity pieces written by Alma Whitaker, *Los Angeles Times* journalist (Lorna Moon Author File; see Notes for Chapter 10, "Author Questionnaire").

1 / HIS FATHER'S BOY

3   Song—Tommy was improvising on Edward Lear's *Mrs. Blue-dickey bird*.

4   Agnes George de Mille—born 18 Sep 1905, died 7 Oct 1993; see References for some of her published accounts; AGdeM unpublished comments as told to RdeM.

4   Katie—Katherine Paula Lester de Mille Quinn, born 29 June 1911 in Vancouver, died 27 Apr 1995 in Tucson; married to Anthony Quinn 1937–65; 5 children; *NYT* lists 19 films, 1934–47.

5   House too quiet—Vancouver *Sunday Times*, 20 Mar 1977. Tony Quinn liked

to tell stories about his life, some of which were not true and many of which told more about him than he knew. In *One Man Tango* (Anthony Quinn with Daniel Paisner, HarperCollins 1995), his second autobiography, he avers that Katherine didn't work for 10 years after the wedding (143, 186), but *NYT* shows 5 films in the first 4 years; that his marriage to her was "empty" (289) because she wasn't (and hadn't claimed she would be) a virgin on the wedding night; that his second wife's constancy and devotion drove him away (292); that his "one true love" (218) had been Suzan Ball, a young actress whose early death relieved him of love's responsibilities. He said (UPI, 14 Nov 1978): "I know about architecture because I studied with Frank Lloyd Wright"; but in 1995 he reports only two interviews with Wright. He said: "I believe in monogamy"; interviewer answered: *"What!"* (Alex Witchel, The Number It Takes to Tango, *NYT*, 6 July 1995:B1–2; see also, Anthony Quinn, *The Original Sin*, Little, Brown 1972).

5   Toni Quinn—Witchel 1995; next century (Quinn 1995: photo caption before p. 215).

5   Simple and real—Katie was honest, loving, loyal, devoted, and understanding. Her eldest daughter, Christina, said (5 July 1985): "Sometimes nice doesn't pay off. You need a bit of temper." Katie made the tragic mistake of falling in love at 26 with a tall, dark stranger, 22, who didn't know what loving was and couldn't learn it in 27 years; who would someday write: "To be loved is the triumph of living"—not to love, to *be* loved (1995:289). Agnes de Mille said Tony was "a carnivorous egotist," whom she admired as an actor and whom she rather liked but who revealed himself as "something of a pig" when he wrote about Katherine.

9   While that which is pardonable—R. De Mill 1908:392.

9   Ralph Samuel—Another famous descendant was CBDeM's second cousin, Sir Herbert Louis Samuel (1870–1963), British statesman-philosopher, leader of the Liberal Party.

10 School—Beatrice's catalogue, *The Henry C. de Mille School for Girls*, 1898.

13 Skeezix—Frank King, *Gasoline Alley*, 14, 18, 21, 22, 27 Feb 1921. The doctor who comes to examine the baby only guesses at the birth date and is not the "good authority." Walt's halfhearted attempts to give the baby away arise from his being a bachelor; he keeps the baby because he is in fact the baby's father. The note in the basket is a fake. The "good authority" is the mother, purportedly unknown, who knows Walt well enough to give him a baby that looks just like him. An unconvincing cover story later proposes Colonel Coda and Madam Octave as the parents. After artist Frank King died, the strip was taken over by Dick Moores, whose genial letters to RdeM (quoted here by permission of Dick Moores) were most informative; Dick Moores died in 1986. On 17 July 1984 he wrote: "I think Frank had it in mind all along to . . . reveal that Skeezix was Walt's son, but the mores of the times just didn't permit it. . . . I do know that I have a difficult time having Skeezix address Walt as 'Uncle' Walt!"

2 / A MARRIAGE MADE ON EARTH

18 Shot in a basement—Dmitri Volkogonov, *Lenin: A New Biography*, translated and edited by Harold Shukman, Free Press 1994.

20 Dearest Gretchen—CBdeM ltr to CAdeM written near Thoreau NM c17 Dec 1913; abridged; spelling and punctuation corrected; reproduced by permission of Cecil B. DeMille Trust and Cecilia de Mille Harper Trust; the omitted remainder poetically describes places where Cecil and Constance might live.

22 Henley—Or Ever the Knightly Years Were Gone, *Echoes*, 1888.

24 At seventy-four—Constance's notes reproduced by permission of CBDeM Trust and CdeMH Trust.

3 / THE INTELLECTUAL OF THE FAMILY

25 Title—"Bill was always the intellectual of the family" CBDeM 1959:37.

25 Lead the people—WdeM 1939:309; the dramatist can be a powerful source of public thought, who leads and elevates his audience (WdeM, Our "Commercial" Drama, 1913 ms).

25 My Hunting Story—CBdeM 1890 ms, abridged, some punctuation added, original spelling retained, reproduced by permission of CBDeM and CdeMH Trusts.

26 Biplane—Art Ronnie, It Was a Great Race, *Westways*, Jan 1973:42–44.

27 Fifty-nine and ten tenths—Told to RdeM by CBdeM.

27 Shake hands with a Negro—Agnes Notes.

28 Goethe—WdeM July 1909 ms.

30 Nothing I wrote—WdeM 1939:61.

30 Suddenly in 1913—AdeM 1952:5; WdeM 1939:58–59, 26, 63.

31 Real owners—"The art of drama is owned in common by the whole people" (WdeM, Our "Commercial" Drama, 1913 ms p. 5).

31 Film historians—Scott Eyman, *Film Comment*, Mar–Apr 1992:46–47; Kevin Brownlow, *The Parade's Gone By*, Knopf 1968:267.

31 Elected—As president of the Academy of Motion Picture Arts and Sciences, William presented the best-actress award to Mary Pickford for *Coquette* (1929), her first talking picture. In 1907 at thirteen Mary had played the daughter in William's play *The Warrens of Virginia*. Everyone including Belasco thought she was a very promising youngster, but when the play closed in 1909 "the poor kid" met D. W. Griffith and in 1911 told William she was going into the movies. Horrified, he tried to persuade her not to throw "her whole career in the ash can" and bury herself "in a cheap form of amusement" in which there would "never be any real money" or "anything which could by the wildest stretch of imagination be called art." The "stubborn little thing" said she knew what she was doing. "So," William wrote, "I suppose we'll have to say goodbye to little Mary Pickford. She'll never be heard from again and I feel terribly sorry for her" (ltr to David Belasco 25 July 1911, quoted in *Masquers 50th Anniversary Book*; abridged in Mary Pickford, *Sunshine and Shadow*, Doubleday 1955:146).

32 Impossible to do creative work—WdeM 1939:183.

32 Mice—Frances Beranger Notes.

32 No further need—AdeM 1990:188.

32 Flexibility—"[Cecil] DeMille had a prescience that Griffith lacked; he was able to estimate the shifting states of audience interest." (John Fell, *A History of Films*, Holt, Rinehart & Winston 1979:108).

32 Innovation—"Cecil is much more [than William] the innovator" (Eyman 1992:47).

32 "Cecil was tough"—Agnes Notes.

32 Magic years—WdeM 1939:231, 27, 166–68, 256, 159, 266, 310–11, 296.

32 Wife—Anna Angela George de Mille, born 2 Oct 1877, married 1 Mar 1903, divorced 1927, died 17 Mar 1947.

32 Drove everybody crazy—AdeM 1978:263; 1990:178, 189, 196.

33 Fiction in the daytime—Agnes Notes.

33 Unseen guest—Beulah Marie Dix Flebbe (1876–1970), novelist and screen-writer, wrote five scenarios for CBDeM, including *The Road to Yesterday* (1925), based on her play, and *The Affairs of Anatol* (1921); see her daughter's charming, informative book (E. F. Scott 1972:21, 173).

33 Georgist play—WdeM, The Chances of a Single Tax Play, c1913 ms, p. 3.

33 Plumy tail—Scott 1972:128.

33 Innocent fiancée—Agnes Notes.

34 Knowing nothing about sex—AdeM 1978:264.

34 Close bond—WdeM 1939:165.

34 Printzlau—For CBDeM Olga wrote one film adapted from a story by Wil-liam, *Why Change Your Wife?* (1920).

34 Mistresses—AdeM 1990:183.

35 Met to sort it out—Agnes Notes.

35 Anna and William after separation—AdeM 1978:263–67.

35 Wanted a son—AdeM 1973:7–8.

36 Tuna Club—Founded in 1898 by Charles Frederick Holder, who wrote *The Channel Islands of California* (Hodder & Stoughton [London] 1910).

4 / THE CAT THAT WALKS BY HIMSELF

38 Natalie—Natalie Visart Schenkelberger, later Visart, DeMille costume de-signer.

42 Belasco's technique—Mary Pickford, *Sunshine and Shadow*, Doubleday 1955:98.

42 Adoption—*Los Angeles Times*, c10 Feb 1940; Decree of Adoption No. AD 1926, filed 25 June 1940, Superior Court, County of Los Angeles.

45 Margaret Belgrano—"Talented. . . . strikingly beautiful, her gifts are along histrionic lines"—Mildred Brown Robbins, *San Francisco Chronicle*, 20 Mar 1946.

5 / THE FUNERAL

46 Clara Beranger's family—Frances to RdeM. In plays by Chekhov, Ibsen, and contemporary writers, Frances used the names Lynn Beranger and Frances Dorgeval.

47 Every penny—AdeM 1973:10.

48 *Queen of Queens*—Koury 1959:218–29.

48 Greatest philosophers—WdeM 1939:244.

48 Drama Department—In 1990 the Drama Department, "founded by Wil-liam de Mille," became the School of Theatre (*USC Chronicle*, 26 Feb 1996).

William's students included Joe Flynn, Marvin Kaplan, and Art Buchwald (Comments by James H. Butler, Professor of Drama, USC, 1982).

49   Agnes on William's decline—AdeM 1991:158–59; 1990:189.

50   Brothers' correspondence—Cecil's letter was dated 9 Aug 1952; William's answer is misdated 9 Aug also; it is handwritten, postmarked 25 Aug. At the end of the letter William regrets not having been able to attend Cecil's golden wedding celebration, which occurred on 16 Aug.

51   Loyalty oath—Imposed on civil servants by President Harry S. Truman.

51   Fire the Reds—AdeM 1990:188.

51   Settle into their stride—WdeM 1939:22. William wrote: "There is probably only one country in the world which would kill a master musician for his political convictions" (309); he meant Nazi Germany. He tolerantly compared the Soviets to Hollywood's "masterminds of finance," who had replaced artistic individualism with a "Soviet system" of collective movie production (309). In 1939 neither William nor Cecil could know that "Russia" would not "become less insistently propagandist" until 50 years and 60 million murders later, but Cecil suspected the worst, and he was right. In the same year Aleksandr Solzhenitsyn, like William forty years before, decided to make writing rather than engineering his profession. In 1941, when William became chairman of drama at USC, Solzhenitsyn was drafted into the Soviet army. In the spring of 1953, when William retired from USC because of cancer, Stalin died, and Solzhenitsyn, suffering from cancer, was released after eight years of imprisonment in Gulag. In 1954, both of them were close to death. Solzhenitsyn survived. Twenty years later he sounded an alarm the West had long needed to hear. Had William lived to hear that warning, I believe he would have been deeply impressed by the moral strength of Solzhenitsyn and would have learned from that great man that even a Jeffersonian Democrat could have enemies on the left.

51   Janet Stevenson—Lecturer in drama at USC 1951–53; named as Communist, *New York Times*, 30 Sep 1952:4.

51   Progressive organization—Independent Citizens Committee of the Arts, Sciences, and Professions, a Communist front organization, which enlisted the help of Hollywood liberals (*Guide to Subversive Organizations and Publications*, Committee on Un-American Activities, U.S. House of Representatives, 3 Mar 1951); Frances to RdeM.

52   Dollar—CBDeM, host of the very popular weekly Lux Radio Theater, was permanently banned from radio when he refused to pay a one-dollar political assessment to the American Federation of Radio Artists to be used against a ballot proposition he was for, Proposition 12, to abolish the closed shop in California (CBDeM 1959:367, 384ff). Two years later, the Taft-Hartley Act made the closed shop illegal, and Senator Taft said that the law would not have been passed if CBDeM had not called attention to the issue by refusing to pay the dollar. As things work in the legal world, the passage of the law did not bring CBDeM's job back.

52   RdeM's first marriage—1943–54 to Rosalind Jane Shaffer, ballet dancer, devoted mother of William Cecil de Mille (1945–64), and professor of dance at Smith College.

6 / TWILIGHT OF DEMILLE

57   Body viewed—NYT 19 Sep 1921.

57   Taylor murdered—NYT 3 Feb 1922. Minter's mother suspected (Cari Beauchamp, *Without Lying Down*, Scribner 1997:422).

58   Death near for Lorna Moon—*Los Angeles Herald*, 28 Oct 1929.

59   Ran up ladder—CBDeM 1959:428.

60   Labor hearing—House Subcommittee on Labor-Management Relations, transcript, 16 June 1958: 313–81.

61   Read in the Bible—Psalm 22:19,11; 2 Timothy 4:7; John 17:4.

61   Mormon librarians—Cecil B. DeMille Collection, Arts & Communications Archives, Lee Library, Brigham Young University, Provo UT.

63   Forgiving—CBDeM 1959: 265, 58–61, 38–40; Koury 1959:108.

64   Hall of the Slain—Valhalla.

65   *Quo Vadis?*—Novel by Henryk Sienkiewicz, 1846–1916. According to legend, Peter, the apostle, fleeing martyrdom, met Jesus on the Appian Way and asked: Whither goest thou [*Quo vadis*]? Jesus replied: To Rome, to be crucified again. Peter returned to Rome and was crucified.

7 / AN UNEXPECTED BROTHER

66   Lioness, cat, sparrow—This metaphor summarizes two wills and several trusts. In Father's will, a public document executed in 1958, Katie and John and I were treated equally, like sparrows, but ten years earlier Father had established a modest trust for me, which recognized my peculiar status in the family and caused my instant growth to cat. In 1960 Cecilia and her children inherited all of Mother's large estate under a will written in 1954, when Mother was no longer able to judge such matters; the will of 1954 does not tell us what Mother would have wanted to leave to her adopted children if she had been sound of mind after Father died in 1959. There were also large gifts to charity through the CBDeM Trust.

66   Helped him write the will—"I'm sure Grandfather's whole will was written at Mother's instigation," Cecilia Presley quoted by Anne Edwards, *The DeMilles*, Abrams 1988:174.

68   Del Valle—AdelV interview, 2 Apr 1993.

70   Hedda Hopper—Professional name of Elda Furry Hopper, actress in some 80 films, including CBDeM's *Reap the Wild Wind*; gossip columnist, autobiographer (*From Under My Hat*, Doubleday 1952:64, 107, 108, 187, 257, 280); close friend of screenwriter Frances Marion (*Off with Their Heads*, Macmillan 1972:38, 99, 319), who was Lorna Moon's closest woman friend in Hollywood. Hedda's rival columnist was Louella O. Parsons.

70   *Juno*—Easton 1996:367–68.

71   Dear Cecilia—N. S. McCarthy ltr 27 Feb 1959, reproduced by permission, 17 Jan 1983, from Mary Beich McCarthy, Michael M. Gless, and Marjorie Gless, sole proprietors under the will of Neil Steere McCarthy.

73   You were brought—Rosemary McCarthy Bullis, interview, 9 Oct 1982.

73   Wonder Baby Not Worrying—Alma Whitaker, *Los Angeles Daily Times*, 8 Nov 1922, II-6; Foundling Finds Home in De Mille Mansion, *Los Angeles*

Examiner, 14 Nov 1922, I-5, with photo; Infant Boy Adopted by Cecil De Milles, *Hollywood Daily Citizen*, 14 Nov 1922:4.

73 N. S. McCarthy (1888–1972)—Famed lawyer dies of stroke, *Los Angeles Times*, 26 July 1972. McCarthy's association with CBDeM began in 1914 (CBDeM 1959:117).

74 *The Kid*—Charles Chaplin, *My Autobiography*, Simon & Schuster 1964:242, 295, 501. There is reason to suspect that baby Skeezix may also have come from *The Kid*. *The New York Times* reviewed *The Kid* on 22 Jan 1921. Three weeks later, on 14 Feb 1921, Walt Wallet found baby Skeezix on the doorstep. Both the kid and Skeezix were visited by a doctor and both were taken to an orphanage. Both Walt and the little tramp tried at first to give the baby away, then acted as father. A note found in the kid's clothes said: "Please love and care for this orphan child." A note in Skeezix's basket said: "Please care for and give baby a good home." The kid was reunited with his own mother; Skeezix was mothered by Auntie Blossom; each retained the father he knew.

75 John adopted—Superior Court in Los Angeles, 21 Mar 1917; the last known address of Gus and Ada Gonzales, man and wife, was said to be 551 West C Street, Colton CA, a rural district near San Bernardino. "Gonzales" is as common as "Smith"; "Ralph" in Spanish is "Raúl." Ada is a Teutonic name, little used by Spanish-speakers. Neil liked historic names; Father's great-great-grandfather was Ralph Samuel (1738–1809) of Liverpool.

75 Origins—Louise, John's wife, was understandably avid to discover her husband's and children's antecedents. She asked Father, who (she said) answered: "Don't stir up a nest of bees." (Presumably he said: "Don't stir up a hornet's nest.") She asked Mother, who (she said) told her to drop the subject. Years later, after Cecilia died, Louise told me with confidence that John was Father's natural son, born in Wyoming to a Spanish woman after Father went there to make a movie. Unfortunately for this bold and, to some, satisfying scenario, John was born on 17 Sep 1913. This means the Spanish woman got pregnant in Dec 1912, at which time Father was in New York writing his play *The Royal Mounted* and wouldn't sit down with his friends Lasky, Goldfish, and Friend at the Claridge Grill to talk about going West to make movies until late summer 1913. Father arrived in Hollywood in Dec 1913, when John was three months old (WdeM 1939:35–51; CBDeM 1959:68–72). Sometime during her first year in Hollywood, Mother became aware of a cute, dark-skinned baby boy in need of a good home. No clues survive to tell us how this came about or who the parents were. Where then did the Spanish woman of Wyoming come from? "Spanish," of course, came from Mother's calling John "a Spaniard." "Wyoming" came from *The Squaw Man*, Father's first film, and Hollywood's first feature film, a story photographed in 1914 in southern California but *set* in Wyoming. Art imitates art.

76 *Green Grow the Lilacs*—Which later became *Oklahoma!* (Scott 1972:174).

76 Javits—Jacob "Jack" Javits, opportunist U.S. senator from New York, a Democrat's Republican, usually found on both sides of the tough issues, "a hustler for the high ground of public life" (*NYT* obit 1986).

8 / N O B O D Y ' S   B A B Y

78   My sister Mary—Born 9 Jan 1914 at 655 Maryland Street, Winnipeg.

78   *Sign of the Cross*—Play by the English actor, playwright, and producer Wilson Barrett (1846–1904).

79   *Bunty Pulls the Strings*—Graham Moffat's quaint comedy (reviewed by C. Hamilton, *Bookman*, Dec 1911, 34:366–67) about a family of Lowland Scots in 1860.

81   *TLS*—14 Oct 1926:700. ". . . quiet ironic pathos . . . lively humour . . . lack of restraint here and there."

81   Arnold Bennett—*Evening Standard*, 4 July 1929 (Mylett 1974:282).

81   V. S. Pritchett—"Miss Moon has cut a romantic collection of grotesques who are quite convincing when they do not drop into the melodramatic or the sententious" (*Spectator*, 3 Aug 1929, 143:166–67).

81   White Ship—There was a White Ship Inn on Water Street in Strichen.

81   You could stick a pin—DS114. Some dictionaries call "like sixty" US Colloquial, but OED gives it as British slang from 1860, meaning "at a good rate."

82   One night Snowey—DS294–337.

83   Marcy—Everett Charles Marcy was born in Olean, Cattaraugus NY, 13 Oct 1904, died at 43 in Pasadena CA, 5 Jan 1948; he was 25 years old when he visited Mary Moon; he was a writer at M-G-M in 1945 and a member of the Screen Writers Guild 1946–47.

83   Strichen—From Gaelic *strath uigin*, valley of the *ugie*, or little water, originally known as Mormond Village. Mormond means big hill, Gaelic, *mor*, big, *monadh*, hill. Mormond Hill rises just NE of the village to a height of 768 ft.

83   Ashes—Articles clipped most likely from the *Buchan Observer*, 4 May, 8 June 1930.

83   Sunny afternoon—Probably Tuesday, 3 June 1930. Eva Skea (Evelyn Scott, ES), ltr to *Leopard*, 12 Dec 1980; Margaret Cameron Bremner to David Clark (DC, RdeM's researcher) June 1983.

85   White Horse—126 ft high, 162 ft nose to tail, modeled on the prehistoric White Horse of Berkshire.

85   Martin Wood—A grove, later destroyed by a storm, on the side of Mormond Hill between the Neuk (nook), Aunt Sadie's house on Burnshangie Road, and the White Horse Monument.

85   Hunter's Lodge—Built in 1779 by order of Captain Alexander Fraser of Strichen, son of Fraser of Strichen, Lord Strichen (ltr Gen. Sir David Fraser, 13 June 1995).

85   Proceeds—Lorna's heirs, determined by the California court, were: Mary Moon, Bill Hebditch, and Bill's father, in equal shares. Cash in Lorna's estate was less than $8600 before payment of debts. Accrued royalties added $540. Mary's share, less than $3000, was sent to her guardian, Walter Moon, who must have sent it to Leeds; whether Aunt Nellie gave it to Mary or used it to repay herself for years of nuisance and expense, is unknown. Four years later, Mary received about $4000 (1934 dollars) from the sale of Lorna's house (see Notes for Chapter 24, "Deed").

86   We were quite good friends—Sonia Dresdel (1908–76), six years older than Mary, played Mrs. Baines in *The Fallen Idol* (1948), which starred Ralph Richardson.

86   I told him he had to—HM to RdeM.

87   Made me a star—A flattering exaggeration; Chaney starred in *The Hunchback of Notre Dame* in 1923; Lorna's popular *Mr. Wu* was written four years later.

89   What is your religion?—This and most other details of this affair I learned from the pseudonymous Harry Parfit, to whom I am grateful.

90   Novel—Eva Bruce, *Call Her Rosie*, Washburn (New York) 1942, Hammond, Hammond (London) 1944. "heart-warming first novel . . . earthy humor . . . lively, satisfying story" (Charlotte Dean, *New York Times Book Review*, 4 Oct 1942:14). Author Bruce told a reporter (*Foley Trail: A History* . . . , Pembina Lobstick Historical Society 1984) she had graduated from the University of Aberdeen, which was false (see Chapter 14).

91   Prickman—*National Review*, 1 Apr 1977:376. Copyright 1977 by National Review, Inc., 215 Lexington Ave, New York NY 10016. Reprinted by permission granted 26 Mar 1993.

92   I spent my first day—MM ltr 24 Aug 1977.

9 / DADDY AND TIGER

94   HOLLYWOODLAND—Name of a real estate development, large white letters standing on the side of Mount Lee since 1923, shortened to HOLLYWOOD when LAND fell down.

94   Coconut Grove—A nightspot where the big bands played; portrayed in *Bombshell*.

95   Rod—Rod Bugiardo, Casanova's, Lisetta, Fred Wimpel, and Jack Palter are pseudonyms.

96   We had lunch—Helen Lampson Fischer, interview 4 Jan 1982.

97   Stanley Holloway—Well-known English actor (*The Titfield Thunderbolt*, 1953) and singer (*My Fair Lady*, 1964).

97   You surprised me—Dawn Day Berkshire, interview 23 Mar 1993.

98   Damsel in distress—Whom CBDeM had secretly helped 20 years before (See Notes for Chapter 8, "Proceeds").

98   Little Prince—John Lowe, *Edward James, Poet-Patron-Eccentric: A Surrealist Life*, Collins 1991.

99   Kathryn Kuhlman—(c1910–76) faith healer and Pentecostal preacher 1926–76.

99   Hi Sis—I have corrected Bill's phonetic spelling and nonexistent punctuation. Ashton Creek is near Enderby BC.

101   Tiny mother—On the Bobbs-Merrill Author Questionnaire, Lorna wrote: "I have red hair, golden brown eyes with green in them, am 4 [ft] 11½ inches tall, weigh 108 pounds."

102   Less than nothing—EB ltr 27 Nov 1967.

102   Witch on wheels—Though Cousin Don was normally very circumspect, from 1970 to 1978 he confided family secrets and gossip (which he loved) to Mary, who passed some of them on to RdeM. Herself a great letter writer, Mary exchanged letters 1948–70 with Eva Bruce, 1966–69 with Annie Lyall,

sharing many of them with RdeM. Dorine, Don, Bertie, Bill, Beryl, and Eva also wrote to me. Such letters, quoted or not, form the basis of much of this account. All letters quoted are quoted with permission. RdeM interviewed many of the persons named.

104 Articles by Mary Moon—*BC Motorist*, Nov–Dec 1972, Nov–Dec 1973, Jan–Feb, Mar–Apr, May–June 1974; Vancouver *Sunday Times*, 13, 20, 27 Mar 1977.

106 Travel books by Mary Moon—*British Columbia Calling*, Tad 1973, photography by Ted Czolowski; *Washington Calling*, Tad 1974, photography by Willie C. Clarke.

107 *Ogopogo*—Moon 1977.

107 Follow-on article: "Ogopogo, Canada's lake monster, oft seen, never snared," *Smithsonian*, Nov 1978:173–85; collected in *Great Mysteries of the West* (Fulcrum, 1993:31–37) by editor Ferenc Morton Szász, professor of history, University of New Mexico.

108 Unwanted Children—*National Enquirer*, 14 Mar 1978.

108 Safecracker—"Bobby Sutton" is RdeM's pseudonym for the adventurer's pseudonym. The manuscript, found in Mary's apartment, and a photograph of Bobby with Barbie, suggest that the story is at least partly true.

108 Freedom of Information Act—Mary Moon was a U.S. citizen, naturalized in 1952.

110 Milarepa—Story told in *National Review*, 13 Oct 1978:1294–95; related earlier by Dwight Goddard (*A Buddhist Bible* 1938:568).

10/OLD PICTURES

116 George Sand's biographer—Curtis Wilson Cate.

116 Five years—Canada had a longer war than the US did and rationing lasted longer after the war.

118 Toxima—Toxemia.

119 William Center—*Leopard Magazine*, Jan 1981:15; Aberdeen *Evening Express*, 28 Feb 1984.

119 Half a croon—Half crown, a silver coin a little smaller than a US silver dollar, 1904 equivalent of 1990 US $20.

119 Buchan dialect—A Lowland Scots dialect, called the Buchan Doric; OED (1933) defines Doric as "a broad or rustic dialect of English, Scotch, etc. 1870." Christian Watt (1833–1923), eloquent chronicler of "the Broch," that is, Fraserburgh, descendant, wife, and mother of fishermen who lived in the same house in the village of Broadsea for 2½ centuries, says the "mother tongue" she learned before English was "Buchan Doric" (Fraser 1988:4, 88, 28).

119 District of Buchan—The district has produced other notables. Three miles southwest of Strichen, at Whitehill of New Deer, during Lorna's childhood, lived a poor tailor, one of whose ten sons became a newspaperman, conceived an interest in finance, and came to New York in 1904, where in 1917 he founded a business magazine bearing the family name, *Forbes*; the founder was Bertie Forbes, who was succeeded by Malcolm, his son (Jack Webster, *Another Grain of Truth*, Fontana/Collins 1989).

121 Granddaughter—Evelyn Scott (ES), younger daughter of Aunt Sadie.

121 Author Questionnaire—The Lorna Moon Author File and Lorna's letters to her editors are in the Bobbs-Merrill Manuscripts collection at the Lilly Library, Indiana University, Bloomington. Most of Lorna's letters cited or quoted here are in that collection, but others are in RdeM's possession. RdeM is the sole copyright owner of *Doorways in Drumorty, Dark Star*, "Broken" (a poem), and all unpublished poems, letters, and other literary properties created by Lorna Moon, aka Nora Low Hebditch, by assignment from William Hebditch recorded at US Copyright Office, 1 Nov 1982, Volume 1943, Page 225; and by assignments from Bobbs-Merrill Company, Inc., Grace G. Shaw, Publisher, 12 Oct 1984.

122 The sweet, the pure—Blackmore 1989:271, 127.

122 Winds up the clock—Margaret Bremner to DC; born 2 Apr 1906, Margaret Bremner taught school in Strichen 1929–30, later worked as a journalist.

123 Dad had spoken out—Eva Bruce letter 11 Nov 1962.

123 Sovereign—a gold coin of 7/8" diameter, with a portrait of Queen Victoria or Edward VII, equal in 1935 to £1 in gold or US $4.80, equal in 1993 to about US $90. A heap of gold sovereigns was a worthy sum in a country village in 1905.

123 David Toulmin—Pen name of John Reid. Born in 1913, 27 years after Lorna, Toulmin was a farm laborer from the age of 14. Silent movies inspired him to write stories of country life. Having been schooled like Lorna through the eighth grade, he read nearly all of Shakespeare and developed a graceful literary style. After he was 50, his stories and novels began to be published and praised (Webster 1989:103–8). Using the information available to him, Toulmin wrote admiring introductions for the 1980–81 editions of Lorna's books, unfortunately marred by errors. For example, he wrote (*DD* 1981:8–9) that Lorna's parents "banned her books" in Strichen and that "none of her family took any real pride in her composition." No evidence supports the first contention; good evidence and testimony contradict the second. Though a literary man, Toulmin allowed ancient rumors to distort his reading of Lorna's story "The Funeral" instead of using the story to test the rumors. Toulmin the novelist should have known that a man who mixes mortar in his daughter's casket does not keep her books for 20 years, safe, clean, and whole, ready to be photographed for a new edition.

123 Publisher friend—Jock Rennie, proprietor of Gourdas House.

123 Friend in Oxford—Rodney Needham, professor of social anthropology at All Souls College.

123 Man in Buchan—David Clark (DC), who did fine work. I am also grateful to Dot Bennett of the Anderson and Woodman Library and Institute in Strichen, the Margarets McLeman, mother and daughter, TV producer Michael Steele, novelist David Toulmin, journalist and biographer Jack Webster, and numerous informants who spoke to David Clark or me in Scotland.

124 Cabbages—Paul Hawken, *The Magic of Findhorn*, Tao Publications (Boston) 1974.

124 Troch story—Toulmin, *Leopard*, Nov 1980:23–24; Webster 1989:117–18. Maggie Whyte Watson, a Benzies cousin, said to DC: "That troch story. Never, never. He [Charles Low] wasn't a man like that."

124 Father was very proud—AL (Annie Lyall) ltr 6 Feb 1967.

124 I was coming back—Margaret Bremner to DC.

125 Bandeen flatly denied—To Evelyn Scott (ES ltr 12 Dec 1980).

125 Nora's casket—Inches 6½h × 6½d × 9½w, rosewood (?), metal identification disk "Hollywood Crematory, 2337, Los Angeles," brought to Strichen
26 May 1930 by E. Marcy, kept by Charles Low until he died in 1952,
preserved by his housekeeper, Margaret McLeman, who on 10 June 1984
gave it to RdeM, who examined and photographed it, finding no scratches
or other signs of rough use, and next day gave it to the Anderson and
Woodman Library in Strichen.

125 Divinely gifted—Toulmin, Introduction to *Dark Star* 1980:3.

125 Reputable villagers—Jack Webster ltr to RdeM 20 Nov 1992.

125 Libel suits—Eva Bruce ltr 5 Dec 1961.

125 Niver kent—I never knew rightly what was ado with him (*Leopard*, Jan
1981:15).

11/TEN DOWNING STREET

126 Robb Gibb's Contract—I am grateful to Donald A. Low of the University
of Stirling for his letter (26 Feb 1996) identifying Robb Gibb.

127 Cocky Low—Maggie Whyte Watson to DC. MWW lived in Strichen from
the age of two to 35, 1904–37.

127 Terrible place—Margaret Bremner to DC.

127 Havering—Foolish talk.

128 Boothby—Forty years younger than Charles Low, Robert Boothby (1900–
86) was called a fearless rebel, intelligent, humane, warmhearted, and possessed of erratic brilliance. "His claim to parliamentary distinction, superb
oratory apart, was his fearless and prescient espousal of ideas" (Biffin 1991).
It should come as no surprise that Charles Low and Bob Boothby, two
outspoken advocates of unpopular ideas, would take pleasure in each other's company (Robert Boothby, *Recollections of a Rebel*, Hutchinson [London]
1978; Alistair Horne, *Harold Macmillan*, Viking 1989; John Biffin, Boothby,
the Perennial Backbencher, *Guardian Weekly* [London], 28 July 1991:28).

129 Philophonical—Liking the sound.

129 Bad investment—When Da Low's 100 shares of Eileen Alannah were sold
in 1952, they brought £3/16/8., or about $10. The Lows' financial fortunes
varied. On North Street, they scraped along. At the Temperance Hotel they
were comfortable. On High Street they had money for time of need. "She
had to keep the house. But they used to have money, because when he
recuperated from his operation [1930], he was in Kepplestone Nursing
Home in Aberdeen, which was private and expensive" (Margaret Bremner
to DC). "There always seemed to be money when it was needed! They
had a very small pension, 7/6 weekly. . . . Mrs. Low worked very hard
herself, kept lodgers and had the tea room. . . . However, with failing health
and the war years I thought they were quite poor. . . . Da Low was failing
for a lot of years" (McLeman Notes). When Charles Low died, on 12 Aug
1952, in his house at 13 High Street, his estate was valued at £1606/6/5,
comprising securities worth £856/6/5 and buildings at 11/13 High Street that

brought £750 when sold. His will provided a bequest of £100 for his house-keeper, Margaret McLeman, and a bequest of £200 for each of his living children (Annie Lyall and Eva Bruce, who were not specifically named).

130 Grandson in Canada—Charles Murray McCallum Lyall (1907–51), son of Annie Low Lyall; Maggie Low's ltr 12 Aug 1939; Charles Low's ltr 14 July 1939.

131 Sculptor—Douglas Bissett; the bust of Charles Low is in the Strichen Library.

131 School—Strichen Higher Grade School, called Strichen School, three blocks south of 13 High Street on Market Terrace, near the railroad track.

133 Ramsay MacDonald—Mary Hamilton, *J. Ramsay MacDonald*, Thomas Seltzer 1924; Lord Elton, *The Life of James Ramsay MacDonald*, Collins (London) 1939; David Marquand, *Ramsay MacDonald*, Jonathan Cape (London) 1977.

133 Charles Low's mother—Mary Ann Low was born on Castle Street in Fraserburgh in 1834 or 1835, a contemporary of Christian Watt (Fraser 1988). Charles Low was born at 18 White Conduit Terrace, Islington West, London, 19 Oct 1861. On 29 Apr 1875, Mary Ann Low, 40, married Samuel Flint, widower, a London police constable; their daughter, Eva Flint, married another policeman, who contracted syphilis from prostitutes and passed it on to her; she went blind and was known in Strichen as "blind Eva." Blind Eva's son Ted died 23 June 1936 in an auto accident near Doncaster in Yorkshire on his way to holiday at his home in St. Neots; traveling with him, his cousin Sadie Low Scott, 41, mother of Jean and Evelyn, also died.

133 Balmoral—Balmoral Castle was purchased by Prince Albert in 1852.

134 No wonder—"James McDonald Ramsay" (sic), *John Bull*, Sep 1915 (Marquand 1977).

134 Braes—Slopes. Charles Low took pride in the White Horse and would climb Mormond Hill with granddaughters Jean and Evelyn Scott to pull weeds that obscured its form, then sit down to picnic with the girls in the Horse's eye and tell them the fanciful local legend of how it came to be there (Jean Scott, "The White Horse," BBC 1948); in later years he would pay village boys to climb up and pull the weeds.

134 I am humiliated—An old clipping, They Call It 10, Downing Street, from an unidentified NE Scottish newspaper, 28 Aug 1950, preserved in Canada by Charles Low's great-grandson C. J. C. Lyall.

135 A splendid woman—Charles Low's reverie is constructed from research data. Young Charlie Low, the Lows' second child, worked in construction in New Zealand, didn't marry, apparently left no children, and died in his sixties when a building block fell on him (Dorine Bruce ltr 13 Apr 1983).

1 2 / P U T T I N G   O N   A I R S

137 They had an air—Quotations from Cousin Evelyn combine selections from letters, interviews with DC, and conversations with RdeM.

137 She'd a likit—*Leopard* Jan 1981.

138 Big one, little one—LM ltr in Among Our Contributors, *Century Magazine*, July 1922 (permission to reproduce letters written by Lorna Moon and comments on them by editors published among the unnumbered advertising

pages of *Century Magazine*, Dec 1921, July, Nov 1922, Jan, Nov 1924, given by *Current History*, 30 Dec 1992).

138   Annie and Sadie had blue eyes—Eva Bruce ltr 10 July 1966.

139   Legitimize—Sarah Anne Low (Annie Lyall) was born on 9 Jan 1883; her parents, Charles Low and Maggie Benzies, were married on 30 June 1883.

139   Porridge—Annie Lyall quoted by Margot Heimburger ltr 16 June 1975.

139   I don't remember any caresses—Eva Bruce ltr 5 Dec 1961.

140   Mrs. Low was—Margaret Bremner to DC.

140   Dad and I were very thick—Account constructed by RdeM from LM ltr late Feb 1929 and DS65–67 (see *Citations* at the beginning of the Notes).

141   I dinna know—*Leopard* Jan 1981.

142   Muckle gowk—Great half-wit.

143   Pebble in the boot—Since the butler's contribution was at most a donation of sperm, he would presumably wish to remain anonymous. After having his scoundrelly way with trusting Mary Ann, or hiding his honorable disapproval while the laird exercised his *droit du roué*, the butler may have married and great-grandsired respectable folk, who would not now welcome a blot on the patriarchal salver. History, however, demands one vital fact: the register of births does name the butler, and his name was Charles. Can one doubt that Mary Ann must have loved the butler if she named the baby Charles? But soft!—the wise man leapeth not into the wrong bed of sin. Charles is a great name in Scotland. Suppose the Deeside laird himself also was named Charles, after the king or the Bonnie Prince. Mary Ann's unplanned child might then have been a proud inheritor of the laird's great first name, noble blood, and blue genes. In the miniseries, the laird addresses the butler by his family name, while the butler answers with "Your Lairdship." Only the passionate Mary Ann calls the highborn rascal Charlie, for a few feverish seconds in the dimly lit grip of ill-advised affection.

13/A PERSON OF THE BETTER CLASS

145   Talk of turning in one's grave—AL ltr 22 Mar 1953 to McIntosh & Hamilton, Fraserburgh.

145   Strichen Higher Grade School—The literacy of a college graduate in the United States today does well to equal that of an 1890s Scottish 8th grader. Normal Correspondence College, 110 Avondale Square, London SE, 1903.

146   Given to Annie Low—CJCL ltr 26 July 1983.

146   Banker—James Murray Lyall, born a twin 6 Jan 1883 in MacDuff, NE Scotland, lived in nearby Banff; was a banker in Turriff, 15 miles west of Strichen; came to work in Strichen and met Annie; they were married c1906; emigrated to Canada c1910; left home 1934; died 8 June 1935 in San Diego.

147   He was a charming little lad—AL ltrs 6 Feb, 22 Nov 1967, 13 Apr 1953.

147   One evening—Eva Bruce ltr 11 July 1966.

147   Alpine Club—Mary Biner, *Calgary Herald*, 1968; clippings, photos, letters, and other mementos saved by Annie.

148   Annie Lyall Blvd—F. S. Morley, The Voice of One, newspaper, no name or date.

148 Eva Bruce came—A cotter is a poor Scottish tenant farmer. Peats are pieces, or bricks, of bog moss, to be dried and used for fuel.

149 Divorce—"My mother told me that my grandfather committed suicide because my grandmother wouldn't give him a divorce" (Ingrid ltr 9 Feb 1993). "Grannie's husband left her for another woman" (PL ltr 1 Feb 1976).

149 Six months later—San Diego Union, 9 June 1935, II-1 and Classified announcement; James Lyal (sic) death record, State of California. Newspaper story supplied by Rhoda E. Kruse, San Diego Public Library, to whom I am grateful. Gunn and Goodbody are actual names.

149 Annie felt much better—Letters from and interviews with Charles James Calhoun Lyall (CJCL) & Penelope Maeve Lyall (PL); Registration of Marriage, Province of Alberta, 3 Apr 1929, Record No. 273.

151 Spoke like someone raised in London—"Nana's [Annie's] Scottish accent came and went depending on whom she was talking to" (CJCL interview 1 Dec 1992). "I remember asking my mother why Nancy [Annie] spoke with an English accent if she was a Scot" (Ingrid ltr 31 March 1993).

152 $1.25 an hour—AL ltr 25 Jan 1967.

152 Five languages, hobnobbing—AL ltr 25 Jan 1967.

153 You say you are writing—Quotations from letters written by Ingrid to RdeM.

158 Name change—"Irene" was not the first new name. In Vancouver and at the Alpine Club and ever after in Alberta, Annie Lyall chose to be known as "Nancy," a name she may have judged to be more English and more genteel than "Annie." Cousin Charles called her "Nana." To simplify the reader's task, I have called her only "Annie."

When Da Low died in 1952 he was a man of modest means. His will provided bequests of £200 for each of his living children (determined after his death to be Annie Lyall and Eva Bruce). The remainder was £945/16/4 to be divided (£157/12/8 each) among his living grandchildren (deemed to be Jean and Evelyn Scott, Dorine and Don Bruce, and Bill Hebditch) and subdivided (£52/10/11 each) among the children of his dead grandson, Charlie Lyall (Ingrid, Charles, Penelope). Nora's second and third children did not receive anything, Mary because she was a misbegotten Moon and Richard because he was not only illegitimate but also hardly more than a 30-year-old female rumor with a silver spoon in its mouth—not the sort of heir unapparent one sends money to, or even a copy of the will, which the poor fellow had to beg 30 years later from his respectable, magnanimous big brother Bill. In 1953, Annie wrote to the lawyers in Scotland (AL ltr 22 Mar 1953 to McIntosh & Hamilton) saying she hoped the money would come soon, because she needed it to pay for treatment for her arthritis. She didn't give them Ingrid's address, so they sent Ingrid's share to Annie. I asked Ingrid if she remembered receiving £52/10/11 from the estate of Charles Low. She replied: "Until your letter I had never heard of Charles Low or of the pounds, shillings, and pence he thoughtfully left to his great-grandchildren. Annie never mentioned it. She told me I was strong and could always take care of myself. In her will she left a thousand dollars to each of my children, but she told me to my face that there was nothing for me." Penny said: "Grannie had tags on everything, and she said some of her things were to go to Ingrid," but Ingrid recalled: "After Grannie's death, Dr. Margot was so incensed by her treatment of me that she packed up her bedroom suite, her glass-front secretary, mink stole, copper kettle, and Wedgwood tea set and shipped them all to me at her own expense. She didn't say that Grannie had wanted me to have them. She said Grannie 'had a lot to be forgiven for.' "

158 Just had a visit—AL ltr to MM, fall 1969.

14/A WITCH ON WHEELS

159 A fine portrait—The photograph of Maggie Low is in the Anderson and Woodman Library in Strichen.

159 Dropped from the family—McLeman Notes.

160 Malevolent females—EB ltr 1942.

160 Bob Bruce—Robert D. Bruce, born 31 May 1882 in Ontario, came west to Edmonton, in Alberta, where he and two friends, Charles McPhee and Fred Elsie, worked in the Hudson Bay Store. Friday 13 Mar 1908, Bruce, McPhee & Elsie, General Merchants, pitched a tent in Entwistle, on the Pembina River, and went into business for themselves. Entwistle was named after Jim Entwistle, a locomotive engineer who bought the site for a railroad settlement. When the steel tracks came to Entwistle, the partners went westward setting up tent stores across the plains and forests ahead of the Canadian Northern Railroad. From these tents they purveyed dry goods and tobacco to the construction crews, then came back and built a proper store in Entwistle (*Edmonton Journal*, 5 May 1952; *Foley Trail: A History. . . .* Pembina Lobstick Historical Society 1984, Hazel Fausak, editor, Box 85, Evansburg). On 7 Oct 1913 Robert married Eva Low at New Westminster BC, in the presence of Eva's sister Annie Lyall and of Bob's half-sister from his mother's first marriage, Lilian MacKay. Other half-siblings were Rose Mackay and Peter John Mackay. In 1895 Peter Mackay had married Isabel Ecclestone McPherson (1875–1928), "Auntie Belle," the poet. In 1918 Bruce, McPhee & Elsie built a store in Evansburg; in 1927 the Bruces moved to Evansburg. In 1940 on Robert's doctor's orders, the Bruces moved to Vancouver. In 1941 they bought a house on Galiano Island. Robert worked in Burril's store, which he and Dorine's husband, Ed Wilson, bought and operated. In the late 1960s the Bruces moved to Campbell River on Vancouver Island, where Dorine was living. Robert died at 90 on 1 July 1972. Eva died at 92 on 22 Oct 1983.

160 On some winter days—EB ltr 19 Sep 1969.

160 It was a wonderful place—This and other quotations by permission from Dorine are from letters written 1978–91. Dorine died at 79 in Campbell River on 21 Feb 1994.

161 Kidnapped by her father—"She did write me one time that she had borne a daughter to DeMille" (Eva Bruce ltr to McIntosh & Hamilton, Solicitors, Fraserburgh, 24 Apr 1953); "a daughter she had to Cecil B. DeMille" (Annie Lyall ltr to McI. & H. 22 Mar 1953).

161 I published—EB ltr 1942. Pyjamas, *Chatelaine* (Toronto), June 1932:19, 42, 44; Making Over Mary, *Chatelaine*, May 1933:14, 15, 32, 37.

161   A piece of fluff—LM ltr 2 May 1929. Wedding of the Wheat was posthumously published in Feb 1932, Eva's Making Over Mary in May 1933.

162   Eva's novel—*Call Her Rosie* 1942:106, 126–27.

162   Lively and satisfying—Charlotte Dean, *New York Times Book Review*, 4 Oct 1942:14.

163   Without the pipes and drums—EB ltr 1942.

163   Why was Eva cast out—ES to RdeM 1984.

163   *Braes o'Mar*—A poignant song recalling Mar's Rebellion, led by the ill-advised Earl of Mar, who on 6 Sep 1715 defied the English king, George I, by raising his blue rallying flag, or standard, at Braemar on the river Dee (DS112).

164   Banana—ES to RdeM. Anna and Nanna did get a younger brother (Charles Low ltr 14 Feb 1947) but his name was not Banana.

164   Whether Henry thought—*Call Her Rosie* 1942:25, 97.

165   Death was not a doorway—EB ltrs 8 Nov, 5 Dec 1961; 27 Nov 1967; 14 May, 23 Nov 1970.

15 / GETTING AWAY

167   Eulogies—Bobbs-Merrill Author Questionnaire, 1928.

167   Plotting to get away—In *Dark Star* Nancy Pringle dreams of escaping parental authority (DS47).

167   Dark-haired—Blackmore 1989:xix–xx, 2, 19, 61, 64, 65, 149, 234, 363, 377–79, 387, 496, 505, 509, 547. *Lorna Doone* was first published in 1869.

168   Gorse—Lorna Doone's "scent of the gorse" (Blackmore 1989:363) finds an echo in Lorna Moon's "bitter scent of broken bracken stems" (Flat on My Back, 1929).

168   Silvery voice—In *Dark Star*, Nancy's "laugh, dancing like a silver ball on the face of the cliff, rose up to him . . . she called, with many silver voices" (DS267). *Lorna Doone* and *Dark Star* show other parallels. In both stories a boy and a girl meet in a rocky, mossy, sylvan retreat by a waterfall, first when she is a child, later when she is grown. One fascinates the other. The fascinator is an orphan and ward of Chancery, who will be rich when old enough. The fascinators are Lorna Doone and Harvey Brune; both have distant ties to Italy. Lorna Doone is "of an ill-starred race." Nancy Pringle was born "under a dark star." (Blackmore 1989:59, 63, 123, 489, 493, 509, 510; DS57, 60, 100, 212.)

168   Unschooled Lorna Doone—Though Nora Low was a healthy child, who went to school in Strichen for eight years, Lorna Moon told Bobbs-Merrill (Questionnaire 1928): "I was fortunate enough to escape 'schooling' almost altogether on account of poor health. I read endlessly, but since my only source of reading was an old library, I was restricted to the classics, with a weekly fling at the Bible!"

168   This Mortal Sappho—Lorna had many women friends, but there is no sign that she ever desired a woman. A woman attracted to women would not choose to spend eight unmarried years in bed with the vain, unsubtle Walter Moon, or give away her female child and never see her or exchange a word with her again. She described her book as "the intimate journal of an

amoureuse" (LM ltr 15 June 1929) and may have seen Sappho as a woman like herself. One can hardly believe she would terrify her publisher with a lesbian novel, however subtle or poetic. Radclyffe Hall's restrained *Well of Loneliness* had caused a scandal the year before, and Lorna's editor had changed "breasts" to "bosoms" in *Dark Star* (DS311). Born twenty years after Lorna, not in a Scottish village but in sophisticated New York, Agnes de Mille saw Sappho as a model for creative women. Indignantly she defended her against accusations of sexual misconduct with the women of Lesbos. Baseless defamation, she said, a whispering campaign by "the boys in Athens" (1958:214), envious men who wanted to disparage women's achievements. So much for honey-voiced love songs to adorable girls.

168   Bob Dingwall—AL ltr 6 Feb 1967.

169   The arrival of the new watchmaker—DS70–71.

170   Circuses—ES to RdeM.

171   Facing the wind—DS15.

172   At Entwistle on train days—LM picture postcard to "Miss Low" (probably Sadie) at the Temperance Hotel; no date, salutation, or signature; given to RdeM by ES.

173   Will knew little—"Will knew nothing about farming. I think he pictured himself hunting and fishing on his acres. Indeed, he brought rods and guns with him for the purpose—a gentleman of leisure!" (AL ltr 6 Feb 1962).

173   When the money—AL ltr 6 Feb 1962; MM notes on interview with Bill Hebditch at Kelowna BC (27 Sep 1977).

174   Lonely, cold, and hungry—Told to Annie by Bill Hebditch (AL ltr 6 Feb 1962).

16/THE CAREER WOMAN

175   Lorna demoted—As told to Alma Whitaker (Bobbs-Merrill PR release, 1928). Alma Whitaker (1881–1956) was an English newspaperwoman who was on the staff of the *Los Angeles Times* for many years. Only 5 years older than Lorna, she apparently believed she was 18 years older, and she acted like a big sister, helping Lorna to publicize an imaginary story of her life, most of which RdeM supposes Whitaker believed. When RdeM was "discovered" in the foundling home (see Notes for Chapter 7, "Wonder Baby Not Worrying"), Whitaker reproduced Neil McCarthy's fanciful tale of the baby's origin but called the note found with the baby "unconvincing," which suggests she suspected something else was going on.

175   Sunshine Society—*Winnipeg Telegram*, 5 Jan 1914:9.

176   Journalists—Lorna's letter to Bobbs-Merrill (10 Dec 1925) suggesting reviewers for *Doorways in Drumorty* mentions many journalists; in Winnipeg: Col. Garnet Clay Porter, Genevieve Lipsett Skinner, Knox W. McGee, M. E. Nichols, and Mollie Glenn, all of whom are listed as journalists in Henderson's Winnipeg City Directory, 1914. I am grateful to Gail M. Coyston, Library Dept, City of Winnipeg, for help with research.

176   Acted in plays—In view of stories Walter told Mary Moon, it does seem likely Lorna acted in *The Sign of the Cross* and *Bunty Pulls the Strings* in Winnipeg, but she told Alma Whitaker that "Bud Bainbridge of the Shubert

Theater [in Minneapolis] decided she would be an ideal 'Bunty' . . . and persuaded her to become [for the first time, that is] an actress. She toured with this show quite successfully." No record of the tour has been found or of *Bunty Pulls the Strings* at any Minneapolis theater while Lorna was living there. I am grateful to Robert A. Epstein for research in Minneapolis.

176   Accounting job—For Peters Home Building Company; promoted to Vice President and Treasurer in 1920. Walter and Lorna Moon lived in Apt 2, 1119 Franklin Ave (Davison's Minneapolis City Directory, 1919:1271, 1920: 1401); Lorna is listed as "writer."

176   Syndicated editorials—LM ltr in Among Our Contributors, *Century*, July 1922.

176   Review of *Male and Female*—No review of the film was found in the *Minneapolis Journal*. Two favorable reviews in the *Minneapolis Tribune* (8, 22 Feb 1920) are unsigned; neither is stylish enough to be by Lorna, and one calls Scottish playwright James M. Barrie "the eminent English author." Lorna (ltr 10 Dec 1925) suggested Carlton Miles to review *Doorways*; Miles reviewed plays in the *Minneapolis Journal*; "where they like my red hair" (LM ltr 14 Mar 1929).

176   Babylonian orgy—William Ernest Henley's Babylonian theme makes a brief literary appearance in Barrie's play; CBDeM brought it to graphic flower in the movie.

176   Met DeMille—It is unlikely that CBDeM visited Minneapolis 1917–20 or that Lorna met him anywhere before going to Hollywood.

177   *Affairs of Anatol*—Six writers got screen credit for the movie story, though of course CBDeM was the author-in-chief: "Scenario by Jeanie Macpherson, Beulah Marie Dix, Lorna Moon, and Elmer Harris, suggested by Arthur Schnitzler's play *Anatol* and the paraphrase thereof by Granville-Barker." For a list of films written by LM, see Lorna Moon Filmography, after the Notes.

177   "Divorce"—AL ltr 13 April 1953. Lorna had only one husband, Will Hebditch, from whom she was never divorced.

177   You know, I practically—RdeM interviews Helene Moon (1904–86), 16 Jan 1983.

178   Snobbish critics—*Motion Picture News*, 24 Sep 1921; Robert Sherwood, *Life*, 18 Sep 1921; both quoted by Ringgold & Bodeen 1969:197. Sherwood became a noted playwright.

178   Sigh for the moon—AL ltr 22 Mar 1953.

178   Convinced that I was—LM ltr, Among Our Contributors, *Century*, 104, July 1922.

178   Lorna Moon, the scenarist—*NYT*, 12 Dec 1921:20.

179   Decorated it herself—LM wrote: "I like decorating houses and have real talent for this" (Bobbs-Merrill Questionnaire 1928, Hobbies).

179   A busy year—Paramount advertisement, *Vanity Fair*, June 1921:20.

179   Olga Printzlau—*Morning Telegraph*, 1 May, 18 Dec 1921; 24 Dec 1922. Olga's first photoplay was *The White Faun* for D. W. Griffith in New York; her one-act play was *Window Panes* (Academy of Motion Picture Arts and Sciences Archives).

180   Watch out—Rita Weiman, a New York writer (Frances Notes).

181   William's lecture—Ideas drawn from WdeM, Speeches and Essays, 1905–13, ms.

182   Fran-Sis—RdeM ltr to Frances Beranger 21 Nov 1983.

17/OUR LADY OF DEFINITE OPINIONS

183   So long ago—Conversations 1981–93 with Agnes de Mille.

184   Father sired—AdeM 1990:184.

188   Confiscation of public rights—AdeM 1990:188.

188   Votes stolen—Lothrop Stoddard, *Master of Manhattan: The Life of Richard Croker*, Longmans, Green 1931:84–86, 179–82.

Henry George proposed to take in tax all of the land's "natural value," which other economists have said is equivalent to its productive potential or rental value. Later Georgists proposed to reduce the tax percentage. "Potential rent" or some other arbitrary calculation appears to be required for tax assessment when a confiscatory Single Tax drives the price of land toward zero.

A just society, George said, requires "association in equality." The Single Tax, he believed, would fairly redistribute wealth without damaging the market, but—like labor, capital, and entrepreneurial talents—land is an economic resource, whose price reflects alternative uses. Taxing changes in its value would lead to significant misallocation of resources (Walter E. Williams, Professor of Economics, George Mason University, personal communication, 31 May 1994).

Henry George believed that as the government's only tax the Single Tax would limit government spending and keep government small. He did not reckon with the insatiable appetite of career politicians and bureaucrats for higher taxes, bigger government, greater power, and more intrusive social rule, or their deviousness in working their will on the trusting taxpayer. His theory erroneously assumes that politicians and bureaucrats will impose taxes with restraint, will act less selfishly and less dishonestly than businessmen, and will be able to make economic decisions that are as sound as those made by free markets. A hundred years ago such assumptions seemed reasonable to many idealistic improvers of society, including Ramsay MacDonald, and George Bernard Shaw, who said Henry George had made the speech that converted him to social reform. (Charles A. Barker, Henry George, *International Encyclopedia of the Social Sciences*, 1968:151–55; *New Palgrave Dictionary of Economics*, 1987; Henry George, The Single Tax, in AdeM 1973:386–91; Charles Hooper on Henry George, in David R. Henderson, editor, *Fortune Encyclopedia of Economics*, 1993.) I am grateful to David R. Henderson for critical review of an early draft of this discussion.

188   Theoretically most defensible—Stephen Kresge and Leif Wenar, editors, *Hayek on Hayek: An Autobiographical Dialogue*, University of Chicago Press 1994:63. Friedrich Hayek (1899–1992) and Milton Friedman, free-market economists, received the Nobel Prize in Economics.

190   Interested in money—Agnes Notes; AdeM 1990:166. Agnes apparently didn't know that Father took no money from *The King of Kings* and assigned his income from *The Ten Commandments* (1956) to a charitable trust. Of all

his films he was proudest of *The King of Kings*. He strove to put God's word on the screen and believed that God approved of his efforts. He believed that Christ had come to save sinners, and hoped his sins would be forgiven. To Agnes, Father's piety was either hypocritical pretense or foolish belief in quaint myths, though of course religion had inspired much great art.

190   Griper—Eddie Salven, CBDeM's able assistant director for many years.

190   Pottenger—Francis Marion Pottenger, M.D. [1869–1962], *The Fight Against Tuberculosis: An Autobiography*, Henry Schuman 1952:130–37; Cora ltr 18 Sep 1923.

191   Wouldn't appoint her—Easton 1996:82.

191   I never heard—AdeM 1990:174; Easton 1996:82, 100–15. Easton refers to Agnes's "arrogance" (345) and insolent pride ("hubris," 306) in professional relations. I reminded Agnes that Father had endowed a chair of drama at USC, whose first occupant was William; she had forgotten that, and she added it (AdeM 1990:189).

192   Richard de Mille disagrees—AdeM 1990:191. At my suggestion Agnes removed several errors of fact and some insupportable opinions from her essay, but she persisted in saying that the name de Mille is "French or Dutch depending on how you read the family history" (1990:159). The error comes from her having heard Father spinning tales about his (French) Huguenot ancestors; he may have had Huguenot ancestors, but their name was not de Mille (see Chapter 1).

192   Neglected William—AdeM 1990:190.

192   Somehow—AdeM 1990:160.

193   Opinionated—Agnes called herself "a highly opinionated woman" (Easton 1996:377).

193   President shot—AdeM 1991:191; *The Man Who Dared*, 1933; *NYT*, 17 Feb 1933:1. In 1933, Giuseppe Zangara fired five times at President-elect Roosevelt, hit four other people instead, and fatally wounded Mayor Anton Cermak; in 1981, John Hinckley nearly killed Ronald Reagan. Agnes received the Medal of Arts in 1986. At the luncheon after the award ceremony, she said to President Reagan: "You're a much better actor now than when you were in the movies." Presumably he smiled. He was always a gentleman. The following year Agnes completed the manuscript of *Martha* (Easton 1996:452, 463).

193   Hounded—*NYT*, 5 Feb 1982, II-8.

194   Un-American—Easton 1996:448–49.

194   Publicity photo—Anne Edwards, *The DeMilles*, Abrams 1988:135.

195   Incontrovertible fact—AdeM 1990:184.

18 / THE LOVE AFFAIR

196   I remember—See Notes Chapter 7, "Dear Cecilia."

196   It was much later—The diary crisis occurred in 1946, 18 years after William and Clara's wedding in 1928, 25 years after William's affair with Lorna, which had ended 7 years before William and Clara were married; William was 68, Clara was 60, Frances was 37. Frances told Margaret about it in 1959.

199   Cliver quine—Clever lassie.

199   Gather ye rosebuds—Robert Herrick (1592–1674), To the Virgins, To Make Much of Time.

199   Despises Christian Science—"PERSONAL DISLIKES: I can't stand an English accent, fat men, little dogs, Christian Scientists, and people with a bedside manner" (Bobbs-Merrill Author Questionnaire, 1928).

201   True to Lorna—Lorna could not have "broken off with William," as Agnes put it, before mid-May 1921. She left town during the summer and may have seen him as late as August or September. Clara's first picture with William, *Miss Lulu Bett*, was completed in November; the writing must have begun months earlier. This suggests at least a period of weeks when William could have been seeing Lorna while working with Clara. Sixty years later Frances recalled: "When Paramount sent Mother out to do scripts for William, it was a very, very few months before they became lovers." Frances's inexact memory and the facts as they are known are not sufficient to prove the case either way, but I think William's sense of what a gentleman would do and the practical difficulties of managing two mistresses, going home to a wife, and directing movies all at the same time make two-timing unlikely. Agnes needn't have skipped a year to protect her father's claim of being faithful in his infidelity.

19/THE CONSPIRACY

202   Gleaming forth—F. H. K. de La Motte-Fouqué, *Undine: A Romance*, 1811, which H. C. de Mille read aloud to his family. William had written children's books and was entirely at ease with water sprites and fairy queens (William C. de Mille, *Christmas Spirit & Votes for Fairies*, John Martin's House 1913; *The Forest Ring*, G. H. Doran 1914).

203   Twenty years ago—"Most people who are infected with the tubercle bacillus have a latent or subclinical infection, and most of them will not develop the disease unless something stresses their immune system." (*Science News*, 6 Feb 1988:92–93.)

204   TB and pregnancy—F. M. Pottenger, Tuberculosis and Pregnancy, *International Abstract of Surgery*, Nov 1921:353–58; The Psychology of the Tuberculous Patient, *Diseases of the Chest*, Jan 1938:8–10; *The Fight Against Tuberculosis*, 1952.

      "Under no circumstances should a mother with active tuberculosis nurse her child. In a case of open tuberculosis the safety of the child demands immediate removal from contact with the mother. . . . One pregnancy is usually stood all right—in many instances two; but I have seen an increasing number of patients break down after a third or more." (F. M. Pottenger, Indications for Therapeutic Abortion in Tuberculosis, *JAMA*, 22 Dec 1934: 1907–10.)

206   Defer formal filing—It was deferred for 18 years; Neil liked to keep the client's options open (see Notes for Chapter 4, "Adoption"). I am grateful to Andrew H. Swartz for his critique of Neil McCarthy's presentation to his client, which, like other conversations given without quotation marks, is constructed by inference from the known facts and the characters of the participants.

206   Castelar Creche—A one-story foundling home (Creche means nursery) at 818 Castelar Street, near City Hall, Los Angeles.

206   *The Woman*—William's 1911 play; see Chapter 3.

208   Speed, bonnie boat—*Skye Boat Song*, Harold Edwin Boulton, 1859–1935. In the Author Questionnaire (see Notes for Chapter 10) Lorna listed the name Flora Macdonald as one of her own.

209   Warlock—A thing or person that doesn't use human reasoning (DD91).

209   Frances Marion—1888–1973, maiden name Marion Benson Owens; married Fred Thomson 1919 (Cari Beauchamp, *Creative Screenwriting*, Fall 1994:55–66; *Without Lying Down: Frances Marion and the Powerful Women of Early Hollywood*, Scribner 1997). I am grateful to Cari Beauchamp for sharing her research.

20/THE SHORT-STORY WRITER

211   Lorna's first story—Silk Both Sides (*Century* 103:191–95, Dec 1921).

211   Lorna Moon quarries—Augustus Muir, quoted in publisher's promotion, 1925.

212   Dear old whimsical—LM ltrs 6 Jan 1929, 9 May, 10 Dec 1925.

212   Buried as Barried—DLC ltr to English agent, 9 Mar 1926.

212   The boldest knight—Barson Maith, "A Woman's Heart."

213   Freeze the rivers—Penciled lines found with old pictures kept by Sadie.

213   Second story—Feckless Maggie Ann (*Century* 103:877–86, Apr 1922).

213   Fifty readers—Among Our Contributors, *Century* 104, July 1922.

213   Third story—The Sinning of Jessie MacLean (*Century* 104:385–93, July 1922).

213   Empty arms—Among Our Contributors, *Century* 104, July 1922.

214   Dear Mr. McCarthy—LM ltr 28 Sep 1922. The enclosed pitiful note has not been found. Photos of the baby were taken at 7 months by Dr. Pottenger to show the prospective parents that he was normal, healthy, and in good spirits. Still, they ran some risk. In the 1920s the only paternity test was family resemblance, a test I passed as I grew older, but when Father made the decision he had to rely on his judgment, formed while Lorna was working for him, that, however headstrong she might be, he could trust her solemn word, and on William's belief that he was the father of the child. Once the boy was in his house, Father would have to keep him.

215   *Los Angeles Times*—Oct 1922: contest (12, 29), Conan Doyle (15), shot (25), paint can (16), abandoned infant (24), son finds mother (25), *Lorna Doone* (28); winner announced (12 Nov).

215   Nine months—*Hollywood Citizen*, 14 Nov 1922.

216   Fourth story, Kirsty—The Corp' (*Century* 105:91–97, Nov 1922).

216   Engine trouble—Among Our Contributors, *Century* 107, Jan 1924.

216   Lost a year—Two years of hospital isolation, 1923 and 1924, followed the transfer of the baby, but Neil McCarthy would write to Cecilia that "some weeks" after the transfer Mrs. McCarthy heard from a friend that "at a luncheon party Lorna had told the entire story to the guests at the table and that she and Bill were the parents." As Rosemary McCarthy said, Neil could really dream stuff up.

216   Fifth story, young love—The Tattie Doolie (*Century* 107:448–61, Jan 1924).

217 Sixth story—The Courtin' of Sally Ann (*Woman's Home Companion* 52:27ff, Oct 1925). Written May 1924.

217 Big deaf face—DS217.

217 Broken I am—"Broken" (*Woman's Home Companion* 51:24, July 1924; rights reverted to author's estate, assigned to RdeM, see Notes for Chapter 10, "Author Questionnaire").

218 Seventh story, one-armed woman—Wantin' a Hand (*Century* 109:15–18, Nov 1924). Last story written at the Pottenger Sanatorium, July 1924 (LM ltr 30 Apr 1925).

219 Bind her to us—In his memo to editor Howland (26 Feb 1925), Chambers added: "Make her like us and don't let anyone else cut in."

219 Up-and-coming—LM ltr 30 Apr 1925.

219 Eighth story, money that came too late—The Funeral of Jimmy McBride (*Century* 112:526–31, Sep 1926). Written in San Francisco.

220 Swept the whole male sex—LM ltrs 27 May, 12, 22 June, 10 Dec 1925.

220 Photograph—*San Francisco Chronicle*, Sunday, 18 Oct 1925.

220 Anesthetic—Research suggests general anesthesia also harms the immune system.

220 Bonny corp—Bonny corpse (EB ltr to RdeM 8 Nov 1961).

21 / THE NOVELIST

221 Pay the rent—Lorna received no contractual advances from Bobbs-Merrill. *Dark Star* brought substantial royalties, on which B-M paid minor incidental advances when Lorna told them she was broke and needed money. Help from the DeMille office was confined to times when she was too ill to be employed. When she was well, she was on her own.

221 M-G-M screen credits—See Lorna Moon Filmography, after the Notes.

221 Thalberg's favorite writer—Samuel Marx, *A Gaudy Spree* (Franklin Watts 1987:22); a colorful source but not accurate about the life of LM.

221 Beulah—Scott 1972:69.

221 Writing on the sand—Cari Beauchamp, *Creative Screenwriting*, Fall 1994:55.

221 A very great friend—Marion ltr to RdeM 10 Jan 1973; Marion, *Off with Their Heads*, Macmillan 1972:204.

222 I hired myself—LM ltr 15 Nov 1926, ellipse omitted.

222 Lorna's rate—Lorna's highest weekly salary at M-G-M was $650, in 1927. Frances Marion's salary was $3000, the highest rate for writers (David Chasman, Vice President, M-G-M, personal communication; Turner Broadcasting System Legal Department). To appreciate the value of 1927 salaries in the currency of today, multiply by six or more.

222 Lorna's house—Lot 381, Tract 1504; book 9937, page 151; a small Spanish California house; 2541 Graciosa Drive; the houses have been renumbered.

223 *Ars gratia artis*—Art for art's sake, on the arch over the lion's head.

223 Studio secretary came—Marion Rodgers, editor, *Mencken and Sara: A Life in Letters, The Private Correspondence of H. L. Mencken and Sara Haardt*, McGraw-Hill 1987: 327. Dull and ordinary; This afternoon [6 Nov 1927] I am riding (327). Sara Haardt Mencken died of TB in 1935 at 37.

223 *Los Angeles Times*—Mentioned in DLC ltr 16 Aug 1927.

223 Don't let repayment—CBDeM telegram to LM, 12 Jan 1928. These transactions were not for public view. In a memo (18 July 1930) to Russell Treacy, CBDeM's business manager, Gladys Rosson states: "From Mr. deMille's personal Bank account, of which you have no record on the books, he advanced from time to time certain sums to Lorna Moon amounting in all as follows: In 1928, $5000; in 1929, $500; in 1930, $1500; in 1922–23, $3000." Reimbursements from William to Cecil, whatever they may have been, do not appear in the record; after divorce and tax levies William had little money.

224 It is revolting—LM ltr 6 Jan 1929.

224 Here and there—Arnold Bennett, French Audacities: The Art of Proust, 24 Feb 1927 (Mylett 1974:26–28).

224 "Flutes and Lovers"—In 1954 Bobbs-Merrill offered to send the manuscript to the author's widower. At seventy-six, Will Hebditch knew as much as he cared to know about his fugitive wife's notions of romance; he didn't answer the letter; the manuscript is lost. On 13 Dec 1956 Will Hebditch accepted payment from Loew's Inc. for renewal of a contract dated 18 Apr 1930 transferring motion picture rights in *Dark Star* to M-G-M (Turner Broadcasting System Legal Department).

224 She was growing; She fought him—DS129, DS134.

225 Your letter found me—LM to DLC 23 Jan 1928. Most of LM's surviving letters are long scrawls written in bed, many during fever. She wrote without apostrophes: dont, wont, cant. I have edited, condensed, occasionally reordered. A *chil* is an Indian kite, or hawk, whose cry is a rattle.

226 Dear Cecil—LM ltr to CBDeM 2 Mar 1928. Father Denis J. Falvey (Msgr. Francis J. Weber, archivist, ltr 21 June 1985).

226 What does he mean—LM ltr 16 Mar 1928.

227 I'm shooting—LM ltr 20 Mar 1928.

227 Be a good girl—DLC ltr 26 Mar 1928.

227 Every night I pray—LM ltr 31 Mar 1928.

227 If ever I rise up—Found with a letter kept by Eva.

228 I've started—LM ltr to G. Rosson June 1928.

228 I can't get any work done—LM ltr to CBDeM 9 July 1928.

228 I'm fed to the teeth—LM ltr 5 Aug 1928. Mehitabel the cat has a lowercase *m* because archy, her biographer, is a cockroach and can't press the shift key on the typewriter (Don Marquis, *archy and mehitabel*, 1927).

229 Journal—LM Author File.

22/A ZEST FOR LIFE

230 Secretary typed—Marion 1972:204.

230 You are a great darling—Father was moving from the DeMille Studio. He wrote on Lorna's letter (LM ltr 18 Oct 1928): "Tell her about my bungalow." Answering Lorna, Gladys Rosson wrote: "Mr. deMille is building a perfectly magnificent bungalow on the M-G-M lot, where he can have all the luxurious trimmings that amuse and interest him so. We hope that you will soon be up and about, and that we may receive you in these new offices. Our new picture, DYNAMITE . . . is to be an all talkie. . . . Mr.

deMille is happy to have been of some assistance to you during the past year, and sends you, as always, his very best wishes" (GR ltr 26 Oct 1928). This formal, delegated response was typical of Father's correspondence with persons outside the family, whether or not they used terms of endearment when writing to him.

230   Your wire and letter—LM ltrs 4 Nov, 28 Dec 1928.

231   Laddie, hold me—Marion 1972:205.

231   *New Yorker*—Harold Ross, editor (LM ltr 14 Feb 1929; Thurber 1984).

231   The Curtises—LM ltr 7 Nov 1928. Lorna here implies she was 24 at the Pottenger Sanatorium, where she was 35–39.

232   Vance is in a tailspin—LM ltr 9 Nov 1928.

232   I have tried the book out—LM ltr 18 Nov 1928.

233   If we publish—LM ltrs 10, 16 Dec 1928.

233   Laurance, you are; knockout—LM ltrs 15, 28 Jan 1929. James Branch Cabell (1879–1958) was the author of *Jurgen*, a daring, briefly suppressed novel (1919). Goatee in LM Author File.

233   Blue-eyed gent—Frances Marion told Mary Moon that Dorothy Parker had an eye for Everett Marcy (LM ltr 8 Mar 1929; MM ltr 1 Oct 1967). *Dark Star* was not reviewed in *The New Yorker*; Geoffrey Hellman reviewed it in *The Bookman* (Sep 1929:99–100).

234   Stallings has been drunk—LM ltr 3 Feb 1929. Laurence Stallings was a well-known playwright and novelist, working in Hollywood.

234   *Dim Star*—LM telegram 24 Jan 1929.

234   Hooey—LM ltr 3 Feb 1929.

235   I'm going to Francie's house—LM ltr 14 Feb 1929. In 1926 Lillian Gish had played Hester Prynne in *The Scarlet Letter*, directed by Victor Seastrom, scenario by Frances Marion (Marion 1972:130, 133–35). George Jean Nathan (1882–1958), prominent literary critic, founder with H. L. Mencken of *The American Mercury*.

235   Highest hill—Marion 1972:111.

235   Much temp—LM ltr 17 Feb 1929.

235   Publicists—AJ ltr 26 March 1929.

235   The Wedding of the Wheat—Bored rich American college girl and dedicated penniless Austrian nobleman reunited by botany and love in Siberian wheat field after silly misunderstanding (*Hearst's International Cosmopolitan*, Feb 1932:74–76, 79–80). Science ("glumes") and purple writing ("the heart of the world stood still listening to a wordless song").

A story with a similar tone, possibly written at the same time, is Lorna's Lipstick Lady, a fluffy sophisticated tale of a divorcing couple reunited by the wife's wily manipulations and the husband's dogged devotion. Lipstick Lady was included in *Too Gay!*, a 32-page booklet published in England in 1945 without a date (Clifford Lewis, Newcastle-under-Lyme) as a 6-penny "novel." *Too Gay!* reads like a 1920s movie melodrama (jealousy, murder, blackmail, fatal accident, heroic act, confession, happy ending). Each "chapter" bears a silent-film title: "She Looked Too Fast / He Would Be Blamed / She Had to Save Him / She Meant to Be His Wife / Giving Her a Bad Name." The style is not up to Lorna Moon's and may have been adapted by another writer from a movie scenario.

One wonders how these two stories came to be published in England 15 years after the author's death. The disposition of Lorna's personal property is unknown. She deeded her house to CBDeM, but he did not receive her personal property (GR ltr 5 Aug 1930). Frances Marion had a key to the Graciosa house (GR ltr to FM 23 May 1930), but when she met Mary Moon 20 years later she had few mementos of Lorna to give her (FM ltr 10 Jan 1973). Lorna had said she wanted the crucifix behind her bed to go to CBDeM (N. S. McCarthy ltr 23 June 1930), but Everett Marcy kept it, saying Lorna had promised it to him (E. C. Banta for N. S. McCarthy ltr 25 July 1930), and he may have kept other items as well, such as manuscripts.

235 Steep price; agent's commission—Price was $1000 (Mildred Temple, assistant to Ray Long, ltr 24 April 1929).

235 Book had "it"—Clara Bow, "the It girl," had "it," meaning sex appeal, in her 1927 movie titled *It*.

236 PEN—Poets, Playwrights, Essayists, and Novelists, professional association.

236 Fishmonger—LM ltr 8 Mar 1929.

236 Most notable—LM ltr 14 Mar 1929; Lionel Stevenson, Atherton *versus* Grundy: The Forty Years' War, *The Bookman*, July 1929:464–72.

236 The way I was involved—Virginia Parsons Massey ltrs 19 Oct 1982, 10 Feb 1983. Art teacher, Sophie E. Harpe (HSG, *The Inkling*, 1925).

237 I have five novels—LM ltrs 2 May; 5, 15 June 1929.

23/GO CHINA BY LORNA MOON

239 An awful thing—A story told by LM in ltrs 12, 19, 20 Feb; 4, 14, 22 Mar 1929; adapted by RdeM.

24/LAST RITES

243 Collapsed—George Shively ltr 26 June 1929.

243 Life is a trackless waste—LM ltr to Anne Johnston 15 Aug 1929.

243 What could prove my devotion—LM ltrs to DLC and GS 1 July 1929.

244 Irish nurse—Reported by Adelaide B. Cannon, who described Lorna as "my dear friend whom I have the pleasure of serving now and then in a secretarial capacity" (ABC ltrs to DLC 10 Oct, 2 Nov 1929).

244 Short and not sweet—LM ltr 9 Oct 1929.

244 Houri in a convent—"Like a most unrepentant Mary Magdalene," LM ltr 15 Aug 1929.

244 Flat on My Back—Lorna's title, changed by the *Cosmopolitan* editor, was I Am Sorry for My Friends (LM Author File).

245 I have never met—LM ltrs 5 June, 9 Oct 1929.

245 Thursday—*Los Angeles Times*, 30 Oct 1929; Tom Shachtman, *The Day America Crashed*, Putnam's 1979.

245 Lorna Moon, red-haired girl—Gilmore Millen, Death Near for Lorna Moon, Author (*Los Angeles Evening Herald*, 28 Oct 1929:1, 17), selected and condensed by RdeM from 15 column inches.

246   My Sweet Lamb—LM ltr 13 Dec 1929.

246   Your lovely yellow roses—LM ltr 31 Dec 1929.

246   Decided not to die—*Herald*, 2 May 1930.

247   Gamest person—ABC ltr to DLC 10 Oct 1929.

247   Mabel Normand—*NYT*, 24 Feb 1930.

247   It's so wearying—Jeffrey Meyers, *D. H. Lawrence: A Biography*, Knopf 1990: 379–80. Lawrence was born 11 Sept 1885, nine months before Lorna; he died 2 Mar 1930, two months before her.

247   How I hate to write—LM ltr 18 Feb 1930.

247   Macabre and my cough—LM ltr to AJ 14 Mar 1930.

248   It's anything but gloomy—Marion 1972:206–9.

249   Deed—On 21 Apr 1930, ten days before her death, Lorna deeded her house to CBdeM to repay unsecured personal loans amounting to $10,000 1922–30 (GR ltr 5 Aug 1930). After CBdeM sold the house, Mary Moon received about $4000, as if from Lorna's estate (see Notes for Chapter 8, "Proceeds"). Nothing in the record suggests that CBdeM knew that Lorna had an older son.

249   Alexina Brune—*Los Angeles Evening Herald*, 2 May 1930. Mrs. Alexina Brune lived at 2020 Pinehurst, in Hollywood (Los Angeles City Directory, 1928–29). Brune is not a frequent name in America or Scotland; *Dark Star* features Harvey Brune, who may have got his name from Alexina. In July 1928, Lorna stayed with a friend named Edith (last name unknown) at 302 South St. Andrews Place, Los Angeles (LM ltr 18 July 1928).

249   History—LM Certificate of Death 406, State of New Mexico, 2 May 1930, signed by Carl Mulky, M.D., a noted TB specialist. My thanks to Melba Clark, medical librarian, St. Joseph Medical Center.

250   Instead of going to church—LM ltr 17 Oct 1928; *Aberdeen Press & Journal*, 25 Apr 1928.

250   Sky was blue—*Albuquerque Journal*, 1, 3 May 1930. First talking picture, *General Crack*. Information provided by John Vittal, Albuquerque Public Library.

25/LORNA MOON AT THE BELASCO

251   By a strange coincidence—*Los Angeles Times*, 3 May 1930:II-10; 4 May 1930: II-5; combined and condensed by RdeM.

251   At the age of thirty—*Publishers Weekly*, 24 May 1930:2626.

251   Killed in the War—*Variety*, 3 May 1930.

252   Collaborating—Los Angeles *Record*, 6 May 1930.

252   Save the project—Victor Gollancz ltr 19 May, DLC ltr 31 May 1930; no advance had been paid; no later letters refer to "Macabre." The manuscript has not come to light.

252   Unsavory version—Mordaunt Hall, *NYT*, 24 Nov 1930:26.

252   Tie-ins—LM Author File, ltrs 30 Jan, 17, 19, 26 Feb, 3, 9, 19 Mar, 7, 10 Apr 1930. Tie-in editions of *Dark Star* from Readers Library, London, and Dédalo, Madrid.

253   *Golden Boy*—In the screenplay (1939) Barbara Stanwyck says: "I'm just a dame from Newark."

253   Frances Farmer—*Frances*, 1982. In *Will There Really Be a Morning?*, a Canadian television movie (broadcast 22 Feb 1983), Susan Blakely played Frances Farmer playing Lorna Moon.

253   Biography—Margaret Brenman-Gibson, *Clifford Odets, American Playwright: The Years from 1906 to 1940*, Atheneum 1981; citations from pp. 107, 116–17, 163, 467.

254   Correspondence—RdeM ltr 15 Nov 1982; Brenman-Gibson ltr 2 Dec 1982; Luise Rainer ltr 25 Aug 1983; Virginia Rowe (speaking for Kobland) ltr 27 June 1983.

254   Ads for Lorna Moon's *Dark Star*—*New York Times Book Review*, 24, 31 Mar; 7, 14, 21, 28 Apr 1929; *Saturday Review of Literature*, 30 Mar 1929:842.

254   Reviews of Lorna Moon's *Dark Star*—*New York Times Book Review*, 7 Apr 1929:2; *New York Herald Tribune Books*, 31 Mar 1929:4; New York *World*, 31 Mar 1929:11m; *Nation*, 1 May 1929:527; *Saturday Review of Literature*, 11 May 1929:996.

255   Elsie Smith—L. C. Smith, Underwood, and Royal were makes of typewriter.

26/HER SON'S IMPRESSIONS

257   Bowr of earthly blisse—Milton (OED).

259   Fastidious lover—"She was a great conversationalist and had been romantically involved with George Jean Nathan, or was it Mencken? She was an intellectual aesthete in her choice of male partners"—Frederica Sagor Maas, screenwriter (*Silk Legs*, Dec 1927), comment supplied by Kevin Brownlow, to whom I am grateful.

259   Dorothy Ellington—LM ltr 18 Feb 1925; *NYT*, 16 Jan to 27 Aug 1925.

260   Tricky tales; Already *Dark Star*; Mr. Curtis—LM ltrs 2 May, 15 June 1929. *Orlando* (1928), a novel by Virginia Woolf, *The Bridge of San Luis Rey* (1927) by Thornton Wilder, modeled on a French novel.

261   Arnold Bennett—Mylett 1974:xvi–xxviii. Arnold Bennett (1867–1931) died at 63 of typhoid fever, 11 months after Lorna Moon.

261   It is captivating—Arnold Bennett (*Evening Standard*, 4 July 1929; reprinted in Mylett 1974:282–84, 387).

261   Noted critics—*TLS* (14 Oct 1926:700); Henry Seidel Canby (*Saturday Review of Literature*, 13 Apr 1929:876); V. S. Pritchett (*Spectator*, 3 Aug 1929: 166–67). St. John Ervine (*Daily Express*, 11 July 1929) said: "very nearly a great book of great quality." *New Statesman* (29 June 1929:378, 380) said: "For a change we have a 'first novel' which is not 'promising'; it is an achievement." I am indebted to J. S. G. Simmons, Deputy Archivist, Codrington Library, All Souls College, Oxford, for identifying several British sources.

262   Emperor Charles—CBDeM 1959:4.

262   Bristly—Scott 1972:101.

263   Fanciful account—The author (Anne Edwards, *The DeMilles*, Abrams 1988: 77, 81–82) also proposes that Lorna went to Albuquerque by car (she went by train); that I was found in a basket on Neil McCarthy's doorstep (he went to the sanatorium to get me); that after I was born, Lorna attempted

to care for me for nine months (we were never together after I was born).
263　I know all these people—LM ltrs 24 Dec 1928, 12 Feb 1929; LM Journal.

I am grateful to Saundra Taylor, Curator of Manuscripts, Lilly Library, Indiana University, Bloomington, to librarians at the Santa Barbara Public Library, Westmont College, and the University of California, Santa Barbara, and to others named in the Notes, for unfailing helpfulness. Numerous members of my several families have been generous with consultation and permission.

Lorna Moon Filmography

(Sources: *American Film Institute Catalog*; Ringgold & Bodeen, 1969.)

The Affairs of Anatol. Famous Players Lasky Paramount, September 1921. Romantic comedy, "suggested by" Schnitzler play. Directed by Cecil B. DeMille. Scenario by Jeanie Macpherson, Beulah Marie Dix, Lorna Moon, & Elmer Harris. Wallace Reid, Gloria Swanson.

Don't Tell Everything. Famous Players Lasky Paramount, November 1921. Comedy-drama. Directed by Sam Wood. Lorna Moon story; Albert S. LeVino scenario. Wallace Reid, Gloria Swanson.

Too Much Wife. Realart Paramount, January 1922. Comedy-drama. Supervised by Elmer Harris. Directed by Thomas N. Heffron. Lorna Moon story; Percy Heath scenario. Wanda Hawley.

Her Husband's Trademark. Famous Players Lasky Paramount, February 1922. Society melodrama. Directed by Sam Wood. Lorna Moon adaptation of story by Clara Beranger. Gloria Swanson.

Upstage. M-G-M, November 1926. Romantic drama. Directed by Monta Bell. Lorna Moon story & scenario. Joe Farnham titles. Norma Shearer.

Women Love Diamonds. M-G-M, February 1927. Society melodrama. Direction & story by Edmund Goulding. Lorna Moon & Waldemar Young scenario. Edwin Justus Mayer titles. Lionel Barrymore.

Mr. Wu. M-G-M, March 1927. Melodrama. Directed by William Nigh. Lorna Moon adaptation & continuity from a play. Lotta Woods titles. Lon Chaney.

After Midnight. M-G-M, August 1927. Society drama. Direction & story by Monta Bell. Lorna Moon scenario. Joe Farnham titles. Norma Shearer.

Love. M-G-M, November 1927. Tragedy. Adapted from *Anna Karenina*, with alternative sad and happy endings. Edmund Goulding producer-director. Lorna Moon adaptation; Frances Marion continuity; Marian Ainslee & Ruth Cummings titles. Greta Garbo, John Gilbert.

Min and Bill. M-G-M, November 1930. Drama. Directed by George Hill. Scenario & dialogue Frances Marion & Marion Jackson. "Based on Lorna Moon's novel *Dark Star*." Marie Dressler, Wallace Beery.

References

American Film Institute Catalog.

Blackmore, R. D. *Lorna Doone: A Romance of Exmoor.* 1869, Oxford 1989.

Bruce, Eva. *Call Her Rosie.* Washburn (New York) 1942; Hammond, Hammond (London) 1944.

De Mill, Richard Mead. *The Foundation and the Superstructure, or the Faith of Christ and the Works of Man.* Putnam's 1908.

de Mille, Agnes. *Dance to the Piper.* Little, Brown 1952.

————. *And Promenade Home.* Little, Brown 1958.

————. *Speak to Me, Dance with Me.* Little, Brown/Da Capo 1973.

————. *Where the Wings Grow.* Doubleday 1978.

————. *Reprieve.* Doubleday 1981.

————. *Portrait Gallery.* Houghton Mifflin 1990.

————. *Martha: The Life and Work of Martha Graham.* Random House 1991.

DeMille, Cecil B. *The Autobiography of Cecil B. DeMille.* Edited by Donald Hayne. Prentice-Hall 1959.

de Mille, Richard. Safety Valve. *Astounding Science Fiction,* Feb 1953:59–82.

————. *Put Your Mother on the Ceiling: Children's Imagination Games.* Walker 1967, Viking 1973, Penguin 1976, Gestalt Journal Press 1997.

————. *Castaneda's Journey: The Power and the Allegory.* Capra Press 1976.

————, editor. *The Don Juan Papers: Further Castaneda Controversies.* Ross-Erikson 1980; Wadsworth 1990.

de Mille, William C. *Hollywood Saga.* Dutton 1939.

Easton, Carol. *No Intermissions: The Life of Agnes de Mille.* Little, Brown 1996.

Fraser, David, editor. *The Christian Watt Papers,* 2nd edition. Caledonian Books (Collieston, Aberdeenshire) 1988.

Innes of Learney, Sir Thomas, Lord Lyon King of Arms. *The Tartans of the Clans and Families of Scotland.* Johnston & Bacon (Edinburgh) 1964.

Koury, Phil A. *Yes, Mr. DeMille.* Putnam's 1959.

Lasky, Jesse L., Jr. *Whatever Happened to Hollywood?* Funk & Wagnalls 1975.

Lewis, Samuel. *Topographical Dictionary of Scotland.* Lewis & Co. (London) 1851.

Moon, Lorna. *Doorways in Drumorty.* Bobbs-Merrill 1925, Jonathan Cape 1926, Gourdas House 1981.

———. *Dark Star.* Bobbs-Merrill 1929, Victor Gollancz 1929, Gourdas House 1980.

Moon, Mary. *The Okanagan Mystery: Ogopogo.* J. J. Douglas (Vancouver) 1977.

Mylett, Andrew, editor. *Arnold Bennett: The* Evening Standard *Years, "Books and Persons" 1926–1931.* Chatto & Windus/Archon Books 1974. Introduction by Andrew Mylett, pp. xvi–xxviii.

Ringgold, Gene, & DeWitt Bodeen. *The Films of Cecil B. DeMille.* Citadel 1969.

Samuel, Stuart M., & Lucien Wolf. *The History and Genealogy of the Jewish Families of Yates and Samuel of Liverpool.* [Lucien Wolf] London 1901.

Scott, Evelyn F[lebbe]. *Hollywood When Silents Were Golden.* McGraw-Hill 1972.

Thurber, James. *The Years with Ross.* Penguin 1984.

Further sources are given in the Notes.

Index